Copyright © 1989 by Princeton University Press
Published by Princeton University Press
41 William Street, Princeton, New Jersey 08540
In the United Kingdom: Princeton University Press, Oxford

All Rights Reserved

Library of Congress Cataloging-in-Publication Data

Barish, Evelyn, 1935–
  Emerson: the roots of prophecy / Evelyn Barish.
   p. cm.
  Bibliography: p.
  Includes index.
  ISBN 0-691-06787-2 (alk. paper)
   1. Emerson, Ralph Waldo, 1803–1882. 2. Authors, American—19th
century—Biography. 3. Prophecies in literature. I. Title.
PS1631.B27 1989
814′.3—dc20   89-10291
[B]

Publication of this book has been aided by the Whitney Darrow Fund
of Princeton University Press

This book has been composed in Linotron Monticello

Princeton University Press books are printed on acid-free paper,
and meet the guidelines for permanence and durability
of the Committee on Production Guidelines
for Book Longevity of the Council
on Library Resources

Printed in the United States of America
by Princeton University Press,
Princeton, New Jersey

10 9 8 7 6 5 4 3 2 1

EMERSON

The Roots of Prophecy

EVELYN BARISH

Princeton University Press
Princeton, New Jersey

Contents

Acknowledgments

I AM GRATEFUL to the following for fellowship and other support during the years while this book was in preparation: the National Endowment for the Humanities; the City University of New York Faculty Awards Program and its successor programs; the American Philosophical Society; the Bunting Institute, Harvard University; Edmond L. Volpe, President of the College of Staten Island, City University of New York.

Debts to individuals and colleagues are pleasant to acknowledge. Taylor Stoehr was an invaluable reader and unfailing supporter during the years of my work in Cambridge. Marion Kilson, as head of the Bunting (now Radcliffe) Institute, made that institution a warm and effective scholarly home. Patricia Craddock and Margaret Neussendorfer helped with their knowledge and enthusiastic response. Members of various seminars have contributed useful criticism: Jerome Hamilton Buckley made the Victorians Seminar at Harvard a hospitable group; so were the members of Aileen Ward's Biography Seminar at New York University and the members of the Seminar on the History of Psychiatry directed by Theodore Carlson, M.D., at New York Hospital–Cornell Medical Center. My colleague Mason Cooley has offered patient and insightful comments on the manuscript. I am especially grateful to Gay Wilson Allen, one of my early teachers, who has read many of my manuscripts over the years and had faith in them all. Alfred Kazin read this work and encouraged me in it at a critical time, and I am glad to thank him.

Materials from the Emerson family papers and *The Journals and Miscellaneous Notebooks of Ralph Waldo Emerson* (Cambridge, Mass.: Harvard University Press, 1960–82) have been quoted by permission of the Houghton Library and the Ralph Waldo Emerson Memorial Association. I am grateful to the late Mrs. Ward Gregg for her permission to print the papers of Mary Moody Emerson. Mr. Richard J. Wolfe, Curator of Rare Books and Manuscripts in the Countway Library of Medicine, Harvard University, led me to unfamiliar sources. Mrs. Marcia Moss, Curator of the Concord Free Public Library, was helpful with local materials. Miss Carolyn Jakeman, of the Houghton Library, gave valuable assistance.

Abbreviations of Frequently Cited Works

Ahlstrom
> Sydney E. Ahlstrom, *A Religious History of the American People* (New Haven, Conn.: Yale University Press, 1972).

Allen
> Gay Wilson Allen, *Waldo Emerson: A Biography* (New York: Viking Press, 1981).

Barish, "Magician"
> Evelyn Barish, "Emerson and 'The Magician': An Early Prose Fantasy," *American Transcendental Quarterly* 31, supp. 1 (Summer 1976): 13–18.

Barish, "Angel"
> Evelyn Barish, "Emerson and the Angel of Midnight: The Legacy of Mary Moody Emerson," *Mothering the Mind: Twelve Studies of Writers and Their Silent Partners*, ed. Ruth Perry and Martine W. Brownley (New York: Holmes & Meier, 1984), pp. 218–37.

Bercovitch
> Sacvan Bercovitch, *The Puritan Origins of the American Self* (New Haven, Conn.: Yale University Press, 1975).

Bishop
> Jonathan Bishop, *Emerson on the Soul* (Cambridge, Mass.: Harvard University Press, 1964).

Buckminster
> Joseph Stephens Buckminster, *A Sermon Delivered at the Interment of the Reverend William Emerson* (Boston, 1811).

Cabot
> James Elliot Cabot, *A Memoir of Ralph Waldo Emerson*, 2 vols. (Cambridge, Mass.: Riverside Press, 1887).

Cheyfitz
> Eric Cheyfitz, *The Trans-Parent: Sexual Politics in the Language of Emerson* (Baltimore: Johns Hopkins University Press, 1981).

Cooke
> George Willis Cooke, *Memorabilia of the Transcendentalists in New England* (Hartford, Conn.: Transcendental Books, 1973). Reprint of Cooke's "Historical and Biographical Introduction" to the Rowfant Club reprint of *The Dial*, 1902.

CW
> Ralph Waldo Emerson, *The Complete Works of Ralph Waldo Emerson*, ed. Edward W. Emerson, 12 vols. (Cambridge, Mass.: Houghton Mifflin, 1903–04).

Despland
> Michel Despland, *Kant on History and Religion* (Montreal: McGill-Queens University Press, 1973).

EIC
> Edward W. Emerson, *Emerson in Concord: A Memoir* (Boston: Houghton Mifflin, 1889).

Ellis
> Arthur B. Ellis, *History of the First Church in Boston: 1630–1880* (Boston: Hall & Whiting, 1881).

Ellison
> Julie Ellison, *Emerson's Romantic Style* (Princeton, N.J.: Princeton University Press, 1984).

Emery
> Sarah Anna Emery, *Reminiscences of a Nonagenerian* (Newburyport, Mass.: Wm. Huse & Co., 1879).

"EP"
> "The Present State of Ethical Philosophy: An Early Essay of Emerson," in *Ralph Waldo Emerson: Together with Two Early Essays of Emerson*, ed. Edward Everett Hale (Boston: American Unitarian Association, 1902), pp. 97–135.

Evelyn Barish Greenberger, *Clough*
> Evelyn Barish Greenberger, *Arthur Hugh Clough: Growth of a Poet's Mind* (Cambridge, Mass.: Harvard University Press, 1970).

Evelyn Barish Greenberger, "Phoenix"
> Evelyn Barish Greenberger, "The Phoenix on the Wall: Consciousness in Emerson's Early and Late Journals," *American Transcendental Quarterly* 21 (Winter 1974): 45–56.

Gregg
> Edith W. Gregg, ed., *One First Love: The Letters of Ellen Louisa Tucker to Ralph Waldo Emerson* (Cambridge, Mass.: Harvard University Press, 1962).

Greven
> Philip Greven, *The Protestant Temperament: Patterns of Child-Rearing, Religious Experience, and the Self in Early America* (New York: New American Library, 1979).

Handy
> Robert Handy, *A Christian America: Protestant Hopes and Historical Realities* (New York: Oxford University Press, 1971).

Haskins
> David Greene Haskins, *Ralph Waldo Emerson: His Maternal Ancestors With Some Reminiscences of Him* (Boston: Cupples, Upham & Co., 1887; reprint, New York: Kennikat Press, 1971).

Heimert
    Alan E. Heimert, *Religion and the American Mind: From the Great Awakening to the Revolution* (Cambridge, Mass.: Harvard University Press, 1966).

"HDS"
    Ralph Waldo Emerson, "Harvard Divinity School," *Complete Works*, 1: 119–51.

HMS
    Manuscripts in the Ralph Waldo Emerson Memorial Association archives, Houghton Library, Harvard University.

Hollander
    Joseph L. Hollander and D. J. McCarty, eds., *Arthritis and Allied Conditions*, 8th ed. (Philadelphia: Lea and Febinger, 1972).

Holmes
    Oliver Wendell Holmes, *Ralph Waldo Emerson* (Boston: Houghton, Mifflin, 1885).

Hume, *Dialogues*
    David Hume, *Dialogues Concerning Natural Religion*, book 3 of *Treatise of Human Nature. The Philosophical Works of David Hume*, 4 vols. (Boston & Edinburgh: Little, Brown & A. C. Black, 1854).

Hume, *History*
    David Hume, *History of England*, 6 vols. (London: A. Millar, 1754, 1756).

Hume, *NHR*
    David Hume, *The Natural History of Religion*, vol. 2 of *Essays and Treatises on Several Subjects*, 2 vols. (Edinburgh: Bell & Bradfute, 1804).

J
    Ralph Waldo Emerson, *Journals of Ralph Waldo Emerson 1820–1876*, ed. E. W. Emerson and W. E. Forbes, 10 vols. (Cambridge, Mass.: Houghton Mifflin, 1909–14).

JMN
    Ralph Waldo Emerson, *Journals and Miscellaneous Notebooks of Ralph Waldo Emerson*, ed. W. H. Gilman et al., 16 vols. (Cambridge, Mass.: Harvard University Press, 1960–82).

Klebs
    Arnold C. Klebs, ed., *Tuberculosis: A Treatise by American Authors on Its Etiology, Frequency, Semeiology, Diagnosis, Prognosis, Prevention and Treatment* (New York: Appleton, 1909).

L
    Ralph Waldo Emerson, *The Letters of Ralph Waldo Emerson*, ed. Ralph L. Rusk, 6 vols. (New York: Columbia University Press, 1939).

Matthiessen
> F. O. Matthiessen, *American Renaissance* (Oxford: Oxford University Press, 1941).

Miller
> Perry Miller, "From Edwards to Emerson," in *Errand into the Wilderness* (Cambridge, Mass.: Harvard University Press, 1956).

"MME"
> Ralph Waldo Emerson, "Mary Moody Emerson," *Complete Works*, 10: 397–433.

Morison
> Samuel Eliot Morison, *Three Centuries of Harvard: 1636–1936* (Cambridge, Mass.: Harvard University Press, 1936).

Morton
> Samuel George Morton, *Illustrations of Pulmonary Consumption* (Philadelphia: Key & Biddle, 1834).

Mossner
> Ernest Mossner, *The Forgotten Hume: Le Bon David* (New York: Columbia University Press, 1943).

NHHA
> New Hampshire Historical Association archives.

Newman
> John Henry Newman, *Apologia Pro Vita Sua*, ed. David DeLaura (New York: W. W. Norton, 1968).

Packer
> B[arbara] L. Packer, *Emerson's Fall: A New Interpretation of the Major Essays* (New York: Continuum Publishing Co., 1982).

Paul
> Sherman Paul, *Emerson's Angle of Vision: Man and Nature in American Experience* (Cambridge, Mass.: Harvard University Press, 1952).

Peabody
> Andrew Preston Peabody, *Harvard Reminiscences* (Boston: Ticknor & Co., 1888).

Pochmann
> Henry A. Pochmann, *German Culture in America*, (Madison: University of Wisconsin Press, 1957).

Pommer
> Henry F. Pommer, *Emerson's First Marriage* (Carbondale: Southern Illinois University Press, 1967).

Porte
> Joel Porte, *Representative Man: Ralph Waldo Emerson in His Time* (New York: Oxford University Press, 1979).

C. Porter
Carolyn Porter, *Seeing and Being: The Plight of the Participant Observer in Emerson, James, Adams, and Faulkner* (Wesleyan, Conn.: Wesleyan University Press, 1981).

D. Porter
David Porter, *Emerson and Literary Change* (Cambridge, Mass.: Harvard University Press, 1978).

Robbins
Sarah Stuart Robbins, *Old Andover Days: Memories of a Puritan Childhood* (Boston: Pilgrim Press, 1908).

Robinson
David Robinson, *Apostle of Culture: Emerson as Preacher and Lecturer* (Philadelphia: University of Pennsylvania Press, 1982).

Rowe
Henry K. Rowe, *History of Andover Theological Seminary* (Newton, Mass., 1933).

Rusk
Ralph L. Rusk, *Life of Ralph Waldo Emerson* (New York: Columbia University Press, 1949).

Sanborn, *Personality*
F[ranklin] B. Sanborn, *The Personality of Emerson* (Boston: Chas. Goodspeed, 1903).

Sanborn, *Sixty Years*
Franklin B. Sanborn, *Sixty Years of Concord: 1855–1905*, ed. Kenneth W. Cameron (Hartford, Conn.: Transcendental Books, 1975).

Simpson
Lewis P. Simpson, *The Federalist Literary Mind: Selections from the Monthly Anthology and Boston Review 1803–1811*. ([Baton Rouge]: Louisiana State University Press, 1962).

Stephen
Leslie Stephen, *History of English Thought in the Eighteenth Century*, 2 vols. (New York: G. Putnam, 1876).

Stewart
Dugald Stewart, *Dissertation [on] the Progess of Metaphysical, Ethical, and Political Philosophy*, vol. 6 of *The Works of Dugald Stewart*, 7 vols. (Cambridge, Mass.: Hilliard & Brown, 1829).

Thayer
[James B. Thayer], *Rev. Samuel Ripley of Waltham* (Cambridge, Mass.: [privately printed], John Wilson & Son, 1897).

Tyack
    David B. Tyack, *George Ticknor and the Boston Brahmins* (Cambridge, Mass.: Harvard University Press, 1967).

Wardrop (1813)
    James Wardrop, "On the Effects of Evacuating the Aqueous Humor of the Eyes, and in Some Diseases of the Cornea," *Medico-Chirurgical Transactions* 4 (1813): 142–87.

Wardrop (1819)
    James Wardrop, "Account of the Rheumatic Inflammation of the Eye with Observations on the Treatment of the Disease," *Medico-Chirurgical Transactions* 10 (1819): 1–15.

"What"
    Ellen Tucker Emerson, "What I Can Remember About Father," HMS.

Whicher
    Stephen E. Whicher, *Freedom and Fate: An Inner Life of Ralph Waldo Emerson* (Philadelphia: University of Pennsylvania Press, 1953).

Wright
    Conrad Wright, "The Early Period (1811–1840)," in *The Harvard Divinity School: Its Place in Harvard University and in American Culture*, ed. George H. Williams (Boston: Beacon Press, 1954).

Abbreviations of Names

CCE	Charles Chauncy Emerson, brother of Ralph Waldo Emerson
EBE	Edward Bliss Emerson, brother of Ralph Waldo Emerson
ETE	Ellen Tucker Emerson, first wife of Ralph Waldo Emerson
JCE	John Clarke Emerson, brother of Ralph Waldo Emerson
MME	Mary Moody Emerson, aunt of Ralph Waldo Emerson, sister of William Emerson, Sr.
RE	Ruth Haskins Emerson, mother of Ralph Waldo Emerson
RWE	Ralph Waldo Emerson
SABR	Sarah Alden Bradford Ripley, aunt of Ralph Waldo Emerson
WE	William Emerson, Sr., father of Ralph Waldo Emerson
WEjr	William Emerson, Jr., brother of Ralph Waldo Emerson

EMERSON

Introduction

THIS BOOK began as an attempt to understand a silence. Asked to contribute to a collection of essays about Emerson a "consciousness study" comparing his early and late journals, I became aware of two things. The first was the absence of almost any reference to his father, who had died when the boy was seven. The journals, kept from an early age and richly inclusive, referred frequently to his family— his brothers and aunt especially. But there were no comments about his father, William Emerson, no memories, no quotations handed down by mother or aunt—no vision at all. Apparently there was no curiosity.

I did not understand this, both because of personal experience and because the world around the growing boy must have been full of reminders. From boyhood, he had chosen the profession of his dead father; like five generations before his father, he wished to become a minister in a city where that calling and descent gave title to a sort of aristocracy. He attended the same college his father had. He was surrounded by cultural institutions his father had helped to found and knew the men who had valued and trusted his father with the city's most prestigious pulpit.

Why then was he silent? More than silent. On several occasions, as the editors of the voluminous *Journals and Miscellaneous Notebooks* (*JMN*) have pointed out, young Emerson had taken the bound manuscripts of his father's sermons, cut out the contents, and used the covers and stubs of pages to encase his own writings.[1] The discarded pages were not preserved. Even in an ordinary family this would have been inappropriate. But this was a logocentric family where writing the Word was a vocation to which every son at one time aspired. Clearly, Emerson's behavior was significant, but what it encoded I did not know.

When I undertook a wider study of Emerson's early life, I focused on the thirty-three years leading up to the publication of *Nature*, a biographical Great Divide. After that, his life became an increasingly public and successful one, but with a few exceptions the events in it constituted a repeated pattern of essays published and lectures

[1] *Journals and Miscellaneous Notebooks of Ralph Waldo Emerson*, ed. W. H. Gilman et al., 16 vols. (Cambridge, Mass.: Harvard University Press, 1960–82), 2:272, 396. Cited hereafter as *JMN*.

3

given. Whatever enabled him to write those essays had already
shaped his voice.

Most biographies passed over his early years rather quickly. Yet
those years were extraordinarily rich, complex, and well docu-
mented. Beginning at the age of sixteen and for the rest of his life,
Emerson kept a journal, whose sometimes daily entries often ran
into thousands of words. A selected edition of these appeared in the
first decade of this century, but publication of the complete text commenced only in 1960. When I began my study, no full-scale new
biography had been published since the additional material had begun to appear. Now sixteen volumes of the *JMN* are available, and
publication of the notebooks is not yet complete; the five volumes
covering Emerson's early years alone number some two thousand
printed pages with notes and apparatus.

Yet for all its fullness, the material resists reading. The journals
seem to include everything, but they constitute neither an analytical
nor a narrative record. Emerson comments fully on his very wide-
ranging intellectual interests, but the connections among his
thoughts were not the issue for him, and one looks in vain for some
conscious schema. (The indexes he made to his volumes suggest
both the value he placed on them and the difficulty, which his readers share, of finding his way through this pathless forest.)

Moreover, the journals say comparatively little about the day-to-
day issues of life. They tell what Emerson thought he was, ought to
be, and might become, but they do not tell how he managed his
income, chose his wife, or taught his school. Except in the special
case of his attraction to Martin Gay, they omit persons. Misery is
referred to generically, so to speak; dissatisfaction with himself is
recorded, but rarely tied to specific incidents. Joy is scarcely mentioned at all, though for Emerson happiness was probably insepara-
ble from the exuberant intellectual energy that overflows from almost every page. He was first of all a writer, and being able to write
was the first and most exigent demand of his being.

For the scholar, then, the *JMN* poses both an unparalleled opportunity and an dilemma. What is most important is hard to perceive
amid an often radiant chaos.

HOW TO READ this chaos became my second question and shaped
my research. Interest in Emerson's early life quickly led to study of
the prose and poetry of his youth and early maturity, and in the process an understanding of his relation to his absent father became a

point of departure, although still an important one, rather than an end in itself. Instead, the main thrust of the study was to trace Emerson's intellectual development against the background of his personal and cultural environment. In this I found myself returning to ground opened earlier in my study of Arthur Hugh Clough, Victorian poet and protégé of Emerson, pursuing the experience of nineteenth-century intellectuals as they struggled in the first post-Enlightenment era of religious and political change.

The first of two guiding principles evolved as I followed Emerson's development. This was that research methods must be adapted to suit the material as his life changed course; a study involving linguistic description and criticism and literary materials would be a necessary but not sufficient result. Work in other disciplines must be consulted for new ways of illuminating Emerson's development. This decision enabled me to explore new areas and make use of materials that had hitherto been underutilized, ignored, or simply opaque. Family documents relating to his mother's childrearing practices could be read in the new light shed by social and family historians such as Joseph Kett and Philip Greven. Hitherto underused but very rich information about his influential aunt, Mary Moody Emerson, profited from the new work on women's history by scholars like Nancy Cott, Carroll Smith-Rosenberg, and others. Psychoanalytic insights were offered by clinical studies into the meaning of loss and grief by such major figures as John Bowlby, Helene Deutsch, Anna Freud, and Sigmund Freud. And all of these studies and perspectives needed to be supported in context by work in American religious history.

One of the most interesting and challenging opportunities was posed by Emerson's hitherto unremarked (or suppressed) study of the philospher David Hume. Reading Hume and his commentators greatly illuminated Emerson's development, for it explained the precedence of doubt over intuitional belief in the early stages of his intellectual growth and demonstrated that he had arrived only late and with conscious irony at his reliance on unmediated religious "sentiment" as the sole source of faith.

Of equal but different significance were the problems posed by the obscure breakdown of Emerson's health in his early twenties. Clues led into the thicket of early nineteenth-century American and English medical history and produced a diagnosis and explanation both of his many symptoms and sufferings and of the shadows in which this period of his life had long been shrouded.

CONCOMITANT with my work, others were responding critically to the echoes in Emerson's mature writings of several of these buried issues. An earlier generation of scholars, including Stephen Whicher and Sherman Paul, had already established the extent to which polarities had marked his thought.[2] More recently Harold Bloom had stressed Emerson's demonic will to power. But, although he was the inventor of the critical concept of literary anxiety, Bloom exempted Emerson from such feelings, for Emerson functioned in his work as the American progenitor, the source for others of their own sense of belatedness.[3]

Critics influenced by Bloom, however, have been conscious of Emerson as one more writer wary of his fallen, or secondary status. Barbara Packer, author of *Emerson's Fall*, is shrewdly intuitive about the extent to which Emerson's "metaphors of oral aggression, which accompany the rebirth of desire, are always a sign of recovered self-confidence." She points out that "no one can possibly understand" his work "who fails to recognize that in all of them Emerson's adversary is fear, and that his therapeutic goal is the development in his hearers of an ego strong enough to resist its crippling influence."[4] (Bloom suggests his own awareness of this aspect of Emerson when he remarks that he is one of the three "doctors-of-the-soul," along with Augustine and Freud, and that self-reliance is analogous to "Freud's 'where It was, there shall I be,' or the progressive displacement of the id by the maturing ego."[5] Or as Matthew Arnold had put it a century earlier, Emerson is "the friend and aider of those who would live in the spirit.")

Julie Ellison's excellent study, although focusing on stylistic mat-

---

[2] Stephen E. Whicher, *Freedom and Fate: An Inner Life of Ralph Waldo Emerson* (Philadelphia: University of Pennsylvania Press, 1953), cited hereafter as Whicher; Sherman Paul, *Emerson's Angle of Vision: Man and Nature in American Experience* (Cambridge, Mass.: Harvard University Press, 1952), cited hereafter as Paul.

[3] Among Harold Bloom's many discussions of Emerson, see "The Central Man" and "The Dialectic of Romantic Poetry in America," in *The Ringers in the Tower: Studies in Romantic Tradition* (Chicago: University of Chicago Press, 1971), pp. 226, 301, 302; "Emerson," in *Figures of Capable Imagination* (New York: Seabury Press, 1976), pp. 54, 60–61; and *The Anxiety of Influence* (New York: Oxford University Press, 1973), pp. 5off.

[4] B[arbara] L. Packer, *Emerson's Fall: A New Interpretation of the Major Essays* (New York: Continuum Publishing Co., 1982), pp. 120, 94, cited herafter as Packer. Packer is one of the few commentators to give more than passing notice to Emerson's reading of Hume (pp. 157–60).

[5] "Emerson and Whitman," in *Poetry and Repression: Revisionism from Blake to Stevens* (New Haven, Conn.: Yale University Press, 1976), p. 239; "Emerson," in *Figures*, p. 55; *The Anxiety of Influence* (New York: Oxford University Press, 1973), p. 50.

ters, nevertheless founds itself on the recognition that Emerson does not in fact write dialectically, for dialectic presupposes eventual resolution of its contrarieties. Emerson's prose "accumulates but does not progress" beyond its dichotomies. Every work, every essay, she points out, is built on the same "unstable" structure of antitheses, and she suggests that Eric Cheyfitz's work, which mixes linguistic with psychoanalytic theorizing, has done much to help move "critical descriptions of fixed polarities toward the problem of why Emerson's antithesis are so unstable."[6] Cheyfitz's stimulating study, based primarily on *Nature*, addresses as a central issue Emerson's "rage" at the missing "FATHER" and reconstructs a "child-hero" who contends also with a maternal figure that is at once beautiful and monstrous, seductive and fearsome. Certain similarities between Cheyfitz's work and mine will be discussed in chapter 4, "Romance," and in the Epilogue.[7]

My sources may overlap those used by such critics[8] and other biographers, especially when the *JMN* is concerned.[9] Most often, however, as a student of Emerson's early years, I have drawn on factual, extrinsic evidence to grasp his achievement in shaping that most primary of all texts, his sense of his own identity.

In one respect, at least, I have tried to emulate Emerson's example, and that has been the second principle guiding this effort. I have aimed to assimilate insights gained from varied disciplines with a minimum of linguistic turbulence, avoiding jargon and producing consistent and readable prose.

[6] Julie Ellison, *Emerson's Romantic Style* (Princeton, N.J.: Princeton University Press, 1984), p. 76, cited hereafter as Ellison.

[7] Eric Cheyfitz, *The Trans-Parent: Sexual Politics in the Language of Emerson* (Baltimore: Johns Hopkins University Press, 1981), cited hereafer as Cheyfitz.

[8] Jonathan Bishop's *Emerson on the Soul* (Cambridge, Mass.: Harvard University Press, 1964), cited hereafter as Bishop, was the first book fully to exploit the *JMN* as its central text, and its success has influenced many subsequent critics, including Packer and Cheyfitz. Other recent and useful critical works are David Porter's *Emerson and Literary Change* (Cambridge, Mass.: Harvard University Press, 1978), cited hereafter as D. Porter, and R. A. Yoder's *Emerson and the Orphic Poet in America* (Berkeley and Los Angeles: University of California Press, 1978).

[9] Among the best known are Gay Wilson Allen, *Waldo Emerson: A Biography* (New York: Viking Press, 1981), cited hereafter as Allen, and Joel Porte, *Representative Man: Ralph Waldo Emerson in His Time* (New York: Oxford University Press, 1979); cited hereafter as Porte. For a different view of Emerson and the problem of identity, see Porte, p. 323. Allen's massive and detailed biography has far more narrative energy and point than Ralph L. Rusk's *Life of Ralph Waldo Emerson* (New York: Columbia University Press, 1949), cited hereafter as Rusk. Both works, like previous studies, deal with Emerson's early years only briefly.

IN ALL of this, it gradually became clear that Emerson was not eager to be known. In some areas he deliberately drew what he himself called "a suspicious silver veil" of silence, "only concealing what is best not shewn." In others he was either too distant from the topic when he did write about it, or still too close for his perspective to be reliable. The result was that over much that was most formative in his early years one finds a smokescreen created of mixed impulses, in part family piety and mythologizing, in part the distancing distortions of humorous defense, Victorian propriety, and the simple urge for privacy. He did not lie—far from it. His attempts to assess himself honestly are frequent and painful. But he probably felt, as his era did, that there was little of interest in one's early years, and that his juvenile thoughts could be of no interest to others and were best left rooted in the past.

In intellectual matters, as distinct from personal ones, "smokescreen" is not an appropriate term, for it implies a deliberate choice that we may grant on grounds of privacy, but must question in matters of belief. What we are dealing with is a subtle and profound process, difficult to render in language. Emerson in my view was the first American thinker both to have the courage and finesse to recognize that he was facing an insoluble conflict, born as he was precisely at the time of the shattering of old beliefs, and to be able to accept that he could not force a new shape upon a patched-up creed. If "transcendence" has any meaning, if it can be agreed that one may profitably pass beyond fundamental conflict without resolving it by recognizing that another ground must be occupied, then the word is embodied in Emerson's development.[10]

The struggle of his life taught him not to deny uncertainty, but to gather the moral strength to live with it. The art of life became, in his own words, the act of skating on thin ice. This is a dark vision, but not a desperate one. I would stress that it is the opposite of hypocrisy, which assumes certain knowledge, concealed for self-interested reasons. "Sight is the last thing to be pitied," Emerson wrote; the tragedy that no one saw more clearly than he was that knowledge of spiritual truth could no longer claim evidentiary support. His intellectual career, on the contrary, was defined by his determination to demonstrate the irrelevance of claims for evidence, to lay bare the autonomous, unsupported nature of Immanence.

The work of tracing the relationship among his varied and puz-

---

[10] For the best discussion of why transcendence is an impossibility, see the Marxist study by Carolyn Porter, *Seeing and Being: The Plight of the Participant Observer in Emerson, James, Adams, and Faulkner* (Wesleyan, Conn.: Wesleyan University Press, 1981), pp. 91–118, cited hereafter as C. Porter.

zling stances was complicated. The anomalies were not transparent, the connections not self-evident. My work became in considerable measure the disentangling of these rewoven threads. Gradually it became clear that whatever Emerson had pronounced from his mature position as American sage, the outgrown selves that had suffered and endured had significantly affected his final—and often ambiguous—message. I found myself writing the history of the making of an American prophet. For it became evident that in some way where there had been silence, there would be prophetic utterance; where there had been emptiness, there would be a prodigal "Enchanter," able through magical will to fill the void with his vision. Where there had been death, there would be "a Magician of Might from the Dead Sea-Shore." It is emblematic of Emerson's early vision that he was capable of re-encoding the letters of the word "funeral" into "real fun." Whatever he had made of himself, it was clear he had done so by crossing borders (or "abysses," to use one of his favored words) that more often remain inviolate, while retaining a distance, or space around himself where others experience intimacy. The process by which he learned to occupy that space became my subject.

His achievement began when he recognized that something or some things essential to life were missing, accepted this as his starting point, and made of his isolation a useable freedom. Accident and personal tragedy led to struggle, but struggle made him an expert in the shaping of such freedom.

"Do not require a description of the countries towards which you sail," he urges, "tomorrow you will arrive there and know them by inhabiting them."[11] If Emerson was a prophet, it was not of certainty but of flux; he uttered his vision not from Mount Sinai, but from the surface of a vast ocean, at once unstable, placental, and serene, where a single soul could feel itself the balance and measure of infinite understanding: "As a soul is connected to the womb of its mother by a cord from the navel, so . . . is man connected to God . . . it is like the hydrostatic paradox . . . the Ocean against a hairline of water, God against a human soul."[12] Emerson's prophetic vision places itself at this umbilical moment, a point precedent to birth, to sexual differentiation, and to speech itself; in that station, where borders are both permeable and intact, and ontology is paradox, the doors of perception are open.

[11] "The Over-Soul," in *The Complete Works of Ralph Waldo Emerson*, ed. Edward W. Emerson, 12 vols. (Cambridge, Mass.: Houghton Mifflin, 1903–04), 2:283, cited hereafter as *CW*.

[12] *JMN*, 3:139.

Chapter 1

PARENTS

"Am happy in Boston."

—William Emerson
manuscript journal, 1799

THE FAMILY into which Ralph Waldo Emerson was born on May 25, 1803, probably seemed a model of prudence, propriety, and good feeling to his father's parishioners. For four years William Emerson had been minister of the First Church in Boston, one of the community's most important congregations socially and politically, and he was filling the pulpit of America's oldest church with success. He was a handsome, graceful man, polished in manner, interested in literature, and soon to be cofounder or sponsor of several philanthropic societies and of America's earliest literary journal. Later, a sister of one of Ralph's classmates recalled the elegance of William's black silk-stockinged leg, deliberately displayed, she thought, as he "placed one ankle on the other knee, for that showed his leg to best advantage," during a social call. He carried a gold-headed cane. With his own poll topped by "thick, smooth, and very fine and shining hair," he had "much more than his share of personal attractions."[1]

He and his wife entertained on a fairly grand scale. There was regularly company for dinner after the "Thursday lecture" when the country clergymen came to town for that traditional gathering, and Ruth Emerson arranged a reception as well every Sunday evening for the deacons and other church members at which wine and spirits were both served. During Election Week in late May there might

[1] Ellen Tucker Emerson, "What I Can Remember About Father," cited hereafter as "What." All manuscripts in the Ralph Waldo Emerson Memorial Association archives, Houghton Library, Harvard University, will be cited hereafter as HMS. Arthur B. Ellis, *History of the First Church in Boston: 1630–1880* (Boston: Hall & Whiting, 1881), p. 230 (cited hereafter as Ellis), quoting Charles Lowell's letter to William B. Sprague, *Annals of the American Pulpit* (New York, 1859–73), 8:244–45.

be twelve ministers to breakfast.[2] His father, the William Emerson who had been minister at Concord, had also been of a sociable temper, but he had spent much of his professional life embroiled in conflicts with his divided and politicized flock.[3] This William Emerson made it a point to get on well with all around him.

Born in 1769, a time of tumult before the outbreak of the Revolution, and bereaved by the wartime death in 1776 of his father, William Emerson nevertheless had made his way into the family profession in which five generations of ancestors had served. No doubt he was helped in this by the fact that his mother remarried in 1780, when she was thirty-nine. Her husband's successor in the pulpit was also successor to the widow. Thus the eleven-year-old William was raised as the son of Ezra Ripley, who was twenty-nine when he became Phebe Emerson's second husband.[4]

Graduating from Harvard College in 1789, William first kept school in Roxbury, where he taught both boys and girls in separate schools. A lively interest in the opposite sex may be adduced from the frequent references in his journals to social calls on a long list of ladies, young and old. He also began to compose a series of formal letters of the improving sort addressed to "young misses," as he called them, calculated to turn their minds away from "forwardness" and toward modesty and deference to the stronger sex.

In 1791 he went to serve as minister in the little village of Harvard, a prettily sited but poor and remote hamlet many miles northwest of Boston, where he worked hard for years while languishing inwardly.[5] "UNHAPPY" the ambitious cleric wrote more than once in his journal during those years. He was lonely, "his spirit did not close with" his flock—the village objected, for example, when he introduced the bass viol into church services and voted down its use in 1797. Intellectually he felt stultified: "I am sometimes a broken-

---

[2] David Greene Haskins, *Ralph Waldo Emerson: His Maternal Ancestors With Some Reminiscences of Him* (Boston: Cupples, Upham & Co., 1887; reprint, New York: Kennikat Press, 1971), pp. 59–60; cited hereafter as Haskins.

[3] Robert Gross, *The Minute Men and Their World* (New York: Hill and Wang, 1978), pp. 21–29.

[4] Phebe Bliss Emerson (1741–1825), married William Emerson in 1766 and married Ezra Ripley (1751–1841) on Nov. 16, 1780 (*JMN* 3:386, 353). They had three children: a daughter, Sarah, and two sons, Daniel and Samuel, the latter and oldest born in 1783. This Samuel was the uncle who later employed the Emerson boys as ushers in his Waltham school. See Kenneth W. Cameron, "Emerson on His Father and Step-Grandfather," *Emerson Society Quarterly* 6 (1957): 17.

[5] Ellis, p. 225; WE, HMS.

hearted and unhappy man," he confided in his journal in January
1799.[6]

It is easy to see him through the nineteenth-century lenses of local
historians, but it is misleading. In a closed and bigoted community—which in a previous generation had stoned and driven away
a community of Shakers—William Emerson with some courage
asked his congregation to "abolish the custom of making public confessions for the sin of fornication in particular"—a custom that must
have filled the church without fail. But they hung onto this privilege,
as they opposed everything else he suggested, including his attempt
to end the appointment of "elders in the church for the purpose of
giving admonition." The village thought William Emerson "proud"
and snobbish; he must have found them ignorant. There was no
room for privacy in the "communitarian" values of these Old Light
Calvinists. When he left them, there was no pretence of good fellowship. He made sure that his written admonition to them was part of
the church record, as he warned them against their tendency to give
way to "*every wind of doctrine*" blown by "the sectary and the enthusiast." The real issue, however, was the same ideological split between the party of the past and the party of the future that was to
widen in the next century until his son saw his career cracked apart
by its crisis.[7]

The call to the First Church in Boston when it finally came later
that year—based at least in part on his literary gifts—must have
seemed a precious opportunity to which he must assiduously fit himself.[8] He named his first son John Clarke, after the last incumbent,

    [6] WE, HMS; Ellis, p. 225. Ellis, pp. 216–19, also discusses the opposition to instru-
mental music in churches that sprang up at the end of the eighteenth century. It became
a classic bone of contention between the more and less progressive parties. Ellis is less
than candid when he says that William Emerson stopped playing the bass-viol out of a
sense of appropriateness. The old-fashioned wanted no instrumental music, only plain-
song. In the more worldly First Church of Boston, Emerson's predecessor John Clarke
had first rented a harmonium and later bought one for the church. Leonard Woods, however, the rigidly neo-orthodox but intellectual professor at Andover, not only permitted
music but lectured publicly on its benefits; see his *Discourse On Sacred Music* (Salem:
Joshua Cushing, 1804). See also Robert Handy, *A Christian America: Protestant Hopes
and Historical Realities* (New York: Oxford University Press, 1971), p. 95.
    [7] See Henry S. Nourse, *History of the Town of Harvard: Massachusetts: 1792–1893*
(Harvard, Mass.: Warren Hapgood, 1894); "A Book of Church Records Belonging to the
Church of Harvard [1733–1822]," manuscript in the town hall, Harvard, Mass. Emphasis is William Emerson's; I have not added emphasis to any quotations in this work.
    [8] Nathaniel Thayer, who presided when Emerson was ordained, told him that "the
general and reasonable expectation is, that you will support brilliancy of literary and pro-

and named another Charles Chauncy after his penultimate predecessor. Chauncy had been a redoubtable opponent of Jonathan Edwards during the ideological battles of the eighteenth century, and one toward whom Emerson felt a "veneration almost unbounded," according to his friend and colleague, J. S. Buckminster.⁹ The portraits of each divine hung in fact over the sideboard of the Emerson house as well, so to speak, as over his opinions, for all had expounded the Arminian doctrine adapted to the upper-class Boston merchants who comprised his flock. God was a loving rather than a distant or awful father. Salvation was gained by good works and civic concern in this world as well as by grace. Minimal personal enthusiasm in religious expression was regarded as more sincere. Loyalty to established forms and resistance to democratizing measures in church and public polity were encouraged.¹⁰

Almost as soon as he had left Harvard and settled in at the First Church, he seems to have known he had achieved his life's ambition. "Am happy in Boston," he wrote at last in the fall of 1799. This Emerson's reach and grasp were well balanced. As a young minister, he had prayed repeatedly that he might learn "order"; it was precisely for his order and method that he was praised on his death.¹¹

At the height of his powers, he seemed to embody the successful Arminian. Caution, prudence, and rationality should order one's life. The good Christian led an exemplary existence, but not an ascetic one. William Emerson did not eschew worldly pleasure or worldly pride, but wanted to stand well in the opinion of other men. His struggles while still in his first parish had not been to subdue the flesh or humble the spirit, but to learn the plain lessons of social existence that would help him gain respect and status. "Am I doomed never to be prudent?" he had written in his diary. "Why can I not assume those airs of gravity and wisdom, which render sage so many fools? For the future I will be more discrete. Let others talk; I will act. Let others declaim, I will write." When young he vowed

fessional character" (*A Sermon Preached at the Installation of Reverend William Emerson* [Boston, 1811], p. 17).

⁹ Joseph Stephens Buckminster, *A Sermon Delivered at the Interment of the Reverend William Emerson* (Boston, 1811), p. 10; cited hereafter as Buckminster.

¹⁰ Haskins, p. 64; Ellis, chaps. 5, 6; Alan E. Heimert, *Religion and the American Mind: From the Great Awakening to the Revolution* (Cambridge, Mass., Harvard University Press, 1966), pp. 16–21, cited hereafter as Heimert; Sydney E. Ahlstrom, *A Religious History of the American People* (New Haven, Conn.: Yale University Press, 1972), p. 400, cited hereafter as Ahlstrom.

¹¹ Buckminster, pp. 9–10.

repeatedly to give up laughing and decried his unministerial liveliness, his tendency to be idle, distracted, and indecorous.[12]

Gravity overtook him fairly rapidly, however, after his marriage, and once in Boston his intelligence and naturally sociable disposition won for him the professional and social standing in Boston's highest society that he had desired. By the time Ralph was born in 1803, after only three years in the city, William was chaplain to the Senate, as well as editor of *The Monthly Anthology* (forerunner of the *North American Review*), a friend of the governor, and on the boards of many new societies established to promote learning. He also became a member of Harvard's Board of Overseers. Upper-class Boston society at that time was still close to the English model and could have had few more prizes to offer him. An "aristocratic" exclusiveness and stress on family descent were the norm, and masters did not mingle even in church with those whom Oliver Wendell Holmes later airily referred to as "the dwellers in the culinary studio" and "children of Israel in bondage." At the First Church, "a gallery ran round three sides of the church [and] this part of the house was occupied by the nicer class of domestics." The less "nice" (probably a euphemism for African-American) domestics presumably worshipped elsewhere. To be termed a "democrat" was a reproach.[13]

The writings of his Boston period suggest that William Emerson may have paid for growing prudence with a narrowing of sympathy. As minister of Boston's First Church—which was literally the oldest church in Boston and therefore in the country—he was conscious of its dignity and undertook to write its history. His comments on Charles Chauncy in that study show not only the "almost unbounded . . . veneration" J. S. Buckminster noted, but also hostile feelings toward evangelical religion, whose ministers appealed, he held, with loose incoherence to their listeners' sensuality. He felt distaste for evangelical emotionality and eventually for democracy as well.[14]

Asked to give Boston's Fourth of July oration in 1802, he told the city that the Revolution, glorious as it was, had been fought to defend property as well as other liberties, and predicted that the country's present drunkenness of spirit would worsen if America followed France's revolution into atheism and license. Similarly, in a

[12] WE, 1795, HMS.

[13] Oliver Wendell Holmes, *Ralph Waldo Emerson* (Boston: Houghton, Mifflin, 1885), p. 35, cited hereafter as Holmes; Ellis, p. 239.

[14] *An Historical Sketch of the First Church in Boston, From Its Formation to the Present Period* (Boston: Munroe & Francis, 1812).

sermon to celebrate a charity called the Boston Female Asylum, he sought to help it not by making his audience think of the orphans actually sitting among them, but by assuring his wealthy listeners that the little girls would be educated only enough to read their Bibles; they would not become enemies of social privilege:

> If you have not blessed them with learning, you have . . . raised them above invincible ignorance. . . . Did you entertain the romantick notion of instituting an order of females in the community with new privileges, or even of conferring gentility on these children who are destined to service, you might with reason accuse us of disturbing the wholesome arrangements of society. But we are not infected with a rage for modern innovation.[15]

("Romantick" was a pejorative word for William Emerson, especially as applied to new privileges for females. When on the other hand he wished to honor the Revolution's leaders, he said "they entertained no romantick notions."[16])

It is useful to compare William's sermon to that of Samuel Stillman, who had preached to the same audience for the same purpose a few years previously. Rather than stressing class distinctions, Stillman had praised the charity for providing care that—he reminded his audience—they, dying without property, might wish should exist for their own children.[17] William Emerson and his family were much closer to that eventuality, for he did so die, leaving almost destitute seven persons who were to depend partly on charity. Emerson forgot too that his own sister Mary had been in a position similar to that of the orphaned or impoverished girls whom he described as "destined to service." Nowhere, unfortunately, does his language suggest consciousness of such mortality.

William Emerson lacked the gift of imaginative compassion; writings like these give credence to his son's memory of him as a "severe" father. But he was not harsh; he believed, in fact, that "the great defect of my nature," as he wrote to his sister, "is a certain milkiness of disposition that incapacitates me from doing my duty inflexi-

[15] William Emerson, *A Discourse Delivered Before the Members of the Boston Female Asylum, September 20, 1805: Being Their Fifth Anniversary* (Boston: Russell and Cutler, 1805), pp. 7–16.

[16] *An Oration Pronounced July 5, 1802 At the Request of the Town of Boston In Commemoration of the Anniversary of American Independence* (Boston, 1802), p. 6.

[17] Samuel Stillman, *A Discourse Delivered Before the Members of the Boston Female Asylum, Friday, Sept. 25, 1801.*

bly."[18] He filled admirably the station to which it had pleased God to call him, his pleasure in so filling it being reflected in the harmony of the life he created around himself.

His wife, Ruth Haskins Emerson, born a year before her husband in 1768, was crucial to the quality of that life. She was the daughter of John Haskins, a self-made man who had gone from barrel making to distilling, producing his rum from molasses that had most likely crossed the sea in casks of his own manufacture. He occupied, that is, at least two legs of the so-called triangle between New England, the West Indies, and Africa on which many local fortunes were founded. Consistent with the customs of the elite merchant class of Boston, he owned a slave. Politically a Royalist, religiously an Anglican, he was known for both probity and formalism, but he lost much of his wealth after the Revolution, having supported at first the wrong side. Ruth, a middle daughter among sixteen offspring, shared her father's diligent temperament and chose his post-Revolutionary Episcopalianism, though she adopted her husband's faith after marriage.[19]

Ruth Haskins Emerson was a less colorful character than her husband when she married at the age of twenty-eight, but the comments of her contemporaries strike a consistent note in praising her prudent, self-controlled, and religious nature. She had long been a friend of William's sister Mary, who had first noticed her as a stranger worshiping in church one Sunday with "fervent Calvinistic piety." Ruth was then seventeen, Mary three years younger. "She conversed on religion from the heart," Mary wrote nearly thirty years later, "and I loved every accent." When William sounded his sister for information about her circle of women acquaintances, Mary had eagerly urged the match with Ruth.[20]

They married in 1796. William had previously courted several young women, including the "amiable . . . beautiful [and] faultless" Priscilla Burr, who in 1790 had "charmed with goodness" the young man of twenty-one. And less than a month before his engagement to Ruth, he had visited a Miss Doubleday, "in whose society I

[18] WE to MME, 1806, HMS.

[19] William Ellery Channing, the austere and highminded "Bishop" of Unitarianism, suffered obloquy when opponents objected that his family fortunes grew out of the distillery and slave trades. See Elizabeth Palmer Peabody, *Reminiscences Of Rev. William Ellery Channing* (Boston: Roberts Bros., 1880), p. 360; Haskins, pp. 3–38.

[20] MME to RWE, 1826, HMS; MME to WE, 1795, HMS.

was happy," he wrote. Nevertheless, three weeks later he and Ruth Haskins were engaged, and in four months they were married. It is unlikely that Ruth had seemed equally alluring, but it is possible that she had brought with her as dowry a loan of two thousand dollars, for with its sudden and unexplained accession William Emerson bought the farm on which they settled. Mary had attested that the informal demand for a marriage settlement was still customary when she had written William some years earlier that in her circle none of the girls was courted because it was "an undoubted fact that with regard to the gentlemen the great question is, is there money?" At any rate, they began life with a debt of approximately two thousand dollars.[21]

But if theirs was not a romantic match, he intended it to be a good one. His first surviving letter to her spoke not of love, but of his desire for a true friendship, based on choice, made by congenial minds and lasting eternally. His wish for a time at least was granted, although the tragic sicknesses that ended his life early and the busy existence of a Boston minister may toward the end have caused some emotional distance between them. Ruth, less articulate than he, summed up her feelings accurately in her frequent formulaic address. He was her "dearest earthly friend."[22]

She kept careful records of expenses for the first few years of their marriage, and the surviving account book reveals a good deal about her. Living in the village of Harvard, the young couple found themselves some sixty-five dollars in debt at the end of their first quarter. They began to farm in earnest in 1797, and Ruth, although city-bred, evidently did a good deal of the significant work. The farm provided them not only with food but with cash—from the sale of milk and the butter Ruth churned and from the boarders she took even in this, the first year of her married life. Boarding alone brought in almost a hundred and fifty dollars. The total of farm produce was worth over three hundred dollars. If much of these sums proceeded from Ruth's own work, as no doubt it did, then her labor provided a significant portion of the family's income as well as the food they

[21] It was normal for country clergymen to be farmers and probably impossible for them to raise a family otherwise. William purchased the farm for $2260 only a week before he formally proposed marriage to Ruth, whom he had known for at least a year. Since there were no known connections likely to provide such a sum to him, it is conceivable that John Haskins himself advanced the mortgage to his prospective son-in-law; WE and MME, 1790, 1795–96, HMS.

[22] WE to RE, 1796, HMS.

ate.[23] Understanding this, one grasps more easily why there was at the back of William's account book a separate section recording loans of small sums from "Mrs. E. to Mr. E." and vice versa. Since both generated income, William Emerson and the businesslike daughter of John Haskins had, as it were, separate accounts.

In the first year of their marriage they lost only eleven dollars, which is to say they lived within their income. How large the household was at any one time is uncertain, for in addition to the few boarders, Ruth's or William's sisters might be visiting, and there was at least one servant. One of the curiosities of this account book is the information it provides about the consumption of alcoholic spirits, then drunk without prejudice by clergy and laity alike. There is no reference in it to the ubiquitous but plebian potion metheglin, then still common in New England. But the parson and his wife tapped a barrel of cider every six to eight weeks and in one quarter purchased a combined total of over ten gallons of rum and brandy, while of wine they secured four gallons. These, with some additional gallons in gifts, or "benefactions," probably provided for the entire year's needs. In addition, they bought among other things sugar, flour, beef, coffee, tea, and chocolate. They fattened their own hogs and no doubt cured or smoked them, so that pork and beef as well as vegetables, eggs, and dairy products appeared on their table largely through the work of their own hands. William's salary had not risen, although he now had dependents, and expenses increased with inflation. He complained often in his diary of their poverty during the early years of marriage.

After what appears to have been a miscarriage in 1797, Ruth gave birth to their daughter Phebe in 1798. The couple seems to have been fond of each other, at least in the early years of their marriage. This is evident in a detailed and affectionate letter William wrote while she was away on a visit; since she had gone, he wrote, no one had sung at church without her. He had realized that she was "the soul of the family, if not to the parish," and while watching the moon set he had wanted to share with her the "pleasing melancholy of the scene."[24]

Ruth was reluctant to move from Harvard when William was called to the First Church in Boston, but she knew that it would

[23] Farm women, but not necessarily ministers' wives, earned money by dairying. See Sarah Anna Emery, *Reminiscences of a Nonagenerian* (Newburyport, Conn.: Wm. Huse, 1879), p. 7, cited hereafter as Emery. See also Mary Bushnell Cheney, *Life and Letters of Horace Bushnell* (New York: Harper & Bros., 1880), p. 27.

[24] WE, 1799, HMS.

advance her husband "in the profession in which he most delights." With a second pregnancy under way, the additional income would be welcome. (Phebe died from diarrhea and a canker in 1800 soon after the move.) The days of supplementing their income by farming and taking in students were over, although they served in loco parentis to at least two young girls who helped in the house, one of whom, as a boarder, also brought some income. Children began arriving in the normal quick succession, less than two years apart, and by November 1807, seven of Ruth's eight children had been born.[25]

Eight pregnancies in ten years together with the painful death of two of these children did not apparently unduly weigh her down, although it was a large household—filled with servants, relatives, and unrelated visitors or boarders—whose total number might fluctuate at around eleven or twelve.[26]

RUTH'S CAPACITY to control this busy and demanding household was undoubtedly strengthened by her devotion to the standards of the evangelical tradition in which she had been raised. Little information has been available until now about Ruth Emerson in studies of her son, whose social context is generally understood to be his father's liberal, upper-class status to which the widow valiantly clung. Ruth, however, despite the nominal Episcopalianism she had derived from her father along with his urge to follow "the turnpike road" upward to gentility, had been molded in a different tradition. Hannah Upham Haskins, Ruth's deeply Calvinistic mother, had inscribed upon her children, as Ruth was to do in turn, the disciplines characteristic of poverty and a "typical puritan family."[27] Moreover,

[25] Haskins, pp. 48, 53, 75. One gains a better idea of Ruth's physical and mental strength by considering the birthdates of the four infants, Ralph, Edward, Bulkeley, and Charles, who were born within a span of 63 months, between May 1803 and November 1807. Ruth was on average pregnant within five months after the birth of her preceding child. During these 63 months she was *not* pregnant only 15 months, a period in which she was probably lactating. For birthdates, based on the family Bible, see Ellis, p. 229.

[26] The immediate nuclear family, allowing for births and deaths, generally numbered some seven. In addition there were also present, in 1807 for example, at least one maid servant, the two additional young women not maids already mentioned, a man who came in to polish the plate and perhaps perform other services, someone to launder and or cook, and frequently at least one aunt from among the couple's numerous sisters. In that year the total number supported by the household might fluctuate at around eleven or twelve. Ruth did not herself act as laundress, of course, but she insisted in classic fashion on personally ironing her husband's ministerial lawn bands. (Haskins, pp. 3–38, 54.)

[27] Haskins, pp. 28, 30, 31, 33–34.

Ruth's influence in these matters was unusually great because of her husband's early death.

Recent research on this tradition sheds useful light on Ruth's childrearing practices, which might otherwise today seem incomprehensible or harsh. Their aim, however, was to instill the kernel of Calvinism in its most fundamental, preverbal form.[28] Philip Greven has sketched a model of the evangelical mother, differentiating her from two other contemporary types, the "genteel" and the merely "moderate" parent. Such a mother was guided by the underlying Calvinistic ethos that, seeing children as innately sinful, conceived it the parents' duty to break their children's wills and curb their appetites at the earliest possible opportunity in order to render the young humble, open to grace, and conscious of sin. They must endow them, in short, with active and all-controlling consciences at the earliest possible age.

It might be painful for a young mother to whip a nine-month-old child, for example, but Jonathan Edwards's daughter boasted that she had done so, "on *Old Adam's* account," for it was unquestionably her duty, even though achieving docile obedience without physical force was the ultimate aim and chief glory of such a mother. (Children's crying was regarded as especially obnoxious and subject to discipline.) Habits of eating, sleeping, and dressing were under strict parental control. In the model family of this tradition, children like those of Susanna Wesley, John Wesley's mother, who wrote explicitly on the subject, were fed very little. If they asked the servants between meals for additional food they might be whipped. Clothing was rigorously plain, and a "regular method of living"—dressing, undressing, changing of linen—was followed. Through unrelenting application of such external controls, children were to be rendered pliable and the household at least superficially untroubled, the children being governable by only a quiet word while they showed a "mild tender treatment of each other."[29]

Ruth Emerson seems to have attempted to live out this ideal in virtually paradigmatic fashion, becoming known as "the best of mothers" through her rigorous consistency and self-control. An unusually detailed record of Ruth's regime is the account of Mary Russell Bradford, who as an orphaned adolescent and the ward of William Emerson lived with the Emersons for five or six years. Her

[28] Philip Greven, *The Protestant Temperament: Patterns of Child-Rearing, Religious Experience, and the Self in Early America* (New York: New American Library, 1979), parts 1–2; cited hereafter as Greven.

[29] Ibid., pp. 32ff., 35–36, 37, 44, 47.

language, while eulogizing Ruth as a "lovely woman, very superior and very religious," is tinged even eighty years later with defensive dismay at the rigor of some of the practices she describes.[30]

Ruth rarely showed affection, and never annoyance, but was a firm, even strict disciplinarian. (This usually meant a willingness to use corporal punishment.) She found time no matter how busy to retire to her room every morning after breakfast to read and meditate. Diligent in the physical care of her children, she was quite conscious of appearances, and a major theme in her correspondence was the state of their clothing. Yet even in her relative affluence when they were young, she dressed them with puritanical plainness day and night in the same yellow flannel that the young Mary felt "was not pretty enough."[31]

Her repression of direct gestures of love is evident in the rather tragic correspondence concerning her oldest son, John Clarke, who at the age of five was sent away to live in Maine with Ruth's sister-in-law, Mrs. Lincoln Ripley. No contemporary explanation is given of John's departure, but informal arrangements were often made in that period within families and sometimes with strangers for children to be sent elsewhere to live for a variety of reasons, from overcrowding at home to economic or temperamental needs.[32] Since John had also had trouble with his eyes when he had earlier gone to stay with his grandparents in Concord for the "purer air," and since he returned from Maine very ill with the tuberculosis that was to kill him by the time he was seven, the most likely motive for his extended journey was his health.[33]

There is no question about Ruth's love for her son, or her pleasure in describing the affection expressed among the brothers when little John finally returned. But her ethos stressed teaching the priority of obedience over love, and she gave or withheld that love according not only to his behavior, but even to his imputed misbehavior. Thus in her first letter, not written until some two weeks after his departure and not received of course until later, she sends him her love through her sister-in-law, whom she instructs, "tell him I only wait to hear from you that he is a good boy, and then I shall write him a letter as I promised him." At another time she praises Mrs. Ripley, saying she is "delighted" that the other had withheld his books in

[30] Haskins, pp. 53–55.

[31] Ibid., pp. 56, 55.

[32] Joseph Kett, "The Stages of Life," in *Rites of Passage: Adolescence in America, 1790 to the Present* (New York: Basic Books, 1977).

[33] WE to MME, 1807, HMS.

punishment. "Teach him generosity and beneficence . . . [do not] inform us of the articles you cause him to give, but make him give, of those things he values most, till he derives pleasure from bestowing." She is glad in April that he is "so hardy as to play without mittens."[34]

Food was a particular source of anxiety in that household, for "what one ate [and] how much one ate . . . mattered profoundly to evangelical parents" whose duty was to harden their children; as the seventeenth-century divine John Robinson had written, "from the first to such a meanness in all things, as may rather pluck them down, than lift them up. . . ." Greven has shown how in Susanna Wesley's household the children were treated differently in terms of diet from the adults, "and never permitted to eat of more than one thing [at a meal] and of that sparingly."[35]

Similarly, in the Emerson home the adults—who presumably had already been adequately schooled in self-denial—might have their regular, formal winings and dinings. These were sufficiently splendid so that Mary Moody Emerson reproached Ruth in later years for the formality and graces of her table, her care for her silver, and her desire to "appear genteel."[36] And the family might attend Ruth's parents' weekly teas, at which in winter the hot alcoholic sangaree was passed in a silver tankard. But the children were kept on short rations. Thus, although Ruth wrote repeatedly of the clothes she was sending to John in Maine, there was only one reference to a personal gift to him—"a few sugarplums," sent four months after his departure. He was to eat what her children ate at home, a "milk-diet," which consisted of bread and milk two meals a day, with coffee or chocolate sometimes substituted for the milk, and a meal of broth or meat not more than once a day.[37] When Ruth's relatives came on Mondays for tea, she served them only tea, bread and butter sandwiches, and a basket of cake. Privately among the Emersons, the breakfast bread was unbuttered.

"This has a simple sound," Mary Bradford wrote in her old age, "but we see the wisdom of Mrs. Emerson as well as economy." They had "good dinners," she noted, and described as "aristocratic" the

---

[34] Haskins, pp. 72, 74–75.

[35] Greven, pp. 42–44.

[36] MME to RE, 1813, HMS.

[37] Haskins, pp. 60–61, 73, 71; James Thacher, M.D., *American Modern Practice: Or, a Simple Method of Prevention and Cure of Diseases* . . . (Boston: E. Read, 1817), pp. 436ff.

"salt-fish dinner" of Saturday nights "with all its belongings of vegetables, melted butter, pork scraps, etc."[38]

"Simple" understates Mrs. Emerson's repressiveness in matters of food and eating. The only extant letter of reproach Ruth ever wrote to any of her sons was penned to the fourteen-year-old William the night after she had received his first letter from college. In it he had dwelt on the ampleness of Harvard's welcoming roast beef dinner. Ruth told him sharply to put his mind on higher things and forget about his "accommodations"—until one consults William's manuscript, the reader assumes that Ruth is referring to furniture. She could not bring herself, it appears, in this context to use the simpler Anglo-Saxon word for food.[39]

THESE ATTITUDES were not universal, but were matters of cultural and personal choice. Contrasting childhood memories of abundant and delicious food may be found in contemporary memoirs from both "genteel" and rural populations.[40]

An ironic perspective, in fact, is gained by comparing what the Emerson children were fed with the menu of the inmates of the Boston Female Asylum—the very charity that their father had praised for its low aims. It had been founded in 1803 by wealthy women to train girls in the domestic arts so that they could work as indentured servants, often in the homes of the same women. (Ruth Emerson, in fact, employed one such girl, Mary Anne McFarlane, who lived with her for some years.) The orphans seem actually to have had a diet that was somewhat more varied than that of the Emerson boys, for at least officially the girls' bread was alternated with hasty pudding, rice and molasses, and other forms of carbohydrates. The girls had

[38] Haskins, pp. 58–59.

[39] RE to WEjr, 1814, HMS. Edward W. Emerson made that assumption, writing that "William had evidently given an account of his new room." *Emerson in Concord: A Memoir* (Boston: Houghton, Mifflin, 1889), p. 21; cited hereafter as *EIC*.

[40] In a "genteel" family a girl of twelve or thirteen might write to her mother describing an all-girls' party at which "our treat was nuts, raisins, cakes, wine, punch hot and cold all in great plenty. No rudeness Mamma I assure you." See Alice Morse Earle, *Customs and Fashions in Old New England* (New York: Scribner's, 1893; reprint, Detroit: Singing Tree Press, 1969), p. 22.

In a farm family of easygoing Old Light country Calvinists (who belonged to the parish that the neo-orthodox Leonard Woods found too permissive about infant baptism when he took it over), childhood memories might include an abundance of roasting turkeys, nuts, and apples eaten before the fire at night, and breakfasts of meat and potatoes. See Emery, pp. 7–9, 12–13, 28–29.

butter on their bread at least once a day, although no more meat and vegetables than the Emerson children. But the asylum was run by genteel and wealthy ladies who were more frightened of democracy than of healthy appetites.[41]

METAPHORS of food and eating were to have a significant place in Emerson's language in later years.[42] In this process of prohibition and denial his father as well as his mother became involved. When Ralph was born in May 1803, William was out attending a dinner given by Governor Strong during the afternoon. His diary mentions Ruth's health but contains no reference to any feelings of his own, only the facts of the birth and the note that after receiving the news he left again to spend the evening as usual at his club. He was now part of Boston's highest social circle, and saw no reason to stay home. An inference of apparent indifference to Ralph's arrival is not unwarranted. As a father, William Emerson seems to have been not untypical for his day, though perhaps somewhat less interested in Ralph, his third son, and the result of Ruth's fifth pregnancy, than in the previous children. Because Ralph's memories of his father were largely negative, and because he never really established warm or useful relations with any other older man, some focus on the facts here is relevant.

From the beginning he seems to have been a hungry child, probably weaned early, for Ruth was pregnant again nine months later. He sucked his thumb. This was unacceptable behavior; consequently, "his mother made a mitten to his nightdress." Evidence of unmet hunger and dependency needs was unacceptable even in an infant in this household. The object of desire had to be veiled and made unpalatable so that even in sleep the infant could not be gratified.[43]

[41] I am indebted to Susan Porter for sharing with me her paper on the Boston Female Asylum, "Mother/Mistress, Servant/Child: The Orphan as Indentured Servant in the Early Victorian Family," delivered at the Berkshire Conference on the History of Women, August, 1978, and for personal communication on the subject. For the menu of the Asylum discovered by Dr. Porter, see *An Account of the Rise, Progress, etc. of the Boston Female Asylum with Rules and Regulations* (Boston, 1810), p. 25.

[42] Evelyn Barish Greenberger, "The Phoenix on the Wall: Consciousness in Emerson's Early and Late Journals," *American Transcendental Quarterly* 21 (Winter 1974): 47–49, 51–52, cited hereafter as Evelyn Barish Greenberger, "Phoenix." See also Taylor Stoehr, "Food for Thought," in *Nay-Saying in Concord: Emerson, Alcott, and Thoreau* (Hamden, Conn.: Archon Books, 1979), pp. 117–142.

[43] Haskins, p. 55.

Food, in fact, and eating seem to have become a crux and symbol of his feeling deprived and unloved. In the memoir written by his daughter, most of Ralph's early memories are negative, three of the five relating to embarrassment caused by hunger or eating. In one story, he tried to buy some long-hoped-for gingerbread, only to discover it took all his money, causing him to burst into tears, and the baker to relent. In another, "at a children's party when the cake was passed, he heard one of the children say, 'Ralph's got two pieces.' " And in a third, he maladroitly refused some wine offered by an adult because he was " 'not thirsty.' " The experiences are trivial; what makes them significant is their importance to him at the time, so great that they predominated in his memory even in his forties or fifties, still the subject of thought, joking, and perhaps an anxiety he needed to share with his own children.[44]

As he grew older, the pattern extended itself. Several anecdotes suggest this, one the well-known story he told his son of having once wandered away from home with his brothers for an unexpectedly long period. On their return, Ruth greeted them saying, "My sons, I have been in an agony for you." " 'I went to bed,' he said, 'in bliss at the interest she showed.' "[45] He remembered the episode because he had not realized before that she cared. Later in his sermons he often asked parents to demand less propriety and order from their offspring. The loss of money meant to buy shoes and his mother's serious anger, the breaking of a salver, the spoiling of a carpet, the tearing of a coat—these childish transgressions and a heavy sense of rejection and punishment for them figure intermittently both in his own memories and in the remarks he addressed to parents. Ruth's defenses were limited to stoicism and denial, and her peculiarly sensitive middle son must have early perceived the pattern. As a young adult he wrote to his brother William ironically that he must "learn like mother to call evil good." Such repression must have been confusing, even depressing to the growing boy.[46]

His habits displeased not only his mother, but also his father, who was critical of Ralph. The mitten had not done its work (although it probably planted the seeds of Emerson's later ambivalence toward food and hunger), and when William's letters refer to Ralph, they anticipate and reprove this failing. Writing on Ralph's second birthday, William noted that he might be kissed but also "reminded that

[44] "What," HMS.
[45] James Elliot Cabot, *A Memoir of Ralph Waldo Emerson*, 2 vols. (Cambridge, Mass.: Riverside Press, 1887), 1:35, cited hereafter as Cabot.
[46] RWE, Sermons, HMS. In 1829 Emerson was quoting *Isaiah*, v. 20.

papa will bring home cake for little boys who behave well at the dinner table." Not yet two when his father had departed, Ralph already was offending him by what seemed to the parent to be greed; it was never too early to manage a child's appetites. He cannot have been pleased to find that four years later the tendency had only bloomed, for when the boy was six William, who was again away on a trip, was again writing that he hoped that Ralph "regards his words, does not eat his dinner too fast, and is gradually resigning his impetuosity to younger boys." Years later, Emerson was to write "I can reason down or at least deny every thing except this perpetual belly. Feed he must & will, and I cannot make him respectable." What he knew at forty-five, he had been made to suffer for as an infant.[47]

It was normal for William in his letters to appear to be one to whom accounts were presented and faults were somehow evident even across great distances. He himself had asked his wife to "tell [him] of [his] sins. *Whom the Lord loves he chastises*." But he treated his children differentially in this matter. To his absent son John Clarke, for example, William might send a similar list of injunctions ("Avoid the company of all bad boys. Never make use of any improper language"). But he would also be sure to give this firstborn such pleasant news as the fact that "John's" cow had calved and was giving "eight quarts of milk a day."[48]

References to Ralph, however, lacked these modifications and seem from the beginning to have been distant, demanding, even denigrating. When Ralph was two and a half, William reported that Ralph "is rather a dull scholar." At not quite three, "Ralph has been sick; but is now so well as to go to school. He cannot read very well yet."[49] To read at all before the age of three is beyond the capacity of most children, but Ralph did not get much credit from his father for this accomplishment.

The connection in William's mind between what he perceived as Ralph's excessive hunger and excessive aggressiveness or "impetuosity" is borne out by more modern insights into the roots of the development of character. Long before Freud suggested that the nursing infant is also aggressively eating up his world, threatening it with annihilation and, therefore, risking retaliation, anger, and danger to himself, a man of William Emerson's generation could per-

[47] WE to RE, 1805, HMS; *JMN* 9:394.
[48] WE to JCE, 1806, HMS.
[49] WE to JCE, 1806, HMS.

ceive intuitively that the springs of self-will were related to the expression of appetite. It followed that both must be curbed early.

Under that pressure, the boy was gradually but surely formed. Emerson told his daughter Ellen only two stories about his father, but both powerfully express the still unresolved tension of their relationship. One was about suffering from a skin eruption, for which the supposed cure was salt water bathing. The tale seems a classic description of oedipal rebellion, so pure is its mythological vision of himself as Adam and his father as the avenging God. "Once," Ellen recalled:

> He said, "No, I don't remember him very well. I know the doctor had advised him to have me go into the salt water every day because I had the salt rheum and he used to take me himself to the Bath-house. I did not like it, and when in the afternoon he called me I heard his voice as the voice of the Lord God in the garden, and I hid myself and was afraid."[50]

Emerson's vision of himself as Adam, a trope often present in his writing, may have had its origin here.

AT THE HEIGHT of these conflicts, William's health failed. In 1808 while preparing for Sunday service, William was suddenly overcome by a pulmonary hemorrhage so severe that it had brought him "in an instant . . . to the gates of death." He recovered, but only temporarily, and for the next three years his life was drained by a combination of tuberculosis and the growth of an ulcerated cancer of the stomach. He endured extreme pain, traveling toward the end perhaps only for peace and quiet. He died at home in April 1811 at age forty-two. Ralph was five when William Emerson became ill, old enough that the oedipal struggle had already set in, and he was seven when his father died, with nothing resolved, no approval gained, no lessons learned. From this loss Emerson was to suffer a great deal.[51]

With William's death, the normal process of Ralph's emotional

---

[50] Webster, 1854, gives salt rheum as the popular American name for "almost all the non-febrile cutaneous eruptions which are common among adults," eczema and herpes included; see *OED*; "What," HMS.

[51] Buckminster, p. 8. Autopsy revealed that the immediate cause of death was not tuberculosis but a massive and ulcerated cancer of the stomach so large it completely obstructed the pylorus. He and Ruth must have lived in dread during the years preceding his death, knowing how short his life would be and how unlikely it was that she could provide for herself and six children.

growth was irrevocably halted. The relationship between William and Ruth had already worsened. Years later his aunt Mary—who was frank about such matters—wrote to Ralph at his request about his parents' marriage and said that William's illness had been "a lingering disease of long endurance and of a kind w'h deadened almost every affection." In addition, William traveled for his health a good deal during the last two years of his life, and these absences coupled with his increasing pain and marital discord while he was at home must have intensified Ralph's sense of conflict.[52]

In the ordinary course of events, the boy's recognition that he could not win in his rivalry with his father would have led him to turn outward toward his agemates, seeking other bonds, even while he would have gained from his father's ongoing support a sense that his own aggression and anger were acceptable and containable emotions, not likely to be repaid by the total rejection of his typological fantasy. But for Ralph, whose father had abandoned him at an age when these fantasies were at their height and before reconciliation could be effected, there was to be a double burden of guilt. For when a child loses a parent by death the child irrationally but inevitably sees this tragic loss as a punishment for his or her own misdeeds; by leaving, the parent seems to the child to have given the ultimate testimony that he or she is bad or worthless. Moreover, the missing parent, though the subject of deep interest and need, is also the focus of much anger, both for the abandonment itself and the punishment it represents. The death of a loved one is one of the most difficult experiences for any human to deal with; for a child, its effects are often deep and disforming.[53]

[52] MME to RWE, 1826, HMS.

[53] The bibliography of works dealing with the meaning of loss to a child is long. Among the most relevant are: Sigmund Freud, "Mourning and Melancholia," *Standard Edition of the Complete Psychological Works of Sigmund Freud*, trans. and ed. J. Strachey et al. (London, 1907), 14:214–58; Helene Deutsch, "Absence of Grief," *Psychoanalytic Quarterly* 6 (1937): 12–22; Robert Furman, "Death and the Young Child," *Psychoanalytic Study of the Child* 19 (1964): 321–33; Margaret Meiss, "The Oedipal Problems of a Fatherless Child," *PSC* 7 (1952): 216–29; Peter B. Neubauer, "The One-Parent Child and His Oedipal Development," *PSC* 15 (1960): 286–309; and John Bowlby, *Attachment and Loss* International Psychoanalytical Library, ed. M.S.R. Khan, no. 79 (London: Hogarth Press, 1969).

In addition to the common responses described above, "dull and apathetic reactions" and "no reactions of grief to the loss of individuals" subsequent to the first loss are also characteristic, according to Helene Deutsch, as quoted by Bowlby. The latter also points out that a splitting of the ego may occur ("Childhood Mourning and its Implications for Psychiatry," *American Journal of Psychiatry* 118 [1961]: 487).

Felix Brown stresses that "the fact that the child at the time [of the loss] shows no

Normally, however, the crippling emotions of guilt and anger are worked through during the mourning process. Mourning has always been understood to be a necessary period during which the survivors come to grips with the reality of their new condition and their complex emotions. Clinical study as well has shown the importance of grieving. What has not hitherto been noticed, however, and what seems both clear and of considerable significance for Emerson's biography, is that in his case—as occasionally happens among children—this mourning process did not occur, and his grieving was as repressed as his love for his father was thereafter. This is evident from the fact that the only other memory that Emerson passed on to Ellen about his father was of his funeral, at which he specifically noted that he had not grieved. On the contrary, he took a childish delight in the pomp of the funeral arrangements:

> Telling of his funeral, Father said it wasn't sad to him. "William and I walked as mourners behind the hearse. He was buried on the First Church's tomb in King's Chapel burying-ground. The Ancient and Honorable Artillery [a private clublike militia that had initiated William's call to that pulpit] turned out on the occasion and marched before the hearse, and as we went up School

---

obvious emotional disturbance is no evidence that he or she is not deeply affected, rather the reverse" ("Depression and Childhood Bereavement," *Journal of Mental Science* 107 [1961]: 769). Helene Deutsch points out that "the process of mourning as reaction to the real loss of a loved person *must be carried to completion*; [otherwise] the painful affect continues to flourish," but the emotional energies will take a distorted form. ("Absence of Grief," p. 21.) W. R. Keeler's "Children's Reaction to the Death of a Parent" found in a group of such bereaved children that depression was the single universal symptom, although depression in chidren is not common and is "difficult to detect"; the second most common symptom was fantasy of reunion with the dead parent. Other findings included identification with the dead parent, suicidal wishes or attempts, anxiety, guilt. (Keeler, *Depression*, ed. Paul H. Hoch and Joseph Zubin [New York: Greene & Stratton, 1954], 109–20.)

Margaret Meiss studied an anxious boy whose neurosis stemmed from the death of his father during his oedipal stage: fearing that his wish to get rid of the father had in fact produced his death, he fantasized a destructive and all-powerful God, a paternal and castrating figure ("Oedipal Problems"). Peter Neubauer holds that the absence of a father creates problems for a boy in the latency period in at least two important ways: a possible tendency to homosexuality and difficulty in forming an adequate ego ideal. "Guilt is engendered by fantasy fulfillment of oedipal wishes when the same-sexed parent dies" (here he paraphrases Fenichel 1931), and "fantasy objects, idealized or terribly sadistic, replacing an absent parent are nearly ubiquitous" ("One-Parent Child," pp. 288, 293).

The findings discussed here are only a summary: the literature on the meaning of such loss runs into hundreds of documents. On the issues mentioned above, there is no contradiction among those studies.

St. it seemed to me a grand sight." . . . He used to smile as he recalled his delight in that funeral.[54]

In what was certainly a repetition of this deep but not digested experience, Emerson as an adolescent produced the startling anagram referred to earlier: "Funeral: Real fun."[55] But one cannot today, of course, take that "delight" at face value. Without mourning, study has shown, a child experiences fantasy and inevitably a delayed reaction, usually in the late teens or early adulthood, characterized by depression, anxiety, and identification with the dead parent. Often the abandoned child still imprisoned in the adult feels a drive to reunite with the parent, as through real or fantasied suicide. Difficulties in relating to other people and the real world are common. In assessing Emerson's willingness to lead the rebellion against—or rather the withdrawal from—the religion of his forefathers, these formative experiences are relevant.

As a child, however, Ralph responded to the catastrophe of his loss by withdrawal. Accustomed to expect little attention or love from his environment, he tended to avoid interaction, concealing his talents except from his brothers' eyes. He was remembered by contemporaries from early childhood as an especially literary and good-natured child, but not a competitive one. One classmate remembered his "gentleness and forebearance" but felt he needed "a few harsher traits and perhaps more masculine vigor." From another, William Furness, who liked to draw and who in fact illustrated one of Ralph's earliest poems, Ralph apparently entirely concealed his own capacity for sketching. Although Emerson's habit of decorating his manuscripts is evident even in his childhood correspondence, he kept his drawings invisible to Furness, who wrote, "I never knew him attempt to draw anything, not even the conventional cat with the triangular face, which almost any boy or girl could do and does do."[56]

In class he was neither "prominent" nor "talkative," speaking only when he had something to say, not for effect, and with the same "courtly hesitation" in manner that marked him as an adult. The lack of aggression his peers noted in his early play was probably the result of depression, for which there is considerable evidence. In the brief manuscript of his "Autobiography" as well as in his daughter's

[54] "What," HMS.

[55] *JMN* 1:245.

[56] W. H. Furness, *Records of a Lifelong Friendship: 1807–1882: Ralph Waldo Emerson and William Henry Furness*, ed. H. H. Furness (Boston: Houghton, Mifflin, 1910), p. xv.

memoir and elsewhere, Emerson's memories of his childhood are almost unrelievedly sad in tone.[57]

His brothers were important to him, but he turned early to books and especially to writing, in which bloody fantasies, violent animals, and magic were dominant elements. By late adolescence his journals are networks of complex, even obsessive fantasies involving both death and a search for the wise man, witch, seer, or magician who will instruct the youth, as a father might have done, "how to guide his steps in life." Earlier that interest in the supernatural or magical is probably reflected in a more primitive fascination with codes—but a fascination whose expression was wittily and delicately worked out. One of his first surviving letters, written at age eleven, is in fact a rebus: long, exact in execution, its images of haystacks and inn signs hang on the page like ornaments on a fairy tale tree of gifts.[58] One of his early memories was of learning that by repeating a word it and the world around him lost all meaning.[59] In a way, the codes, anagrams, and palindromes that punctuate his adolescent correspondence testify to the same recognition that power over words and images may work both to give reality to visions and—like the "Enchanter" whom he later invented—to render the real world illusory.

IN SOME SENSE, Emerson never truly buried his father.[60] The "grand sight" of the funeral procession that he remembered masked his inability to grasp the meaning of his loss, as a variety of episodes suggests. He forgot pictures of him. Once as an adolescent he simply left behind with his younger brother Edward some pictures given him by their mother. On another occasion much later, he criticized

[57] John Lowell Gardner, quoted by Holmes, pp. 40, 39.

[58] *L*, 1:frontispiece.

[59] *EIC*, p. 14.

[60] In "Representing Grief: Emerson's 'Experience,' " Sharon Cameron discusses Emerson's "Experience," written after the death of his deeply loved first son when he found himself profoundly confused at his inability to grieve. She cites Derrida's work on the thesis of Torok and Nicolas, observing that in uncompleted mourning, the "introjected object" is "kept in a secret place [and] the consequence of [this] secrecy is a cryptic text." Such introjection leaves the object "both unavailable and invisible to the self in which it is encrypted." Carrying the point further, I would suggest that this well describes the status of the memory of William Emerson, who may be seen as the original "secret text" whose many copies his son spent a lifetime reconstructing and rereading. This essay is obviously relevant to Emerson's interest in codes, anagrams, palindromes, rebuses, etc. See Cameron's article in *Representations* 15 (Summer 1986): 39.

a print turned up by one of his friends with the remark that it did not resemble William, who had been "a *talking* man."[61]

More odd is the use he and at least one of his brothers repeatedly made of the bound volumes of his father's sermons or notebooks. In his twenties Emerson more than once tore out the contents from such a manuscript volume but kept the binding to serve as a cover for his own writings. He followed this oddly cannibalistic practice even in his old age; the editors of the eighteenth volume of the *Journals and Miscellaneous Notebooks* have pointed out that Emerson destroyed one of William's used notebooks in order to write on the remaining blank pages himself. The stubs of the torn-out pages still reveal his father's words. In a family so conscious of its ancestry, Emerson's misuse of his father's sermons must be considered seriously. Surely, he did not act on his own in dismembering these bound volumes. Had Ruth cared (as she did about every detail, for example, of their clothing), these would have been sacred in their household. Quite possibly, she gave them to him to do with as he liked. In general her silence suggests that she herself was unable to experience fully her own feelings of loss, anger, and grief. Clearly, then, she could not help her children to make real their own grief, accept their loss, and hold within themselves the possibilities of being worthy of love.[62]

Similarly but more articulately, when he was forty-six and at the height of his powers Emerson wrote to his older brother that he had three times that year refused requests to write a memoir of his father: "I have no recollections of him that can serve me. I was only eight years old when he died, & only remember a somewhat social gentlemen, but severe to us children. . . ." (Actually, Emerson was still short of his eighth birthday by thirteen days.) That severity Emerson then illustrated with the anecdote of the salt bath, adding somewhat surprisingly,

> I have never heard any sentence or sentiment of his repeated by Mother or Aunt, and his printed or written papers, as far as I know, only show candour & taste, or I should almost say, docility, the principal merit possible to that early ignorant & transitional *Month-of-March* in our New England culture. His literary merits really are that he fostered the Anthology & the Athe-

---

[61] "You forgot those likenesses of father and I took them home with me and forgot to give them to Mother and have them with me." What Waldo forgot to keep, Edward forgot to part with. EBE to RWE, 1818, HMS; "What," HMS.

[62] *JMN* 2:272, 396.

naeum. These things ripened into Buckminster Channing, and Everett.[63]

Privately, he was even more severe, writing in his journal that "from 1790 to 1820, there was not a book, a speech, a conversation, or a thought in the State."[64]

"Early ignorant & transitional"—one cannot ignore the hostility in that tone, especially coming from the suave and tolerant Emerson.[65] Even more surprising is the remark that neither his mother nor his aunt had ever repeated William's words or sentiments. If true, this is a remarkable testament to the problems of the marriage; if not, it gives a clear insight into the son's need to erase memories that he still could not competently confront. In a bitter remark that appears almost inexplicably in the middle of the Harvard Divinity School address, an essay through which the theme of death runs contrapuntally with assertions about the importance of life, Emerson said that "society lives to trifles, and when men die we do not mention them."[66]

Given his belief in his mother's and aunt's silence about William, this is inevitably a deeply personal allusion, descriptive of a world in which he perceived himself to have grown up, one in which the deepest feelings of loss and despair are denied and masked, and attention to the surface of life absorbs one's energies instead. The inauthenticity of it to a sensitive and perceptive child must have been bewildering and alienating.

JUST BEFORE turning thirty, while enduring the painful anniversary of his first wife's death, Emerson reflected that "my manners & history would have been very different, if my parents had been rich, when I was a boy at school."[67] The statement is odd in more than one way, for Emerson did not have "parents" in the plural sense when he was in school. The real poverty to which he alluded was not as he thought his mother's lack of money, but the insufficiency

[63] *The Letters of Ralph Waldo Emerson*, ed. Ralph L. Rusk (New York: Columbia University Press, 1939), 4:178–79, cited hereafter as *L*.

[64] *Journals of Ralph Waldo Emerson 1820–1876*, ed. E. W. Emerson and W. E. Forbes, 10 vols. (Cambridge, Mass., 1909–14), 8:339; cited hereafter as *J*.

[65] For another discussion of Emerson's "fear, shame, and anger" in relation to "his Godlike father," see Porte, pp. 156, 99–104.

[66] "Address Delivered Before the . . . Divinity College" (cited hereafter as "HDS"), *CW*, 1:143.

[67] *JMN*, 4:263.

of love and the absence of the very father whose fantasied presence was implied by the plural.

Death itself was for a long time a confusing and confused concept, a source both of fantasy and of repressed pain and anger. "Blessed is the child," he wrote in his journal in 1834 about the son of a friend who had just died, perhaps identifying with the child's denial of loss. "The Unconscious is ever the act of god himself. . . . Little Albert Sampson asks when his father will come home, & insists that *his father can't die*."[68] The dead parent of a young child indeed is not dead—not relinquished by that aspect of ourselves that Emerson here presciently names "the Unconscious." "*His father can't die*"— death for Emerson, I think, remained not a true loss or ending, but an open question, a source of possibility, for much longer than is common. When he finally began to let it go, as in the opening pages of *Nature*, his anger at the dead past produced a recoil that was energizing and terrific. Until then he wrestled with it, not always consciously, and it formed a significant, sometimes devastating element in the pattern of his growth.

Many critics, sometimes not sympathetically, have noted the remnants of Emerson's sense of *mauvaise honte* and the attacks of nameless guilt and anxiety with which he struggled even as an adult. He blamed himself for his personal and social shortcomings, and some commentators have been inclined to take him at his word when he excoriated himself for emotional coldness and similar failings. The reality, however, was otherwise, and we will not understand Emerson unless we recognize the extent to which his father's untimely death affected him, leaving him with a lifelong project, an only half-conscious agenda: to find a way through the distortions of vision caused by misunderstanding the meaning of the loss he had suffered. If his father was "encrypted," Emerson never closed his ears to the buried sounds of possible life. "Hear the rats in the wall," he wrote at the end of "History." Something was buried alive. There may be something exemplary, if not heroic, about his persistent and devoted attempt to listen for it and be its witness—awkward or remote as such a pursuit might render him to others' eyes. Warmth and urbanity, those outward signs of inward balance and grace, would long elude him.

He began to emerge in his thirties determined to grasp and bring to others his own hard-won understanding of the primacy and overwhelming importance of living "now." For his daring and generosity

[68] *JMN*, 4:309–10.

he was to be rewarded by wide influence, but study of his first thirty-odd years shows how real was the struggle by which he attained that knowledge. "All cognition of the All originates in death, in the fear of death," the philosopher and theologian Franz Rosenzweig wrote, "Philosophy takes it upon itself to throw off the fear of things earthly."[69] For Emerson, whose philosophy so consciously took it upon itself to combat fear, and whose origins were shadowed so early by the experience of death, that aphorism has peculiar pertinence. In later years, Emerson often quoted the fable of the stag who had reason to curse his horns and bless his feet: the growth of unique strength out of insuperable defects was a process he knew well.

[69] Franz Rosenzweig, *The Star of Redemption*, trans. Wm. W. Hallo (Boston: Beacon Press, 1972), p. 1.

Chapter 2

AUNT

"A good aunt is more to the young poet than a patron."
—RWE, 1834

W ILLIAM AND RUTH EMERSON, however, were not alone in influencing Ralph's growth. Joined to them and deserving nearly equal status was William's younger sister, Mary Moody Emerson, a figure strikingly different from either parent—indeed, from anyone else. She not only visited the family and helped care for the children during her brother's lifetime, but after his premature death she and Ruth together set up the boardinghouse that supported themselves and the six children for several crucial years. Both siblings were intellectuals, but where William had prided himself on being a prudent Christian, she was a self-proclaimed romantic; where he was an Arminian, she was an enthusiast; where he spoke for the social norms, she was a self-invented critic of her culture. Normally, her marginality and secondary relationship would have kept these rival siblings on an unequal footing, but William's death meant that through all of Ralph's years of intellectual growth there loomed the presence not of his father but of his aunt.

Mary is a known figure in Emerson's biography, though she is not always portrayed sympathetically; anecdotes about her figure amusingly in those narratives, and her nephew wrote an essay about her. Nevertheless, the real nature of her presence and influence has yet to emerge. Emerson's own memoir, though charming, reverential, and amused by turns, inevitably depicts her through the veil of a lifetime's memories and the mists of family anecdotes and mythologizing. She was a genuine eccentric, but despite the quirks, which he did not conceal, he saw her to some extent as a representative figure. In conversation with his daughter's teacher, F. B. Sanborn, he acknowledged that while little of what he had learned from his professors was of value, had Aunt Mary not taken part in his training, " 'Ah, that would have been a loss! She was as great an element

36

in my life as Greece or Rome.' "[1] Nevertheless, he never placed her in the broader contexts of her familial and social relations, and he was too close to her to discuss—or possibly even to recognize—the extent of her influence on himself.[2]

Clearly, however, a better understanding of Mary and her contribution to her nephew's thought will enable one to grasp his devel-

[1] See Rusk, pp. 21–68 and passim; Cabot 1:28–38; Allen, pp. 17–24; F[ranklin]. B. Sanborn, *The Personality of Emerson* (Boston: Chas. Goodspeed, 1903) pp. 118–19, cited hereafter as Sanborn, *Personality*.

[2] Emerson's own "Mary Moody Emerson," *CW*, 10:397–433 (cited hereafter as "MME"), is the major source of published information about her, supplemented by the notes of Emerson's son and editor, Edward. See also Rosalie Feltenstein, "Mary Moody Emerson: The Gadfly of Concord," *American Quarterly* 3 (Fall 1953): 231–46; Franklin B. Sanborn, "A Concord Note-book: Sixth Paper: The Women of Concord—I," *The Critic* 48 (Feb. 1906): 154–60; Franklin B. Sanborn, *Sixty Years of Concord: 1855–1905*, ed. Kenneth W. Cameron (Hartford, Conn.: Transcendental Books, 1975), cited hereafter as Sanborn, *Sixty Years*; George Tolman, *Mary Moody Emerson*, ed. Edward W. Emerson (Cambridge, Mass. 1929). Tolman includes portions of Mary's letters and journals or "almanacks." References to her appear in the biographies of Emerson, especially Cabot and Rusk.

The early (1909) edition of the *Journals* preserved a more sharply focused image of Mary's interaction with her nephew than does the more modern and complete *JMN* (1960–82), because the latter omits considerable portions of Emerson's correspondence with his aunt that he copied into his journals, along with hers to him. *JMN* was intended to be complete, but not to include correspondence. His replies to her were therefore eliminated, although portions of her letters appear. This is the more unfortunate, since approximately three-quarters of the correspondence omitted was between Emerson and his aunt; no one else engaged his interest in quite the same way. In 1939, the same deletion had occurred when Rusk omitted many of Emerson's letters to Mary from his edition of the *Letters*. None of hers, of course, is printed there.

The cumulative effect of these editorial decisions, made more acute with each succeeding generation, renders it difficult to reconstruct the actual nature of the relationship. Marginal during her own lifetime (and it seems probable that her anger and "difficulty" are at least partly related to that status), Mary's literary history has been one of gradual, but increasing erasure. One hopes that a new era of scholarship with its greater interest in the role played by women may correct this cultural astigmatism.

The first discussion of Mary's relation to Emerson's fiction was my "Emerson and 'The Magician': An Early Prose Fantasy," *American Transcendental Quarterly* 31 (Summer 1976): 13–18; cited hereafter as Barish. In 1980 I completed an essay on Mary's influence on Waldo's literary and religious style, "Emerson and the Angel of Midnight: The Legacy of Mary Moody Emerson," for the proposed anthology *Mothering the Mind*, ed. Martine Brownley and Ruth Perry (New York: Holmes & Meier, 1984), pp. 218–23, cited hereafter as Barish, "Angel." Phyllis Cole has studied Mary Moody Emerson's religiosity in "The Advantage of Loneliness: Mary Moody Emerson's Almanacks, 1802–1855," in *Emerson: Prospect and Retrospect*, ed. Joel Porte (Cambridge, Mass.: Harvard University Press, 1982), pp. 1–32. Others are now at work editing the almanacks and letters. Should the carefully revised edition of Emerson's letters completed by Eleanor M. Tilton become available, a fuller and more accurate picture of this important relationship will be evident.

opment more readily. It is not too much to say that much of the stress that Emerson placed on individual, even maverick, identity—and much of the mysticism seen by Perry Miller as mysteriously at odds with his liberal heritage—he first met in the little-understood figure of his aunt. It was not from his father that he came to understand a culture of criticism; not from his prudential male relatives did he learn to interrogate the Arminian self-assurance and complacency that dominated upper-class Unitarian thought. Mary was not responsible for his general ideas, nor for his intellectual power. But she was a naysayer, a would-be prophet, and an uncompromising intellectual—the first of these types he encountered. To know him, one must know her.[3]

MARY MOODY EMERSON (born August 25, 1774; died May 1, 1863) was only two when her father, leaving his family in Concord to go as chaplain in the Revolution, took her from his wife's care and gave her to his own mother—after whom she had been named—to be raised. The reasons for this transfer are obscure, although such informal adoption was not unusual at the time. Phebe Bliss Emerson had just had another baby, and perhaps it was deemed that Mary, the youngest and at a difficult age, was the infant best spared if economic factors made the support of five children problematic.[4] William, however, died of fever while at camp, and Mary was not reclaimed. Five years later, as a widow of thirty-nine with four children living in her property, "The Manse"—the handsome house built by William—the desirable widow Phebe married Ezra Ripley.

    Although together they had three children, they did not recall Mary to the family home. Mary remained at Malden with her widowed grandmother and probably an uncle, Joseph, both of whom, however, were dead by 1779. Mary's adult obsession with death caused merriment among her relatives, but it is comprehensible, for by the time she was five she had lost those who had cared for her four times over, first her natural mother and father, and then their

[3] Perry Miller, "From Edwards to Emerson," *Errand into the Wilderness* (Cambridge, Mass.: Harvard University Press, 1956), pp. 184–203, hereafter cited as Miller. George Willis Cooke anticipated and answered this question posed by Miller in 1902, writing that there was a direct line of descent "from Edwards through Hopkins and Channing to Emerson," and that each man was influenced by a part of his predecessor's theology—"the idealism." As T. W. Higginson had put it, transcendentalism was "indigenous." See Cooke, *Memorabilia of the Transcendentalists in New England* (Hartford, Conn.: Transcendental Books, 1973), p. 9, hereafter cited as Cooke.

[4] RWE, genealogy, HMS.

surrogates, her grandmother and uncle. At that point, however, an aunt, Ruth Emerson Sargent Waite, also of Malden, informally adopted her, and with this aunt and her second husband Mary dwelt throughout her childhood and adolescence.[5]

Existence was hard and food short, for Mr. Waite was a "shiftless, easy man," and Mrs. Waite was bad tempered. Mary worked at all kinds of household and farm labor. Since they were in constant debt, one of her duties was meeting and fending off the duns. Although an intellectually gifted, even brilliant girl, she had little or no schooling, and in fact lived without companions, "in entire solitude." A telling story of her nephew was that one of the few books she found on the farm was an old book of poetry that had neither cover nor title page; nevertheless she loved the poetry and learned the work intimately. Only in later years did she learn that her favorite author was Milton, the book *Paradise Lost*.[6]

Undoubtedly Mary was deprived socially by her isolation and poverty, but it is not clear that she suffered intellectually from not attending school. On the contrary, at Newburyport, for example, a large town in the region where her relatives lived, students of both sexes at the common school studied only reading, spelling, the Bible, and arithmetic, while at "Marm Emerson's," a girls' school kept by cousins of Mary, young ladies concentrated entirely on sewing, with a few of the advanced students also learning some grammar. At the common school, one former student recalled, Master Chase "would not permit his female pupils to cipher in Fractions. 'It was a waste of time, wholly unnecessary, would never be of the least use to them.' If we could count our beaux and skeins of yarn it was sufficient."[7]

Raised in isolation, without the socialization normal for her class, Mary learned to be not gentle and gracious but hard-working and independent, characteristics that did not always recommend her to society when she eventually encountered it. A contemporary who knew Mary and her Newburyport relatives wrote much later that Emerson's essay had "represented her all *coleur de rose* [sic]. But such is not the impression she left among her relations here. She was bookish, rather strong-minded, not nice in her habits; would do for these days [1870–1900] better than in the time when women were retired and modest in manners, and had great reverence for the

[5] RWE, genealogy, HMS.
[6] "MME," *CW*, 10:400, 411.
[7] Emery, p. 49. See also pp. 36, 21.

stronger sex."[8] As she said of herself, "Society is shrewd to detect those who do not belong to her train, and seldom wastes her attentions."[9] If both the thought and the pungency of its expression call to mind Emerson's prose, one should not be surprised; such similarities occur frequently, for he was to study her writing and be considerably influenced by it.

When Mary was about seventeen, she was recalled by her mother to Concord, as we know from her earliest dated letters. It is not known whether the rapprochement came because Mary was then old enough to help care for the younger children, or because her period of informal indenturedness (if that is what had existed) was over. Her childhood had been, practically speaking, that of an orphan or rejected child, and while she established friendly relations with her sisters, and strove for dutiful and correct ones with her mother and stepfather, even in old age she could not forget how little she had been wanted. Phebe Emerson Ripley later became bedridden, and while Mary often visited Concord and attended her during her many years of invalidism, she was not inclined to make what she regarded as excessive sacrifices to care for her.[10]

But she quickly established a warm epistolary relationship with her older brother William, who by 1792 was the incumbent in the village of Harvard, a handsome bachelor of twenty-three and eager to marry. He seems to have sounded Mary for her contacts among eligible females, for at different times she wrote him assessments of women acquaintances and their prospects of marriage. Mary was determined that her brother should marry Ruth Haskins, of whom she wrote much later, "She was the first idol in the female line I had." Ruth was then twenty-seven, six years older than Mary. "Should I omit personalities, and aim at description; talk of love, and faintly trace some of the ever-interesting delights which result from the culture of this *animated friendship*. Me thinks it would not relish on your taste, which, not vivified by sensibility, as corrected by understanding, would be disgusted rather than entertained."[11] Already a recurrent theme is stated: fear of disgusting persons of lesser "sensibility" by her enthusiasm—corrected though that was by "understanding." Emerson later wrote that his aunt had the misfortune to spin at a higher velocity than all the other tops, and one senses that in the urgent tone of this letter.

[8] Benjamin K. Emerson, *The Ipswich Emersons A.D. 1636–1900* (Boston: David Clapp & Son, 1900), p. 174.

[9] "MME," *CW*, 10:406.

[10] MME to CCE and RWE, 1822, HMS.

[11] MME to EBE, 1823, HMS; MME to WE, 1795, HMS.

In dealing with William, as with others, Mary oscillated between intense expressions of affection and often harsh criticism. Here her devotion to Ruth is almost palpable: "She is virtues self." Yet despite Ruth's "amiability, understanding [and] propriety," Mary admitted a shred of fault in her: Ruth was a bit dull. "Yet true it is, my dear Ruth, thou dost not possess *those energies, those keen vibrations* of soul which seizes pleasure—which immortalises moments and which give to life all the zest of enjoyment." Nevertheless Mary's matchmaking was fruitful, and William and Ruth were engaged on June 8, less than three weeks after he had felt happy with Miss Doubleday. In October 1796 the couple was married.[12]

No doubt pressed by the demands of his new life, William did not communicate with his previously useful sister for many months. Mary characteristically both felt snubbed and said so directly: in May, seven months after the wedding, she apologized for not answering Ruth's letter of "last dec.," "especially as I think early attentions peculiarly proper to new connections. . . . My best love to my brother and to you sister. The former *has not written to his sisters* since he was married."[13]

Further contacts were followed by further disagreements. When he later became editor of *The Monthly Anthology*, William published four letters Mary had exchanged with a friend on the subjects of literature, natural history, the imagination, and religion (the project was of course Mary's own doing), but she had to "urge" him to print them.[14] Unlike his son, he fundamentally did not care for her writing.

In 1806 he defended himself against her criticism by cataloguing Mary's own faults and errors: "Ascetick and censorious" attitudes promoted by her evangelical religion, which permitted her to say anything under the banner of "disinterested love"; poor judgment, stemming from her "balloon-like" imagination; and unfair criticism of himself for having failed to win a "*splendid*" name. Not least, he disliked the "bloated" and "obscure" style of her writing—and her illegible handwriting. (In the last complaint he was entirely justified.) Though right about her driving ambition for her male relatives, he was less candid about his own, for his years of obscurity had been intensely frustrating to him.[15]

His lengthy letters to her (she saved his; her responses are lost) suggest that they needed each other as antagonists. She called forth

[12] MME to WE, 1795, HMS; WE, 1796, HMS.
[13] MME to RE, 1797, HMS.
[14] MME to WE, 1805, HMS.
[15] WE to MME, 1806, 1807, HMS.

some of his most vivid writing. His basic defense was condescension; he was forebearing, affectionate, and tolerant, a "plain christian," and useful in society, while she was full of vagaries and misshapen by religious enthusiasm, capable of producing "sublime epistles" but too "elevated" above mortal concerns to appreciate the just and simple truths of existence.

But when he needed her help, he knew how to use charm and seduction:

> I know not what you mean by compliments. If it is a compliment to say that I love you, and that your residence in my family until death or matrimony separate us is necessary to my happiness, I confess I have been complimentary, and shall be so continually. Come home my good sister, and help to alleviate the burdens of a minister of religion weighed down to the earth by a consciousness of incompetence to his awful functions.

Ruth needed her, the children needed her, and so:

> Again gladden with your voice and healing attentions our charming boys, who have lame legs, wounded hands. . . . and whose minds and hearts afford a fine field for the display of talents such as their aunt possesses. [Therefore,] Come back, you wandering christian. . . . Adieu! my manor is still beautiful as Tirzah, and lacks nothing but the comely graces of a Moody to irradiate its walls. Do learn Mary, to be a little methodical in the keeping of accounts.

From refrain ("come home") to envoi ("learn . . . to be . . . methodical") William wrote with the buoyancy and love of language of a skillful pleader who knew well how to manage his sister and who was in no way burdened by his purported "incompetence to his awful functions."[16]

MARY was too individual, even eccentric, ever to belong to any particular party, but in her enthusiasm, mysticism, and attachment to her country roots, she occupied a position opposite to William's in the political and religious spectrum. He had called her "romantick" and "ascetick and censorious under the blazing influence of disinterested love." (These were in effect code words for the New Light attitudes of the Second Great Awakening.) She loved him and

[16] WE to MME, 1809, HMS.

needed his approval, but she seldom got it, and so she responded with criticism of her own, focusing on his hauteur, social ambition, and lack of sensibility. During his visit to her in Maine in 1806, she wrote Ruth that "a world of life and sentiment has taken the place of that frigid apathy which had taken dominion of all his features and sat uncontrouled whenever he became a hearer in publick." Years later she wrote at her nephew's request about his mother, praising her character but noting that

> she married one of the finest of men—but their rural Eden was not stocked with fruit enow for him—and the little I saw of the innocent Eve did not answer my expectations of her . . . In a new situation [Boston] w'h tempted the ambition of the Adam she sustained any occasional trial of temper with a dignity— firmness—and good sense that I shall ever respect—and obtained a greater influence than is common over one of the best of husbands. At his death (w'h was preceded by a [lin]gering disease of long endurance and of a kind w'h deadened almost every affection) she behaved with that same dignity.[17]

The ambivalence of their relationship caused her pain, which did not diminish with the years. In 1828, on the seventeenth anniversary of William's death, Mary wrote in her journal: "May 12, This day, 17 years since, was the last day of the man I first loved and admired. Different roads, education, and faith led us to view each other with indifference; but the remembrance of that death, of that day in which I erred—will never cease to pain in this life. While he lay dead, I fasted and prayed—but not with fervor."

Then, thinking of some morning play with the household fowl— and in an astonishing leap that reminds one of Emerson's admiration for the dreamlike boldness of her language—she saw herself and her dead brother as they once had been, with only each other to turn to: "This morning I have been playing with the goslings—how astonishing is nature! They have not parents—yet discover a strange instinct for each other's society, tho' there is no protection from it."[18]

Disappointment of hopes for "protection" in others' society was for Mary not only a religious tenet, but a deeply felt personal wound. Ralph Waldo Emerson and his brothers were, partly through their aunt's aid, to form a more coherent family than any she had known,

[17] MME to RWE, 1826, HMS.
[18] "All her language was happy, but inimitable, unattainable by talent, as if caught from some dream" ("MME," CW, 10:403–4).

but it may be that some of his distrust of the social bond had its origins not only in his mature, rational thought, but also in the tragic sense of experience Mary passed on to them as she assumed a parental role.

Her own religious stance reflected the country regions where she was raised. Modern influences to which she responded were not those of post-Enlightenment Harvard, but the more widespread and evangelistic doctrines of the New Lights, also known loosely as neo-Calvinists, the Andover School, or the neo-orthodox. (Old Lights or Old Light Calvinists were less a school than the uninquiring and often permissive inheritors of the unrevived, pre-Edwardsian Congregationalists.) New Light theologians traced their ideas to Jonathan Edwards, active in the 1740s and after, to his follower Samuel Hopkins, and also to the more austere branch of the early covenanters before Edwards. To the New Light, spiritual regeneration was an immediate need, and neither worldly affluence nor worldly approbation guaranteed spiritual well-being. Salvation would not come by any act of individual merit, or "works"; it was God's free gift.[19] Perhaps because of this emphasis on the rationally impenetrable quality of God's will, an undoctrinal but popular interest among the New Lights sprang up in prophecy, or second sight.[20] Mary seems to have adopted this interest and in turn to have nurtured in young Ralph a fascination with the same subject.

The New Lights clung to the Westminster Catechism with its doctrines of grace by election and its stress on original sin, human depravity, and the mystical nature of the Trinity, while emphasizing God's overwhelming power to do as he wished with a people whose best role was to resign all will and pride over to him. They opposed the Liberals with increasing vigor, establishing the Andover school in that town north of Boston with funds provided in the 1780s by the wealthy Mrs. Philips. By 1808, after a break with Harvard and its liberal tendencies, a seminary was added to the preparatory school, and in 1810 Moses Stuart was hired to teach the true doctrine. Frightened of change, New Lights aimed to prevent the evolution of doctrine, which they saw as having perverted Cambridge

[19] Ahlstrom, pp. 280–86; Heimert, p. 6; Winthrop S. Hudson, *Religion in America* (New York: Scribner's, 1973), pp. 59–74.

[20] Robert Handy, *Religion in the American Experience: The Pluralistic Style* (Columbia: University of South Carolina Press, 1972), pp. 82–83. Handy cites a contemporary account of the prophetic experience: Richard McNemar, *The Kentucky Revival* (Albany, 1808). Robert Richardson, Jr., discussed the intellectual opposition to the use of the Bible as a prophetic document in "The Case against Prophecy in the 1790s," unpublished paper delivered in Concord, Mass., July 12, 1980.

thought, and so the seminary required faculty to sign a kind of loyalty oath, a stringent written contract designed to prevent its signa-
tors from ever changing their minds—in effect, from ever thinking
again. Unrestricted thought had led to the heresies of Harvard and
its intolerable election of Henry Ware, Sr., to a professorship in
1805.[21]

Mary's religious allegiances during this period, coinciding
roughly with the beginning of the Second Great Awakening, were
like everything else about her, idiosyncratic. She was inclined to be
at once doctrinally conservative and spiritually radical, if such a distinction can be made. Many years later she was to write, in a passage
her nephew was conscious of, that "I have in the bottom of my heart
. . . always been much of a deistical pietist. Perplexed about the nature of Jesus, I have sought to be absorbed in the sole idea of an all-
surrounding God alone."[22]

But this late and rare avowal of perplexity did not mean that earlier she had not sought for light among the neo-orthodox at Andover
and its environs. Thus while she rejected the punitive aspects of Calvinism, she attached herself to the conservative minister Elijah Parrish of Byfield, and even lived briefly with him and his family. It
seems also to have been Mary who arranged for Edward, Ralph's
younger brother, to attend Andover, whose faculty, like Leonard
Woods, sometimes carried letters for her on their way from Boston.
And although she was sometimes critical of Moses Stuart, she evidently once thought it at least possible that Emerson as a young
divinity student might study with him.[23] Cambridge's theology, on
the other hand, was her anathema. She approved of Channing, but
she was aware that he had learned divinity not at Cambridge, but as
a private student of Hopkins himself. "Why did you not study under
the wing of Ch[anning]—w'h was never pruned at Cambridge" she
asked her nephew in 1824. Clearly, the Second Great Awakening
gave Mary—as it gave many other women—a strong sense of support in her religious questing.[24]

To be sure, their opponents attacked the New Lights as hypo-

[21] Henry K. Rowe, *History of Andover Theological Seminary* (Newton, Mass., 1933),
cited hereafter as Rowe; Leonard Woods, *History of The Andover Theological Seminary*
(Boston: Osgood & Co., 1885). Because of its widespread rural roots and stress on communitarian values, Alan Heimert (pp. 16–21) has concluded that this and not the more
elite group centered in Cambridge was close to the spirit of the American democratic
ethos. Democratic or not, intellectually it was reactionary.

[22] MME, 1828, HMS.

[23] MME and EBE, HMS.

[24] MME to RWE, 1824, HMS; Nancy Cott, "Young Women in the Second Great
Awakening in New England," *Feminist Studies* 3 (Fall 1975): 15–29.

crites and antinomian sinners. William Emerson, v
tering at Harvard and able to enjoy an unrefined joke,
his journal a satiric slander on New Light teachings, represe
a syphilitic, toothless rake finally come to justice. The opening line
give the robust eighteenth-century flavor of the attack:

> "A rake with long debauches lean and pale;
> "Whose eyes were sinking; teeth began to fail;
> "Gout had struck stiff his fingers and his toes;
> "A dire disease had oversat his nose."

The rake is reproached by a "hopkintonian preacher," but defends himself as a true follower:

> "Stay," says the rake, "I live a wretch, 'tis true
> "But learned this wretched course of life from you.
>
> . . . .
>
> "Sweet was the speech; I took thee at thy word
> "And sinned away to glorify the Lord."[25]

It is worth noting that although Perry Miller attempted carefully to distinguish the subtle changes in the meaning of "Calvinist" and to deflect even from Jonathan Edwards its full force, the term was freely applied at the time, and William Emerson introduced this squib by saying that "Calvinism carried to its utmost limits, is happily taken off" in this verse, which he attributes to a neighboring clergyman.[26]

MOST CULPABLY lacking in her brother's doctrines, from Mary's point of view, was the profound, intense, and overwhelmingly important conviction of the immanence of God. This she cherished and pursued through reading, private meditation and prayer, the writing of her journals, and through seeking out ministers of the faith. Her God, however, was not the comfortable gentleman of the Enlightenment, but a distant, awesome, ineffable presence, infinitely greater than mankind.

The Liberals only less than the Unitarians had deemphasized the importance of Christ. But for Mary, the doctrine of the Atonement, stressed by all the New Lights, was central. Its dynamics defined humans in the universe. Humanity was the fallen worm, God the all-

---

[25] WE, 1795, HMS.
[26] Perry Miller, *Jonathan Edwards* (New York: William Sloane, 1949), and *Errand into the Wilderness*, pp. 49–50.

...sent his son as a token of love to
...ter jokingly questioned her rever-
...ays insisted on Christ's mystical role
...oiding the subject. For if God had not
...en the world was not in need of redemp-
...scarcely have been God's inferior. Out of
...e New Lights continually forecast, atheism

...nodox than her nephew reported, she was open to
...critical of the intellectual capacities of all she met,
...quickly exhausting the small fund of information held by
...ry clergymen she might seek out or meet on her travels.
...eristically, she responded readily to the truths she perceived
...ddhism when she met it, being among the first to share with
...nephew some portions of the Vedas given her by a wandering
...ssionary. She despised the "bigotry" of what she called "coarse,
damnatory Calvinism," as she disliked all smallness.

Mary was also ahead of her time by being in effect an early feminist, though she would have scoffed at the term and felt no sister-
hood toward conventional feminine behavior. By the time she was
thirty or so she had inherited from her Aunt Waite some money,
which gave her a small income. Some of it she invested in a farm
known as "Elm Vale," which she purchased with her sister and
brother-in-law, Rebecca and Robert Haskins, in Waterford, Maine.
With them and their thirteen children she lived much of the time far
in a backwoods region she liked to invoke—realistically—as the
realm of wolves and drifting snow.[27] But when she wished, she could
travel to Boston to stay with Ruth, or to Newburyport to visit another sister, Hannah Farnham. Or she could live frugally as a
boarder in some village to which she might be attracted by a local
minister, or possibly a health cure, for with age grew problems with
eyesight and digestion.

In 1807 she received a proposal from a respectable suitor, but she
rejected him, not liking his ideas about religion and politics and obviously unwilling to surrender her independence in these matters.
She felt thereafter what she described as the want of a "protector"—
that is, the difficulty of being a single woman in a society where
marriage was a woman's only career—but she felt also that she had
a "vocation," and that her "whole life was devoted to one and the

[27] MME to Ezra Ripley, 1828, HMS.

same c

essentia

She c

in a lett

stonecraf

moral ton

rles. By this she

nd meditation.[28]

twenty-five Woll-

o read Mary Woman a

Rights of Woman

e of her theories in-

ed by one of her

ut glory, virtue

f education

in girls

es, and

ates

do-

Miss W's—theology, I think, bad; and som
tricate; but still her pages may be characteri
quotations. "Pleasure was for the inferior kind; b
Heaven for man designed." Were her modes o
adopted, I believe, we should find less of *that softnes*
which lays a foundation for many future ills in their liv
less of that voluptuousness in men, which so often ene
their understandings and gives unreasonable women such a
minion over their passions.

Female "softness" and male passion alike could be rooted out by
proper education; the notion that women should be passive sufferers
was entirely alien to her ideas of education, which made no distinctions in principle between the genders. She paid for the education in
Boston of one of her nieces, Rebecca Haskins, and wrote to Ruth
Emerson with whom the girl was living: "Make her frank, open and
ingenuously confident. Torper [*sic*] and timidity, those foes to all
that is great and pious, she is naturally inclined to, *there* may all your
instructions aim. But of all things don't let her indulge any dear
Babe. I think she is injuring these little ones very much."[29] Women
and men should be equally strong. Mary, to be sure, also had accused herself of spoiling the little Charles—it was clearly her nature
to backslide from her rigorous precepts—but she felt that greatness
and courage, so long as these were accompanied by piety, belonged
as much to women as to men.

Wollstonecraft was only the tip of the iceberg of Mary's wide, self-
directed reading: she had an intimate knowledge of English poetry,
especially that of Shakespeare and Milton and Byron, and had read
a considerable amount of history and of the Scottish Common-Sense
philosophers—who were fundamentally, of course, Protestant theologians. A special niche in her pantheon was reserved for her contemporary, Madame de Staël. To all of them, including the last, she
was to lead the young Emerson.

[28] MME, 1807, HMS; MME to CCE, 1825, HMS.
[29] MME to RE, 1813, HMS.

Moral grandeur, however, could only be rooted in strength, and she sought to establish it. "Aunts only message is 'Be brave,' " as Ralph wrote to Edward once.[30] She reproached herself for taking "the lead" in relation to Ruth, but she felt free to criticize on the ground that she was doing God's work. When William and the sickly John visited her in 1806, for example, she wrote to Ruth that the boy was "defective" in walking and running, and afraid to "swing."

Yet for all her emphasis on hardihood, Mary did not herself bear loss or sorrow well. Her stress on independence from others may have been formed in reaction to her own painful early abandonment; this is the kindest way to account for her tendency at times of crisis or loss to irritate wounds rather than to try to heal them. On the second anniversary of William's death, for example, undoubtedly it was partly her own confused and painful emotions that prompted her to write to Ruth not only describing the weakness of William's faith but also implying that not all his service of virtue had been "disinterested." She took the same occasion to preach to Ruth the spiritual benefits of her "glor[ious]" widowhood and "*weaned life*," while pointing out that since Ruth was endowed with "natural timidity" she probably was not "entitle[d] to much praise" for the decorum and propriety of her manners.[31]

Ruth's widowed humbleness was a settled subject with Mary. She reverted to it in a letter to Charles a decade later in 1822 with her typical unconscious humor: "Glad to hear my Sister had a good journey—but as to her looking so much younger etc there is no advantage. She always seems most amiable when she looks pale. A widow who seems only to live to pray for her children and to desire to rejoin her husband is the most interesting sight of the 'women kind'. . ." Mary had once hoped Ruth would find "an earthly protector"—a second husband. Now she thought Ruth's lowliness was her best claim on election. Regarding Mary Caroline, two years old, she urged, "Caroline—Oh Ruth if her temper is not subdued, if she acquires base and selfish habits O Ruth how great is your responsibility[.] I shall have no part in it."[32] So Mary marked and offered consolation on a mournful anniversary.

Ruth may have been limited, but to have been able to live and cope with such criticism, even when it might be so comically misdirected,

[30] *L*, 1:18.
[31] MME to CCE, 1822, HMS; MME to RE, 1813, HMS.
[32] MME to RE, 1813, HMS.

suggests her strength. It also suggests what Mary meant when she said that her manners were to Ruth, "a kind of crucifiction." Together with her virtues of intelligence, devotion, charm, and esprit, was a strong mixture of ego, pietism, and insensitivity. Her remarks may have expressed the Wesleyan ideal of familial relations, but the will to utter such ideas in times of renewed grief is hard to justify. Her nephew commented much later that his aunt had had a wit like a wasp's—never used for show, only to sting. And when F. B. Sanborn in an anonymous obituary wrote of her that she had been able to say more disagreeable things in half an hour than any other living person, Emerson had merely remarked, "I see that he was well acquainted with Aunt Mary." The family had long since learned that humor was the best response to her faults.[33]

BUT IF she was complicated and difficult, she was also valuable, and Ruth both loved and needed her. A year after William's death came the disaster of the War of 1812, bringing with it fear of invasion and the virtual stoppage of business. After six months of continued salary, Ruth had only a pension of five hundred dollars per year, half of William's original salary. She had no home for her family of seven, which included five growing boys (one of whom, Robert Bulkeley, was mentally incompetent), and the baby girl Mary Caroline, born after William's death.[34] (Mary Caroline died in 1814.)

Poverty stared them in the face. Mary and Ruth cast about for ways of managing, considering various temporary homes for the boys, and for a time Ruth retired to live in Concord while Mary went up to Maine with Charles and Bulkeley. During one of these wartime separations Ruth wrote to Mary's sister Phebe Ripley that Mary must return, for to her, Mary was William's surrogate:

> I do not think her place could be supplied to these *fatherless children* by any one on earth. I pray God to preserve her valuable life & enable me justly to appreciate so great a blessing. She possesses some traits of character that bear so strong a resemblance to my dear deceased husband as render her peculiarly dear to me, & I hope she wil not ever leave me except for a visit or a *good Husband*, while she lives.[35]

With the end of the war, they decided together to move back to Boston, rent a house, and support the family by taking in boarders.

33 "MME," *CW*, 10:403; Sanborn, *Personality*, p. 133n.
34 *EIC*, p. 8.
35 HMS quoted by Rusk, p. 31.

In addition to her physical labor, emotional support, and no doubt her income, Mary added what Ralph called, in a poem requesting her return from a visit, her "peace-commanding voice."[36]

Mary's presence was crucial. Ruth was determined that her sons, especially William, should be ministers. Mary concurred and for this years of expensive education were essential—though the boys, as their aunt said, were "born to be educated."[37] Intellectually, as an example of an inquiring, adventurous, and free spirit, Mary was invaluable. But her place among them was founded essentially on her personal gifts, especially on her remarkable capacity to project for others her vision of the world's excellence, of its natural and moral beauty. She could make the conscious life as intensely exciting to those around her—if they could listen—as it was to herself, and she was generous with this gift.

She could also be generous in tangible, practical gifts of love, which her nephews probably found easier to understand than their mother's more rigorous discipline. When Charles was learning to write in 1816, for example, she wrote him a letter that is at once a lesson in metaphor and an expression of pure love:

> My own dear boy, I send you a little cake, as a remembrance of our sweet friendship. And I would have it answer a noble purpose. Let the milk, flour and eggs of which its constitutent parts are composed represent the solid virtues of your character, the sugar its sweetness—the flavor of its fruit and the fragrance of its spices be emblematical of the ornaments and graces of your soul. But especially let the white incrustation be a type that the lovely veil of modesty will be a cover ever to your virtues. It is this which in-hances the value of goodness itself, and renders it usefull and dignified. If Mother will permit you to go to school the first letter you write with your own hand shall be rewarded by / MME/ Kiss R. Bulkley

Mary could reprove harshly, but she could love warmly. She did not require of Charles (as Ruth had done of John at an even younger age) that he be good *before* she would assure him of her interest. The gift she sent him was not a few belated sugarplums but something she had made herself and rendered richer by the baroque inventions of her language. (The "white incrustation" that should be a type of the eight-year old's modesty was the frosting.) For all her faults, Mary had enchanting freedom and gaiety of spirit and an imagina-

[36] *L*, 1:53.
[37] Cabot, 1:28.

tion that made the attainment of virtue seem rich, sweet—and possible.

It was well that she was among them, for William's premature death created a great deficit among the boys, and in some ways Ralph probably never fully recovered from it. While his fantasy life intensified, outwardly his primary defense was withdrawal, and he did not master the skills of social interaction. "How is it, Ralph," Samuel Ripley, Ezra's son and Ralph's uncle and employer, asked him at thirteen, "that all the boys dislike you & quarrel with you, whilst the grown people are fond of you?"[38] Emerson himself recorded that cruel question; undoubtedly he never knew the answer, for if he had, he could have forgiven himself and forgotten it. But how could they like him? To have lost a father for Ralph was to have lost part of himself, an undeveloped, embryonic part. His energies were engaged, then and to an only gradually lessening degree for many years afterward, in remaking that part, that self which had to appear whole before it could be whole, which had first to grow a skin, as it were, over what was missing. In later years he invented in his journals a scenario in which boys cried out to the passerby they had struck with a ball, "If you had learned how to play when you was at school . . . you would have known better than to be hit. If you did not learn then, you had better . . . learn now. Hit him again, Dick." Even as an adult, attending the town meetings in Concord, he never felt fully at ease among his fellow townsmen.[39]

Emerson always understood that some of such strength came from a father's love, and the evidence is clear that anger at that loss, added to the yet more deeply unconscious anger of the child-rival he had never had a chance to grow beyond, lingered on into Emerson's maturity. After William Emerson's death, his son could not make up for that anger and rivalry by becoming like the man he had so foolishly challenged. This lost opportunity for reconciliation and identification became part of his otherwise inexplicable negation of his father's meaning. William Emerson's untimely death, then, was for his son a wound that never fully healed, and from which he was both to suffer and, in some ways, to benefit.

In this process his aunt played a role. She could not, in fact, provide him with an adequate male model, but in many ways as Ruth testified she was intellectually her brother's surrogate, and what she gave him was, in its own way, invaluable.[40] He loved the poets she

[38] *JMN*, 7:253.
[39] *JMN*, 8:229.
[40] Eric Cheyfitz refers to Mary as "Father Mum," and this term has been adopted by David Leverenz, "The Politics of Emerson's Man-Making Words," *PMLA* 101 (Jan.

quoted, sought out and reported on sermons he knew she would want to hear about, and established his first links to religious language in communicating with her. It was her written prayers and not his father's—although these remained among the manuscripts whose covers Emerson later cannibalized for his journals—that the oldest boy repeated for the household every morning. It was her language, he acknowledged later, that had first formed his own religious and meditative prose and the personal style of such impulses.

> Aunt Mary herself wrote the prayers which first my brother William & when he went to college I read aloud morning & evening at the family devotions, & they still sound in my ear with their prophetic & apocalyptic ejaculations. Religion was her occupation and when years after, I came to write sermons for my own church I could not find any examples or treasuries of piety so hightoned, so profound, or promising such rich influence as my remembrances of her conversation & letters.[41]

He did not, in fact, wait until he wrote sermons to reread her letters. From an early date, he copied long extracts from them into his journal as he received them, and copied drafts of his own replies there. The editorial decision to omit these from the *JMN* is understandable but distorts his development by simplifying it. In correspondence with his aunt he felt uniquely able to express his fundamental intellectual problems. Even in his sixties he went on performing for his aunt what he had refused to do for his father, for he then reread her journals once again but now copied extracts of these and of her letters to him into four new volumes—in effect, editing them. "A good aunt is more to the young poet than a patron" he wrote in later years. A patron in its root sense is a paternal figure; Emerson lacked one as a child and did not find one as an adult. But he had an aunt, and he shortly turned her into a Muse: the growth and freedom of that relationship was to mark much of his adolescence and early manhood.[42]

1986), 45. However, Emerson used the term only once in all their correspondence (*L*, 1:198) and then as a joke about her refusal to write him—her insistence on remaining "mum." Her actual nickname was the anagrammatic "Tnam." See Barish, "Emerson and 'The Magician.' "

[41] *JMN* 5:323–24. Mary wrote to Ruth when William Jr. departed of her wish "that Ralph shall and may gain new advantages and commence the eldest son at home under auspicious circumstances." She understood his need for recognition and arranged for him to have it. MME to RE, 1814, HMS.

[42] *JMN*, 4:371.

Chapter 3

YOUTH

"How do you, deer play Mate?"

—MME to RWE, 1820

I N 1828 Emerson wrote to Charles that in response to questions
from his fiancée and her family, he had "dragged" the four
brothers "over the coals of my vituperations. . . . I cook them up
& shall cook in every form. I roast, broil, fry, & mince. I salt and I
pepper them well. I make sugar candy of their virtues & if they have
said a word against me, I cut them into sausages. So you had best
walk with circumspection." To love for Emerson was also to hunger;
the metaphor's charm lies in the mixture of reckless trust and mock
ferocity he attaches to this ambivalent feeling.[1]

The twin necessities of trust and hunger marked the parameters
of Emerson's youth. It was a short one, compressed into the ten years
between his father's death, when he was barely eight, and his graduation from college at eighteen. His emotional nurture through this
period came primarily from two sources: the affection of his brothers
and the attention and inspiration of his aunt. She made no favorite
of him, but from the beginning their interests and tastes overlapped
in a way that gave play to the creative faculties of both. Together
with Ruth, the seven survivors formed a tight community able to
cope with the consequences of war, personal grief, and major loss of
income. It was a heroic and communal achievement in which Ruth
was central but not unique. Poverty threatened constantly, hunger
sometimes, and bankruptcy at least once.

But while they learned the value of hard work and loyalty, they
were also exposed to excessive pressure. Only Emerson refused to
be molded by it, and while his triumphs at school and college were
few, it is possible that his real achievement during this difficult decade was the invisible but profound one of constructing an inviolable
and private space in which his mind could grow. It was not so for

[1] *L*, 1:254; years later Emerson recorded in his journal that he had never known love
without pain.

54

his brothers, each of whom, in one way or another, ultimately became a victim of the pressures internalized at their mother's urging. The family letters give insight into this important but otherwise obscure development, for they show how differently Emerson reacted to the people they all knew and the environment they shared.

Ruth's first concern was to have her sons educated, if possible as ministers. She had five hundred dollars a year for seven years as the pension from her husband's church, occasional gifts of charity, more or less anonymous, and the use of the parsonage for three years, but this was not enough to live on. The mental incompetence of Bulkeley, her fourth son, had been evident even in his early years to his father, who had predicted that he would prove unable to look after himself. Ruth kept Bulkeley at home for as long as she could, but eventually he required boarding out at additional expense.[2]

There were two major supplemental sources of income: rent from boarders, who numbered not more than a small handful, sometimes only two or three, and wages paid to the boys. William, the oldest son, began to bring in money by around 1815, when as a college freshman of fourteen he began to assist his uncle Samuel Ripley in the school he kept in nearby Waltham. Ralph and Edward were to follow the same pattern. Their earnings can only have been small, but their board, lodging, and occasional extras were arranged for them.

In a time when all garments were made by hand, clothing was a major item of expense, and Ruth showed anxious and unflagging concern for the condition of their shirts and coats. Modern readers may find her zeal in this excessive, but it probably reflected the reality of their loss of status and the danger of public shaming in a society still highly stratified and class conscious. Ralph and Edward for example, had only one overcoat between them. When either went without it, he "had to bear the taunts of vulgar-minded school-fellows inquiring, 'Whose turn is it to wear the coat today?' " Even in today's economy of poverty, mothers often keep their children home from school rather than expose them to such attacks, but Ruth Emerson was obviously tough-minded and determined that her sons should be also. The degree of their poverty sometimes amounted to virtual destitution. Sarah Ripley once visited the home and "found them without food, and Miss Emerson [Aunt Mary] consoling [the boys] with tales of heroic endurance."[3]

[2] The pension lasted until 1818, after which finances suddenly worsened for Ruth; *EIC*, p. 8; Cabot, 1:27–28.
[3] Cabot, 1:28–29.

Not an articulate person, Ruth best expressed her love through the unending material care and spiritual guidance she gave her children. Her letters are brief and unemotional, dealing not with feelings or ideas but with their "cloaths," health, payment of bills, and their awareness that God should be their help and guide. Herself always diligent, she felt required to impress on her sons that no moment or penny could be spared for unproductive purposes, and much of the pressure for achievement felt by the boys must have originated with her. "Let your whole life reflect honour on the *name* you bear," she wrote to William in reply to his first letter from college.[4]

The businesslike daughter of a self-made man, her language, though seldom vivid, is heavy with the metaphors of money and trade. When William told her of visiting friends and attending celebrations for the peace that came in early 1815, she replied to the fourteen-year-old boy, "Do not forget how important are the minutes and hours, as well as the weeks and months of your time now— 'O let not moment pass but in purchase of its worth.' " When he was again invited to visit friends she protested that such intercourse must "not interfere with higher duties—viz, that of obtaining your education which is in short to enable you to get a *respectable living* in the world." She worried with good cause about Edward's health and was aware that the twelve-year-old sometimes studied too late while away at Andover. Yet to him also she wrote, "I hope you will remember how precious your time is, and neglect no opportunity to acquire knowledge in whatever can dignify or exalt your character and qualify you for future usefulness—here and a happy eternity hereafter."[5] The emphasis on "minutes and hours" as well as on "weeks and months" followed from the realization that the sooner the boys were graduated from college, the sooner they would be fully self-supporting, and Ruth's timetable called for Ralph and William to matriculate at Harvard at fourteen. This was younger than the norm, but not unique.

Ruth, however, was not invisible within the small society of Boston, which in 1800 had a population of only twenty-five thousand, and the plight of this relict of the city's most fashionable minister recommended her to charity. Help was forthcoming. When Ralph's schoolmaster, Mr. Gould, brought up the matter with the president of Harvard, John Kirkland, the latter found a remunerative spot for the young freshman to fill as "president's freshman." Sheriff Brad-

4 RE to WEjr, 1815, HMS.
5 RE to WEjr and EBE, 1817, HMS.

ford, a family friend (Sarah Ripley's father), provided Ruth with an anonymous quarterly gift of ten dollars. But this public charity, which was a testament both to their father's former standing and to the boys' own promise, would not have been or remained forthcoming if the mother, aunt, and sons had not visibly been putting forth such efforts.[6]

In later years, Emerson was to write, "Society is a joint-stock company, in which the members agree, for the better securing of his bread to each shareholder, to surrender the liberty and culture of the eater." It is interesting to read this famous phrase in the light of his earliest assessment of his dependent relation to society, which he made while urging his older brother to compete for a literary prize. Ralph offered various arguments—money, fame, family pride, and the like, but in particular he finally noted a strategic consideration that touched his own interests: "And as probably a long period will elapse before our family will be independent of the assistance of society, our Benefactors might be encouraged by a gleam of hope darted *from underneath the locks of the 'Scrof'lous'* " [his nickname for William] and thus inclined to assist the 'other brother' by some future time to *dissert* like his predecessor in favour."[7]

If William were successful, that is, some of his credit might extend to Ralph. The latter was only a few days short of fifteen when he used these circumlocutions to express both his own ambition and his knowledge of how complex are the relations of the weak to the strong and the poor to the rich. The prize, he believed, was not merely an end in itself, but also a means toward social reputation and the general "favour" of "Benefactors." The young boy grasped these dynamics naturally—innocently, one might say—for the realities they were, but one cannot be sure that he understood them without some of the pain that, in the sentence from "Self-Reliance," seems bitter indeed. Aunt Mary's remark to William to be humble but "Never like dependence," is often quoted, but the reality of their dependency was an iron fact of life for them. Both Ralph's perception and his articulateness about these dynamics are striking; his capacity to say these things may have been a way of dealing with their discomfort.[8]

The letters from and to the younger Edward when he was sent to Andover give special insight into both the boys' care for each other

[6] RE to MME, 1817, HMS; *L*, 1:77.
[7] "Self-Reliance," *CW*, 2:49–50; *L*, 1:60–61, 42.
[8] *EIC*, p. 21.

and the process by which all but Ralph seem to have internalized the sometimes damaging pressures to achieve. It had been arranged, perhaps through Aunt Mary and her connections, that Edward be sent away to school, an event for which he was eager. Andover had been founded to educate the sons of the poor in evangelical doctrines. He had a scholarship, but tuition was not free even to students as poor as Edward.[9] Two of the daily meals at the attached seminary consisted of bread and milk, and molasses was sometimes substituted for meat at the third. The dining room and workroom were unheated.

The school proper can have been little better, and Edward suffered there from ill health and lack of money. Embarrassed at being unable to pay his share of the fuel costs, for which he wrote repeatedly to Ruth without avail, he was crowded with three other boys into a single room meant for both studying and sleeping. There was no common or sitting room. Despite the constant colds that eventually led to a settled case of tuberculosis by the time he was twenty, he was unable to secure milk rather than coffee, though both he and his mother wished him to have it. Perhaps that, like the fuel, would have meant payment she simply did not have.[10]

Responsive to expectations, Edward overworked, sometimes studying eight straight hours before dinner, and working again afterward. William, at fifteen, was worrying about being able "to get some situation which will prevent my being a burden to mother," and he passed on his anxiety about success to Edward, telling him to send him his essays for correction, and insisting Edward become "the *first scholar*. . . . Composition is of the greatest importance, especially to the *first scholar*. You must attend with particular attention to that . . . Persevere. . . ."[11]

Edward was malleable to these demands, and in turn later brought them to bear on the younger Charles, intensifying them dramatically: "The getting above or below one or two boys, the sitting at one end of a little school-bench rather than the other, seem indeed a little matter"—but it was not. It meant the difference between "obscurity and fame," success and failure. "Yes, Charley, those few feet,

---

[9] The archives of Andover show that Edward had an early kind of student loan: he received $300 from the academy but was required by bond to repay $145.28 some ten years after graduation.

[10] Rowe, chap. 2; Sarah Stuart Robbins, *Old Andover Days: Memories of a Puritan Childhood* (Boston: Pilgrim Press, 1908), chap. 1, cited hereafter as Robbins; EBE to RE, RE to EBE, 1816–18, HMS.

[11] EBE to RE, 1816, HMS; WEjr to EBE, 1816, WEjr to EBE, 1818, HMS.

which separate in school and in College the first from the fourth, nay even that inch of space which divides the first from the second, will widen inconceivably." To imagine that life itself was different from this competitive hell was a "false notion . . . truly a ravening wolf in sheep's clothes,—both pernicious and stupid, engendering indolence and deceiving oneself."

Edward was, as his relatives knew, "excitable" as well as handsome and talented, but how much of that dangerous excitability had been shaped by these early stresses on the "minutes and hours" one can only guess. He was barely twenty-one when he wrote the above letter to Charles and already a victim of well-established tuberculosis. After another few years of poverty, sickness, and thwarted ambition as a law clerk (although his clerkship was to Daniel Webster himself), he was at twenty-three to suffer a severe mental breakdown of a manic-depressive nature from which he never fully recovered.[12]

Each of Ralph's siblings in turn seems to have undergone a vocational crisis in which the alternatives of religion and the law each seemed to involve them in fundamental dishonesty. It was perhaps not accidental that Edward's breakdown, however aggravated by ill health, occurred during the summer after he was admitted to the bar. William's crisis, the only one generally mentioned, followed his return home from Germany—where he had gone to study theology at great expense and sacrifice—convinced that he had lost too much of his faith in conventional Christianity to go further. Returning home, he became a lawyer, but he had to leave Boston for New York and long years discolored by continued poverty and a longing for a more literary career.

Edward too considered the church, then turned instead to the legal profession, but even before his breakdown he articulated how deeply he disliked it on moral as well as personal grounds. His last, bewildered, long letter to Charles, written from Puerto Rico just before he died in 1834 at age twenty-nine, is tragically apposite with the one just quoted. "From a given point I drew what I thought was a straight line. . . . From some fundamental defect of the moral physical or intellectual part my well laid calculations failed. I blame no one, not even myself, for the disappointment—being as yet in the

---

[12] EBE to CCE, 1824, HMS; MME to RE, 1819 [?], HMS: "I heard with some attention what Aunt Sarah stated in her lamentation—that as he was so liable to excitement it cd. be the most hazardous thing in the world to trust him from home." Again in 1819 Mary wrote that Edward should be at Medford, not Waltham, as "it would not wear out his nervous system."

dark as to the real cause." Unconsciously echoing his earlier metaphor of competition in the schoolroom, he ends, "What matters it?
Whether famous or obscure, in wealth or need the great lessons of
this disciplinary world are learned by us and 'twill make little odds
presently whether the form we sat on were of pine or mahogany."[13]

Charles's case was less dramatic, but he too hesitated a long time
and gave evidence of feeling the same divided spirit that characterized not only his brothers but also the comparable English generations whose religious crises are somewhat better known. He described keenly, for example, the "feelings of nausea . . . in the pure
boy's mind" as he grows into a "big world" and finds that its ethical
standards are greatly different from his own. He wished, he confided
to Ralph, to write about that conflict. He too considered a career in
the church, and in an earlier era he would surely have followed one,
but the dilemmas posed by rationalistic doubts took hold of him as
they had his older brothers. Aunt Mary's toughmindedness informed her response when, learning of his doubts, she warned him
off the church and told him in effect to leave acting to the professionals: "Why need any man preach? There are publick theaters where
talent may be displayed, and much better means of getting a living
than preaching, if it imply no more than many teach."[14]

WALDO, however, reacted differently to these demands. (During
the winter of 1816–17, halfway through his thirteenth year,
"Waldo" began to appear as the signature of Ralph's letters—a metamorphosis that took five years to become consistent, but which this
text will adopt henceforth.) William was in his last year at Harvard,
and Waldo was undoubtedly looking ahead to his own matriculation
there the following year. He had already, in Aunt Mary's phrase,
"commenced the eldest son at home." In this role he thrived, and
one of the responsibilities he undertook was to write regularly to
Edward, who was homesick at Andover.[15] Unlike his brothers,
Waldo seldom preached. Instead, he filled his letters with high-spir-

[13] EBE to RWE, 1827, HMS; EBE to CCE, 1833, HMS.
[14] CCE to RWE, 1827, HMS; MME to CCE 1827[?], HMS. After he had told his
aunt that "devotions were delusions" and had spoken out as a young adult against "enthusiasm," she wrote to Charles, "Now if I had the dearest son I would not advise him to
preach, tho' every drop of my blood were to suffer martyrdom, till I was persuaded of his
own connections with God. Then whether he defended the genuine gospel or not, I
should know his life wd influence the cause—and such a life could not be far from the
truth. But he had better know what he intended to preach before he [ventured?]
[15] L, 1:27, 33ff.; MME to RE, 1814, HMS.

ited chatter, jokes, puns, codes, and anagrams. He liked to tease and gossip—sending a supportive teasing to Edward who worshipped him and his talents, a slightly more pointed set of gibes to his older brother, whom he nicknamed "his Deaconship" and "The Kennebunk Pedagogue" and whose "kind scolding long, letter[s]" he repaid without scolding.[16]

Oddly, for those who know only the mature Emerson's persona, humor—not merely wit, but a stream of good-natured humor and cheer—was from an early date a major resource. Along with it went a freedom of imagination and an independent taste for speculation that was noticed early in the family. All the boys liked to write, but only Waldo wished—until the age of fifteen or so—to be a poet. And only he never swerved from his early clerical ambitions evident already by age thirteen, when he revised his early poem "Fortus" and added to his signature the title "L.L.D." "Inapplicant, time-wasting Ralph," as he called himself parodically in one of his letters,[17] made little stir at school, attracted less positive notice from his teachers than William, and had fewer prominent friends and less public success than either Edward or Charles, both of whom were strikingly handsome. Circumstances were no kinder to him than to his siblings. But the second oldest brother had the capacity to create a more intense inner life, which shielded him from the demands of competition and his mother's emphasis on constant productivity.[18]

Nevertheless, life in a boardinghouse was difficult. The family letters seldom mention their paying guests directly, except when their absence in 1818 threatened Ruth with bankruptcy, or when some, like her relative Dr. Kast and his party, were particularly trying—guests by whom Waldo felt the house had been "infested." But however ignored, the presence of strangers among themselves presented difficulties. The running of a boardinghouse was a much more com-

[16] L, 1:45, 51, 56, 51.

[17] EIC, pp. 11–12; L, 1:40.

[18] Holmes, who admittedly "idealized" him, found Charles "the most angelic adolescent my eyes ever beheld," with "an entrancing voice and manner," and an intellectual "brilliance" acknowledged even by his rivals (pp. 16–19); Cabot, 1:38, quoting George Barrell Emerson.

A school supervisor who had once been taught by him said that Edward Bliss Emerson was "the transcendent reality . . . [a] gift of God to those he taught. . . . His face the mirror of his inward being. Immaculate purity of soul, intellectual greatness, exquisite refinement of feeling, and tenderest sensiblility, were all engaged in limning its wonderful attractions." See Cooke, p. 7. The language of admiration among men brought up in the early nineteenth century was peculiarly cloying; see not only Holmes but also Furness, Abbott, and others.

mon practice then than it is now, but it still involved drudgery and cannot have been a life that the reserved and formal Ruth could have liked. The neighbors of her rented house on Hancock Street were a jail, the Boston Female Asylum, and a graveyard. The best rooms went to the boarders, and Waldo's was in the basement with a dismal view of broken furniture and gravestones. The boys of course were expected to work also, and there in the kitchen he sharpened the knives, among other duties.[19]

How emotionally limited that life was, except among the brothers, is evident in a journal entry written some twenty years later. In it Emerson used a strange metaphor of a kind of animal-servant at work in a boardinghouse to express his sense of a life alienated from the great models of earlier literature. "We live[,] animals in the basement story[,] & when Shakespeare or Milton or even . . . [Carlyle] call us up into the high region, we feel and say 'this is my region, they only show me my own property—I am in my element[,] I thank them for it.' Presently we go about our business into the basement again, cumbered with serving & assured of our right to the halls above, we never go thither."[20]

This animal metaphor, complex in its tonalities, is based on the anomaly of being a servant in a house one owns but cannot afford to enjoy or experience—exactly Emerson's own position as a youth; the boy's unease and touchiness, his helplessness to change or improve his environment, and his desire at once to challenge and learn from the strangers who had taken possession of the house are all superbly caught here. Considerably later, he described society as a "great boarding house in which people of all characters & habits meet for their dinner & eat harmoniously together; but, the meal once over, they separate to the most unlike & opposite employments." Beneath the seeming harmony and communal life of a boardinghouse, in his view, was atomistic loneliness and isolation. Such falsity must have seemed repugnant to a sensitive and lonely child.[21]

They were not confined there, however, for there was also work for their uncle Samuel Ripley (son of step-grandfather Ezra) who kept a boys' school in Waltham. Ripley was a decent, only occasionally irritable minister who after his marriage to the prodigious Sarah Alden Bradford was more than assisted by his scholarly—and ultimately legendary—wife. It was she who coached the rusticated Harvard students in the classics and other subjects, while he taught the

[19] L, 1:84; EBE, HMS; L, 1:19n.; L, 1:28.
[20] JMN, 4:274–75.
[21] JMN, 9:221; see Greenberger, "Phoenix."

younger boys. He needed ushers to help tutor and keep the boys in line, and it was almost a rite of passage for his nephews in turn when they had entered college to spend their Christmas and summer holidays working for him.[22]

Comparing Waldo's and Edward's reaction to their apprentice teaching gives sharp focus to Waldo's superior resilience in the face of hard times. To Edward, his uncle's demands were onerous. "The whole care of 17 boys devolves on me from morning to night" he wrote his mother. "Mr. Ripley has not heard but one lesson since I have been here." Only fourteen, he noted that although the boys had half an hour "for play after breakfast," he was given none. He spent almost a year there off and on, sometimes sick, but the care was indifferent. When it was six degrees below freezing, he reported, the family had a fire but not the half-nephew with a chronic cough and worn clothing who was, at some level, clearly cheap labor. Ripley was not deliberately harsh, and Edward reported that his uncle was "very kind in freeing me from any charge of the boys" while he was sick in bed; he went, moreover, to dancing school "void of expense to you," he wrote to Ruth. But it is unlikely that his mother would have chosen this mode of living for her son had not bankruptcy been a real possibility that winter. Boarders were not in sight and she was "in want of that important little article called *Cash*," as she wrote to William.[23]

Edward's complaints were probably justified, but Waldo took similar problems with aplomb. In the same situation, he had written to Edward not a message of distress but a self-buoying scrap of entertaining fantasy: "Here I am surrounded by my 14 disciples, (Pythagoras &c called their scholars disciples I believe, & modesty forbids me to say how far superiour I think myself to Pythagoras) every little while calling out, Silence! for school is just begun ie ½ after 8—but stop I must hear them read—Hem—." To William he reported, "Since I have been here I have learned to skate, rhymed, written & read, besides my staple commodity—school keeping—& have earned me a new coat! Ah my boy! that's the dasher!!! wear it tomorrow to Mr. Gore's to dinner by invitation from King—his birthday."[24]

Gore was a former governor of the commonwealth, rich and retired now at Waltham, and King was Waldo's classmate at Harvard.

[22] [James B. Thayer], *Rev. Samuel Ripley of Waltham* (Cambridge, Mass.: John Wilson & Son, 1897), pp. 32, 56; cited hereafter as Thayer.

[23] EBE to RE, 1818, HMS; RE to WEjr, 1818, HMS.

[24] *L*, 1:55–57.

Waldo too was worried about money, and it was in this letter that he wrote that it "appears to me the happiest earthly moment" if in future he should have "a home, comfortable & pleasant, to offer to mother," so that after living "on the charity of others" she would "in some feeble degree" be repaid "the cares & woes, & inconveniences she has so often been subject to on our account alone." He envied William, he said, for being able to give Ruth five dollars in cash, for "Mr. R. said I needed a coat & sent me to the tailor's though I should rather have worn my old coat out first. . . ." But he could endure such worries, buoyed by a sense of language and play that let him be by turns Pythagoras among his disciples, a pompous hemming schoolmaster, or Waltham's dandy. These were valuable defenses, and he was able to be concerned less with his own deprivations than his mother's.[25]

Waldo's talent did not go unnoticed within his family. He was engaged in an affectionate but long-running battle with William's more serious, directive temperament, and one of the fourteen-year-old's responses was to assume the persona of the poet and harp upon his senior's disapproval of his lack of diligence:

> William does thy frigid soul,
> The charms of poetry deny,
> And think thy heart beyond controul,
> Of each Parnassian Deity?
>
> This I suspect from that cold look
> Quenching like ice Apollo's fire,
> With which each vagrant verse you took,
> When offer'd from my humble lyre.
>
> Not that in truth I mean to say,
> I ever had a lyre—not I—
> Rhymers you know have got a way,
> To Tell a *bumper*—alias *lie*.—
>
> I love quotations—Dr. Gibbs—
> Or someone else perhaps—has said,
> —Poets have leave to publish fibs,
> And 'tis a portion of their trade—

A delighted William showed the letter to their uncle and then endorsed it in minuscule script with "Judgement of Mr. Ripley; 'Oh! that Ralph's a clever fellow, a clever fellow!' "[26]

---

[25] *L*, 1:57n.
[26] *L*, 1:40, and RWE to WEjr, 1817, HMS.

That he was a poet Emerson seems to have assumed from the beginning. It is hard to overemphasize the extent to which poetry—
either his own or translations—occupied his boyhood mind. Two of
his first three published letters are entirely in verse and the third,
written at age eleven, encloses a complicated rebus. Virtually all the
letters are larded either with scraps of his own poetry, comic or serious, with quotations, or with some allusion to his reading. He was
barely twelve when he wrote to William what may have been his
first critical hunch as he reflected on Dr. Johnson's pejorative comments on Donne in *Lives of the Poets*; the eighteenth-century writer,
after quoting a passage of Donne's work, called it "confusion worse
confounded." Young Emerson liked Donne, however: it is "old fash-
ioned Poetry—I should like to see the Poem it was taken from."[27]

Waldo clearly was able to hold his own against William. Indeed,
William may not have been fully a match for the brother who could
inquire coolly, as soon as William had gone off to teach in Maine,
whether he had yet been "hissed or snowballed out of town perhaps." "These are my fears not wishes," Waldo added disingenu-
ously, "but 'I've heard say' that many a poor youth has been stript of
his school by refusing to speak out of school to those scholars older
than himself. You see I love to advise my young friends."[28]

A wider focus on these dynamics and an insight to the role of Aunt
Mary in the family is revealed in another of Waldo's notes to William:

> If I were Aunt Mary, I should tell you how auspicious an omen
> it was to your future happiness that you had commenced the
> year 1818 in the "delightful task—&c," in the mind-expanding
> air, & piety-inspiring regions of Kennebunk—but being as I am
> less enthusiastic less scientifick Ralph I am glad to find that the
> year commences with Mr. Wm's *earning an honest livelihood* by
> turning village schoolmaster. . . . You see how humble my ideas
> are in comparison with those of what Uncle Daniel calls "the
> etherial incorporeal supernatural immortal soul" of Aunt Mary
> who says in her letter to mother speaking of K[ennebunk]
> "there repose the ashes of some of my honoured ancestors—who
> died triumphing in the faith."

Clearly, Waldo was already studying with considerable amusement
both Aunt Mary's style and the word-slinging of Uncle Daniel, who

[27] *L*, 1:4–7; *L*, 1:frontispiece; *L*, 1:10.
[28] *L*, 1:52.

was evidently a critic, like his father Ezra, of the "etherial" and "incorporeal."[29]

The alliance Waldo made with Aunt Mary was not least among his resources, for her interests and tastes fascinated him, and her instruction was as valuable to him, as he told Sanborn later, as his study of Greece and Rome. To some extent, the untold story of Waldo's adolescent years is the history of his capacity to learn from her, applying what was useful in her practices and point of view while maintaining his balance and sense of his own identity. Where his father, however suave, had been unable to avoid quarreling with his sister or smarting under her reproaches, Waldo as a nephew and no rival was able to acknowledge her special gifts and adopt many of her religious and intellectual presumptions. In the long run he was also to discard many, although not all of these, but in the process he learned how to shape an intellectual and religious stance. He also saw at first hand the great cost of such shaping. For him an aunt was indeed, as he said much later, "more . . . than a patron."[30]

The most striking note in their intercourse was the sense of shared play. From an early age, Waldo learned to mix literature and religion into the romantic sublime. He was only twelve when he arose before dawn one morning and, recognizing that as "the sun has not yet illuminated the arch of Heaven . . . this I suppose is the time to feel inspired," proceeded to describe to her his reading about Massillon, whose sermon to the court of Louis XIV on how few were the number God would save had been so powerful that his audience was seized by a kind of mass fit. Waldo was impressed, but concluded that "night with sable wing approaches and compels me to bid / Adieu . . ." Whether or not night had actually fallen was beside the point. He had in Mary the audience on whom he could try these new literary tropes and who was willing to share her ideas with equal freedom. "How do you, deer play Mate?" she asked in a letter sent when she was forty-five, he sixteen. It might have been their motto.[31]

Part of the fascination she held for him—one might almost say that it was the major gift she gave him—was her interest in prophecy and its related subjects, the imagination, dreams, and magic. This involvement was not separate from her religious stance, but intrinsic to it, for prophecy, as it happens, was a power especially sought by some of the New Lights. It was also, as Robert Richardson has

[29] L, 1:54.
[30] Sanborn, Personality, 118–19; JMN, 4: 371.
[31] RWE to MME, 1816, HMS; MME to RWE, 1820, HMS.

shown, a subject of increasing controversy and, especially as the Bible was involved, the focus of attack by the Enlightenment Liberals.

The neo-Calvinists clung to their claims for such insight, since the capacity to see and commune with God oneself, to be illuminated by him without priestly mediation, was the central mark of the Calvinist mind.[32] Many desired and deliberately readied themselves to receive such illumination. Especially during the Second Great Awakening, as one observer wrote in 1808, many of the "illuminated" were "alleviated" in mind by "*the spirit of prophecy*," some of them "caught up or carried away in this spirit, and remaining for hours insensible of anything in nature—dreaming of dreams, seeing vision,—hearing unspeakable words—the fragrant smell, and delightful singing in the breast." A contemporary observer, Richard McNemar, explained that under the influences of these visions "some would seem to desert the body."[33]

Mary, though she claimed a period of such visionary grace for herself, was both individual and shrewd and did not approve of the more extreme or public forms of such witness. In fact, she had acted vigorously to prevent young Edward while at school from joining the older seminarians at their long prayer sessions, which she feared led to fanaticism and hypocrisy. But McNemar's description is valuable in helping decipher the intent and context of her language and letters, significant portions of which draw on the vocabulary of illumination and advocate its visions. It also helps one see that the differences between William and Mary were not merely temperamental, but exemplified those that other scholars have described between their opposite political and religious parties. William's attack on the asceticism and illusory disinterestedness of Mary's religious stance expressed his upper-class Liberalism, while Mary's contempt for her brother's "barrenness of doctrine" and indeed for all of Cambridge except Channing expressed her ties to an older and more rural set of traditions.[34]

Her influence on Waldo in this area was powerful, for he had a predisposition in his youth to be fascinated by death, magic, and all that could help him probe beyond the threshhold of ordinary life and consciousness. From an early date, Mary provided a model of the visionary stance. When he went off to Harvard she in a sense renamed him; in what may have been an important moment equivalent

[32] Richardson, "Prophecy"; Heimert, p. 6.
[33] Handy, pp. 81–82.
[34] Heimert, pp. 16–21.

to a rite of passage, she endowed him with the identity of "genius." "What dull Prosaic Muse," she wrote, in a heightened tone expressing her illuminated state:

> would venture from the humble dell of an unlettered District to address a son of Harvard? Son of . . . of poetry of genius—ah were it so and I destined to stand in near consanguinity to this magical possessor. Age itself would throw off its gravity for a moment and dream that there was a vestige of fame to attach it to earth—that a name so dear was one day to leave some memorial. Vain wish . . . A name on this flying planet . . . is not matter of sin when viewed by the celestial light of faith. . . . In that great assembly, where human nature is purified from its native dross and ignorance, may the name of my dear Waldo be inrolled.

Recurrent themes that Mary was to impress on her nephew are already present: leaving the earth and seeing by celestial light, Waldo as "magical possessor" of "genius," and a prayer that is virtually a prophecy of his fame.[35]

At other times Mary wrote of his "highest sublunary gifts" or commented that "the spirits of inspiration are abroad tonight," suggesting insight into how the mysterious rites of ancient religions celebrated "more intimate relations between man and an nature than now exist." Long meditation on death, the grave, and the otherworld authorized her to urge Waldo also to abandon the haunts of men and seek solitude in the country; "Would to Providence your unfoldings might be there—that it were not a wild and fruitless wish, that you could be disunited from travelling with the souls of other men, or living, reading and writing, with one vital, time-fated idea—their opinions."[36]

She wished him, in McNemar's words, to "cast anchor upon the thing promised though unseen," a process she illustrated by obliquely describing one of her own visionary experiences, in which "so close was this conformation, that a certain pilgrim lived for some months in an eclipse so monotonous as nearly to discern the disk of her own particular star."[37]

The message in her passionate, intense, and schismatic stance reached Waldo clearly, and he seems to have found some needed

35 MME to RWE, 1818, HMS.
36 MME to RWE, 1821, HMS.
37 MME to RWE, 1824, HMS.

nurture in the sense that his aunt had some special connection with the ineffable, a connection fostered by her hermitlike ways and religious meditations. He might joke about it, as in a letter he wrote to Edward after receiving Mary's references to him as "Son of Harvard, . . . son of poetry of genius": "Only think of my condescension! Here am I a son of Alma Mater & addressing a—a what Why a member of an academy—Oh wonderful I admire my humility!!!" But though he joked, he did not forget.[38]

Another term much associated with her was that of sentiment, or the sentimental, which connoted all that was emotional, imaginative, and intuitive in moral and religious consciousness. She tried to encourage the spirit of imagination in her other nephews as well as in Waldo. "Many thanks for your dream[,] do dream more," she wrote to Charles from one of her wandering journeys when she was staying at the house of the conservative minister Elijah Parrish. She went on to describe her own dreams, suggested by

> this Byfield. . . . this old house with the trees thickly set in the front resemble[s] a ruin, and when the stars shine thro' the naked branches, they remind us of these bright spirits which may be looking on the dark and wandering inhabitants of earth. If they ask how I came to turn aside to sojourn among these strangers, I can hardly say, it seemed so undesigned.[39]

Charles resisted, saying stiffly: "You tell me to send you a thought which never has never will have any connection with my corporeal being." But it made him feel "awkward"—and a little pompous. It would be, he asserted, "a mere prostitution of intellect."[40]

Waldo, however, cherished Mary's talent as a writer whose best things were written without premeditation, and in this letter one sees how effective she might be, as she wanders with inspired impulse among her favored images of stars, the ruined earth, and herself as a bright and vagrant spirit or star. He absorbed, too, his aunt's high value for the concept of "sentiment." Sentiment was not only a romantic attitude, it was the opposite of "fact," of all that was gross, material, and the object of contempt. Thus when Waldo asked for some "facts or news," she replied in a phrase that turned up later almost unaltered in his "History," "What indeed are *facts* to me?"[41] In his youth Waldo tried to use her prescription, unsuccessful with

[38] *L*, 1:150.
[39] MME to CCE, 1822, HMS.
[40] CCE to MME, 1824, HMS.
[41] RWE to MME, MME to RWE, 1821, HMS.

Charles, on a downcast Edward when to cheer him up he urged, "Your next letter—pray let it be a flashy sentimental—Gaze on the stars till you get asleep and then dash off a letter about 'vast concave' etc. . . ."[42]

But it worked no better on Edward. What Waldo and Aunt Mary shared was theirs alone. Waldo wrote later that she had provided for him "treasuries" of religious language. He was not overstating his early debt, for he had acted at times as her treasurer, coining that gold and issuing it.[43] In later years Emerson was to describe in a moving, only partly metaphorical passage of his journals his attempts to communicate his private ideas with his brothers, attempts that ended as he realized the human being's essential isolation:

> Men go through the world each musing on a great fable dramatically pictured & rehearsed before him. If you speak to the man, he turns his eyes from his own scene, & slower or faster endeavors to comprehend what you say. When you have done speaking, he returns to his private music. Men generally attempt early in life to make their brothers first, afterwards their wives, acquainted with what is going forward in their private theater, but they soon desist from the attempt on finding that they also have some farce or perhaps some ear- & heart-rending

---

[42] *L*, 1:62. To one who understood truth intuitively, facts per se were irrelevant, except as they bore analogical meaning. Mary's language was full of dense references, inferences, and allusions—a habitual polyglossia her nephew may have absorbed from her. She liked to refer negatively to those who studied insects or spiders (perhaps alluding to Jonathan Edwards and his youthful treatise on spiders) in order to "find their way to a designing Cause." Her point was that so slow and tedious a process of logic, however high its aim, was unnecessary. Still, she could be entertained by observing such botanizing and its inferences. She wrote Waldo about one such experience, and he appears again to have used her language and ideas directly many years later. A friend had shown her a "peculiar dandelion . . . in each petal or blade hung a perfect flower itself. The little children will soon amuse themselves with seeing its downy leaves fly away. Now my dear Waldo," she concluded, archly pointing up the lesson, "if your imagination wanders into regions of *sentiment*, don't blame me. I will keep to fact."

Many years later when suggesting subjects for Charles's writing, Waldo used identical figures of speech: "Is it not a better inquiry than hunting new minerals or dissecting spiders or counting lobes [counting the lobes of worms was another of Mary's phrases used in this conflation] and petals of flowers to explore the obscure birth of sentiment at the frugal board perhaps of a poor wise man and see how slowly it struggles into fame." The dissection of spiders, the counting of "lobes" of insects and petals of flowers, the slow growth of "sentiment" into "fame" and glory—all these figures had originated in Mary's letters (MME to RWE, 1821, HMS); *L*, 1:246. For a more detailed discussion of her influence on Emerson's style, see Barish, "Angel."

[43] *JMN*, 5:324.

tragedy forward on their secret boards on which they are intent, and all parties acquiesce at last in a private box with the whole play performed before himself *solus*.[44]

It is a mournful, inexorable insight, but undoubtedly true both in relation to the relatives he mentions and to human interaction at large. But for a decade or so of his adolescence and early manhood he came closer to watching the same play with Mary than with anyone else.

When courting his first wife, Waldo mythologized his brothers, "dining out" on them in a conscious way as he made Ellen Tucker acquainted with his personal history. In trying to recapture the essence of Emerson's early life, one must balance the sense of dependency and intimacy in that image, which became part of the public mythology of the family, with this more private metaphor of isolation, absence, and distance. Undoubtedly, the brothers were close, as their mutual financial assistance—a burden actually borne largely by Waldo—suggests. But there was a significant absence for each person in the family, felt especially by the sons and probably—as in this image of the theater—incommunicable.

This void was one that Ruth's devoted hard work and language of the marketplace could not fill up. That was the family tragedy— perhaps even the same "ear- and heart-rending tragedy" that was going "forward on their secret boards." Ruth could not transcend it, nor had she any access to poetry, that "musick of the soul" as Mary called it. The other three boys saw what their aunt mediated as a dangerous luxury: nonmaterial thought might be "mere prostitution of intellect." Theirs was a pre-Gradgrindian world of prematurely balanced books and bills paid before interest could accrue. Waldo also learned discipline, but like his aunt he achieved a harder and more inspired task—to keep space around himself, to reserve a sense of his right to dream and be great. "Thanks for your dream. Do dream more," Mary had urged Charles. He could not respond. But Waldo was a more attentive listener, and for a time at least the empty theater had been filled for him by an urgent and original voice.[45]

[44] *JMN*, 9:236.
[45] MME to ETE, 1829, HMS; MME to CCE, 1822, HMS.

Chapter 4

ROMANCE

"Funeral
Real Fun"

—RWE, *JMN*, 1820

"I WONDER," Emerson wrote to Mary in 1821, some months after graduating from college at age eighteen:

how you can ever have linked a hope to the wayward destinies of a thing like me, to my dream-like anticipations of greatness. Not many indulge this prophecying vein, and yet there is something noble & striking in the attempting of a man to conceive the bent of his fortunes which begin here, and nowhere & never end; it is putting out an arm into the unseen world, and when some have done it, they have felt the reaching and beckoning of somewhat unearthly. But this is denied to the multitude.[1]

His suggestion that his college days were marked more by dreams than academic honors is accurate, although it is not the whole story. Certainly, Emerson's well-known failure to shine while at Harvard was not unnoticed by his relatives. Mary, who took pleasure in defending him, gave an account to Ruth of Ezra Ripley's criticism that captures the flavor of the family dialogue about Waldo and his failure to compete:

First conversation in Mothers chamber which took place at prayers . . . was after this sort. Grandpapa. Where *is* Ralph. Aunt. Waldo [she indicates both that she grants him the courtesy of his chosen name, and that Ripley does not] is at home. G. Ah dear now he finds the evil of not being more studious at C[ollege]. The govt. [college administration] would have recommended. Aunt. The govt *have* recommended him I happen to see Everetts. It is his youth. Gr. They have not so fully [as they might. Others would?] have been after *him* if he had

[1] *L*, 1:105.

been what   [William or another was?] Aunt. He is doing
very well. Keeps close at home and reads. So shortly ended this
converse which I feared would excite temper. I never said anything about Mr. Wm. Emerson's school. . . . Speaking of Wm,
that gentleman is respected here I find. Give my duty to him.[2]

Evidently it was difficult even for family members to judge accurately Waldo's capacities and progress. The reasons for obscurity in
so gifted a youth have not been sought, although they deserve attention. Undoubtedly, some of it resulted from the provincial and backward nature of Harvard itself. Only forty-odd years after the Revolution, the university was still small and intellectually sleepy; it
smarted sometimes under the popular press's accusations of elitism,
but its reforms under Josiah Quincy still lay ahead. The most eager
minds, like those of George Ticknor and Edward and Alexander
Everett, went to Germany for real postgraduate study.[3]

Like the English universities, Harvard functioned as a seminary
whose graduates could readily be ordained, but it did not even have
a separate divinity school when Waldo matriculated. President John
T. Kirkland established one in 1819 to meet the competition from
the seminary at Andover, but the latter remained more vigorous and
better attended. At Harvard, undergraduate faculty like Henry
Ware, Sr., and Andrews Norton shifted easily into the professional
division when needed. In general, its late nineteenth-century historians found it neither well run nor salubrious.[4]

Although far more straitlaced than the prereform Oxford of the
same period, which was still run by the "two-bottle Orthodox," as
John Henry Newman called them, Harvard too reflected eighteenth-century rather than nineteenth-century standards of decorum.[5] Student riots were endemic throughout the first three decades, and it was the norm for relations between faculty and students

[2] MME to RE, 1821, HMS; Cabot reported that it was thought that with a better
record Waldo might have gotten an ushership at the Boston Latin School, 1:72.

[3] Conrad Wright, "The Early Period (1811–1840)," in *The Harvard Divinity School:
Its Place in Harvard University and in American Culture*, ed. George H. Williams (Boston:
Beacon Press, 1954), pp. 13–16, cited hereafter as Wright; David B. Tyack, *George Ticknor and the Boston Brahmins* (Cambridge, Mass.: Harvard University Press, 1967), secs.
1, 2, and passim, cited hereafter as Tyack.

[4] Wright, pp. 23–24; Andrew Preston Peabody, *Harvard Reminiscences* (Boston:
Ticknor & Co., 1888), cited hereafter as Peabody; Samuel Eliot Morison, *Three Centuries
of Harvard: 1636–1936* (Cambridge, Mass.: Harvard University Press, 1936), cited
hereafter as Morison.

[5] John Henry Newman, *Apologia Pro Vita Sua*, ed. David DeLaura (New York:
W. W. Norton & Co., 1968), pp. 24–25, cited hereafter as Newman.

to be the "mutual hostility" that exists between "natural enemies."
Emerson's professor of rhetoric, Edward T. Channing (brother of
the famous minister), a man who undoubtedly helped pare and
strengthen his pupil's style, had himself been a leader in such a rebellion during the first decade. It was regarded as normal for a student to graduate who had been rusticated for three months of each
year for negligence, as long as he appeared at some half of his reci-
tations and was willing to respond, however wrongly, to the questions put to him. There was no bar to hard work—an ambitious and
hard-working student might study sixty hours a week—but a sluggish one might do almost nothing and yet be graduated.[6]

Faculty were not above acting as police: "In the case of general
disturbance, which was not infrequent, the entire Faculty went on
the chase for the offenders . . . but were seldom successful"—the
whole proceedings carried on to the applause of the students. Emerson's dislike of Greek may have been related to the way it was taught
by John T. Popkin, a charming eccentric but well known in the
college for the easy predictability of his methods, which permitted
each boy to calculate in advance exactly which minimal portion of
the lesson he would be called on to recite, so that he learned only
that. English, Latin, and mathematics, according to Andrew Peabody, were among the better-taught subjects.[7]

Food was coarse and student accommodations primitive. Large
rats attended the pig sties that abutted the dining commons, and
youths "accustomed to neat homes and well ordered tables" found
meals there "adequate in quantity but by no means appetizing"—
testimony that makes William's enthusiasm for his first college dinner seem the more pathetic. Breakfast consisted only of coffee, rolls,
and butter, unless slices of meat remained from the previous dinner
after having been affixed to the underside of the table by a diner with
his two-pronged fork. Supper was tea with "cold bread of the consistency of wool."[8]

In this ascetic but otherwise laissez-faire atmosphere, which seems
to have been a subculture governed rather by shame than guilt, a
certain amount of free enterprise flourished fairly openly; the "Re-
gent's freshman" was regularly bribed not to record late returns on
Saturday night. Emerson, as "President's freshman," presumably
filled this office. Edward Emerson—as his namesake recorded—was

[6] Peabody, pp. 202–3.
[7] Ibid., pp. 29, 43, 70, 86–88, 201, 204, and passim.
[8] Ibid., pp. 196–201.

one of those who sold ghostwritten themes on the steps of Hollis Hall for fifty cents—sometimes amid contention about value received. Waldo, through the intercession of Mr. Gould, his schoolmaster, was appointed the president's freshman, a position that gave him free room and required the youth to live in a room directly beneath the bachelor president's chambers, subject to the summoning rap of Kirkland's foot on the floor when he required his subaltern to carry messages or the like. Later Waldo was glad to work as a waiter in the commons, for the work paid three-fourths of his board.[9]

During vacations, he earned money at Waltham and wrote warmly and supportively to his brothers, especially the homesick Edward, to whom Waldo was an overwhelmingly important figure. But at college, his career was indifferent. He submitted essays for various prizes, but his ideas were unconventional, and he took no first place. He joined a few social and literary societies—one of which involved acting—but none of his activities seems to have brought him much visibility. An illustrative anecdote tells that although he was named class poet, seven other men before him had been offered the position and had refused.[10] He began his first journal in 1820 at age sixteen, titling it "Wide World," like the twelve following volumes, and dedicating it to witches, elves, gnomes, and sylphs, whom he called on to "assist [and] hallow this devoted paper."[11] It is important to recognize that however conventional the adolescent romanticism of the language, this is not a record of pleasant hopes or wishes fulfilled. Rather the journal and especially its fictions describes a world full of horrors, magic, imprisoned giants, ravenous wolves, snake pits, and slimy asps. It contains no fair maidens, no towers, no frog princes, and no happy endings. There are no living fathers, only dead or dying ones; no protective mentors, only threatening rulers. Natural or unnatural disasters attend the seeking youths who quest for that revelation of magical power that might relieve them of their loneliness or other burdens.

As for interest in the other sex, Harvard might impose harsh fines on its undergraduates for attending the theater—that was associated with sexuality and dissipation—but there is no evidence that Emerson either attempted such contacts or consciously at this period had to deal with such fantasies. His brother William, a schoolmaster at age sixteen, was teased in the family about his flirtations, but there

9 Ibid., p. 199; *EIC*, p. 26; Cabot 1:50–51.
10 Holmes, p. 35.
11 *JMN*, 1:4.

are no traces of such friendships in Waldo's life. Instead, evidence points to the channeling of most of his awakening instinctual life into his reading, writing, and "dream-like anticipations of greatness." Whether this period was merely one of lengthened latency, or whether that latency shaded—to use Erikson's term, as some evidence suggests—into a period of genuine moratorium, it is clear from these journals that this era in Emerson's life was unusually prolonged and difficult, but also—in terms of creative thought—unusually fruitful.[12]

Emerson's early journals are both too rich and too fragmentary to be discussed here in detail, and his fictions are not all of a quality to merit extended analysis, although two of the longer and most complete tales are striking and deserve attention. The other pieces, however, poetry as well as prose, require more than passing notice, for their preoccupation with the mingled themes of magic and death amounts virtually to an obsession.

Closely connected to magic was his fascination with the codes, anagrams, and palindromes that punctuated his journals and letters, for these forms of word play testified not only to Emerson's interest in language itself, but to his understanding of the power of language to transform reality. He had perceived this transformational power of words almost from the beginning when as a child he had discovered that by repeating a word over and over he could dissolve its relation to meaning.[13]

At seventeen he was still fascinated with such powers, fantasizing that possession of them would distinguish him from ordinary mortals, dull sorts who nauseated his taste and shocked his nerves with their "gaunt lantern countenances" and willingness to "do jobs." By contrast, to the "souls only of the mightiest is it given to command the disappearance of land & sea, & mankind & things, & they vanish. Then," he went on, "comes the Enchanter, illuminating the glorious visions with hues from heaven, granting thoughts of other worlds." All his life Emerson wished at some level to be such an Enchanter. To meet the Enchanter and penetrate the secret of his visions of other worlds was an ongoing dream.[14]

Such magical power was valuable primarily because it permitted

---

[12] *L*, 1:105. Allen, p. 61, believes probably correctly that Emerson's reference to a "nasty habit" implies guilt about masturbation. It seems a question, however, whether the degree of anxiety and guilt Emerson experienced during these years preceding ordination can be explained entirely on that basis.

[13] *EIC*, p. 14.

[14] *JMN*, 1:33–34.

one to penetrate the veil of death. Freud has suggested that magical thinking, obsessive by nature, is a mode of dealing by repetition with material the conscious mind represses. What gradually becomes clear as one reads Emerson's early writings is that his interest in magic and language is inextricable from what amounted to an obsession with death. One of Emerson's anagrams, mentioned earlier, is strikingly apropos: "Funeral," he wrote in his journal—then, centered below, "real fun." If fun is the play that domesticates even painful experience, this translation was not accidental; if a funeral might be re-encoded as something quite other, not tragic but "real fun"— like his memories of his father's funeral, "delightful" in its pomp and circumstance—then there might be only a thin line between the fairy land of dragons and kings, to which Waldo dedicated his first volumes of journals (and in which he preferred for some years to remain), and the land of death.[15]

Two volumes of his journals were actually dedicated formally to death. Opening the fourth volume, he imagined that he saw the bones of dead children, and that "the past lies open before us." His work had not so far produced fruit; therefore he invoked magic. "Some other spell must be chaunted . . . I will devote it to the dead. . . . To these monuments which they bequeathed, and to their shades which watch in the universe, I apply for excitement." Below this was a sketch of a death's head. Wide World 9 he dedicated to "the shoreless abyss,—eternity," and it opens with a yet more grisly invocation: "This night, the worm & the reptile are at work, in ten thousand sepulchral grottoes, upon the pitiful relics of human clay. Ever since the . . . hour when the royal Saturn . . . laid himself down in the tomb . . . this desolate & disgusting corruption has proceeded." Human rage had meantime helped on "with ready officiousness, the carnage of Nature. The past . . . lies open before us . . . the bones of its children lie about and beneath us."[16]

He imagined his own death—"My bosom's lord sits lightly on his throne . . . after a few days more he shall cease to be"—in a context in which human life flickered away imperceptibly into decay. Death was peace: "In the grave, the passions rest peacefully; the riot of pleasure, love, & revenge is silent; and that banquet which life offered to youth and health, is most foully disordered. The distinctions

[15] Sigmund Freud, "Obsessive Actions and Religious Practices," *Complete Psychological Works*, 9:116-27; *JMN*, 1:245.
[16] *JMN*, 1:91; *JMN*, 2:76.

of society are levelled in that stern republic, and the badges of those distinctions are cast away."[17]

Often in Emerson's prose and poetic fictions, he drew on historical models for the descriptions of bloody murders. A single scrap of verse, lacking either preamble or conclusion gives the tone of much of the material:

> Thy hands are reeking with untimely sin
> Thy hands are pledged to push a massacre
> Thy hands are busy now with parricide
> Three things might make a man foreswear the world
> And waste his manhood in a hermitage.

The notion that "parricide" in this fantasy should lead to a retreat from the world of action is not irrelevant to the underlying anxieties with which Emerson was struggling at this period and which produced his depression—or as he called it, "genuine misery."[18]

Close to this entry was a description of the death of one Geralde in the halls of Odin: "He summoned the dead from their coffins to come / And shriek in thy ear their own horrible doom." While it is not necessary to mention all of Waldo's references to murder, one may cite a longer poetic passage in which an Inca king slays an invading Spaniard: "He smote the Spaniard's plumed head / And felled him to his footstool dead / The crowd hemmed in the stranger band / And trod them down in the bloody sand." The treading underfoot of the victim is a repeated theme in these visions, which are almost entirely unrelieved by Waldo's normal sense of the ridiculous—to die struck down beside a footstool did not strike him as silly, preoccupied as he was by gore.[19]

In a similar passage in which the savage race takes vengeance on its civilized oppressors, in a poem set in North America, an Indian chief, "Mas." (possibly Massasoit), vowed death to a white tribe: "Then I will fall upon them like the night / And sing my war song in their ears, and kill / And stain the waterside with crimson foam / . . . . And white men's dying groans lull my last sleep." Interracial war seems to have intrigued him. He quoted the advice given Philip II by a bishop on how to treat the Moors: "The more you destroy the less there will remain." Hannibal, on the other hand, he pointed out, "gathered 3 bushels of gold rings after the battle of Cannae."[20]

[17] *JMN*, 2:81–82; *JMN*, 2:80.
[18] *JMN*, 1:218; *JMN*, 3:13.
[19] *JMN*, 1:219, 284.
[20] *JMN*, 2:134–35; *JMN*, 1:264.

Death by suicide was a frequent theme. "The Maniac's Verse" described a man's plunge into the sea, never more to "pluck the rose" or "climb the rock." On the next page, the poem "Life and death of the little red bobbin-maker" described how "Poor little Robin" twisted his bobbin and broke it, "While singing a song / And the grief did young Robin choke." His dog "Daisy / Quickly ran crazy" and they were buried together. Emerson wrote, too, of Cleopatra's self-inflicted death as she lifted the "slimy asp," and in two poems, one a revision of the other, he related the tolling of a death bell: "I love thy music, mellow bell / I love thy iron chime," each began, the second ending with the acknowledgment that the tolling was the speaker's own death knell:

> And soon thy music sad, Deathbell!
> Shall sing its dirge once more
> And mix my requiem with the gale
> Which sweeps my native shore.[21]

SCENES OF the deathbed constitute another subcategory of this theme. Without context, an odd description appears of a mortal paragon, one who sounds suspiciously like a combination of Waldo's own wished-for genius and his dead father's social success, a man whose "extraordinary mental powers" and "soul as pure & exalted as ever panted for a higher nature" were combined with "burning zeal," sobriety of judgment, and a career "unchecked by the ordinary limits of human thought." The person however, is clearly dead, and this flight of fancy is a trial obituary: "His fellow men have accorded him the sincere praise of comely sorrow."[22]

This unnamed gentleman is generically kin to a group of legendary figures, founders or kings of nations who are observed at their death beds, a point at which they have special visionary powers. Aaron Burr, for example, speaks from that posture, saying "I saw her [America's] Genius though youthful walking like a giant among her mountains nourishing his strength. . . . until his going forth to battle the old & fiery dragon of English tyranny. . . . I saw him when he trampled his enemy underfoot."[23] (That last figure, seen in the episode of the Inca king, reappears in the longer "Uilsa" story, discussed below.)

[21] *JMN*, 1:321; *JMN*, 1:322; *JMN*, 1:231; *JMN*, 2:53–54, 1:303.
[22] *JMN*, 1:50–51.
[23] *JMN*, 1:319.

Another such scene was the death of King Richard, a motif Waldo took up several times. The later "Richard's Confession" again invoked the supernatural, as the king described "the mystery of my conduct," and asserted supernatural inspiration: "There was a voice and a language in the sky which spoke to me; the ground I trod, the air I breathed, the waves where I revelled, uttered a sound to mine ear as keenly as if a thousand harps had been struck."[24]

Perhaps the most mysterious of such death scenes, however, was that of an unnamed puritan founding father, an episode that is introduced under the complex, coded anagram for "On an American."[25] This figure too heard voices, and he asserts that he was admonished by God's visions in the night, "speaking an unequivocal language to bring about the establishment of a nation in the unsettled wilderness." The man's mother, Elspeth, appears to resemble the witch Uilsa, and like Uilsa's son Vahn, the man learned to divine God's language from his mother:

> I traced [the omens] in the . . . ground, & in the trees of the forest, and read them in the evening cloud. You have heard of the mysterious character of my mother Elspeth, for she was known and noticed among all the settlers. She instructed me in sights and omens and all which I saw concurred. . . . And had she never taught men, I must have been blind indeed to the doings of fate.
>
> . . . But I say my life was devoted to Providence to promote this great design and immediately obeyed my weird.

("Weird" in the sense of having second sight is a term Waldo applied both to his aunt and to Uilsa.) The dying man sees the empire he founded now "branching to the skies and mixing with the stars" and adjures the "Young Man" who comforts him to "remember that it was my boast . . . when in the arms of death that the disease which is bearing me away . . . was found first in the diligent labour to plant a colony in America."[26]

"Richard's Confession" ends in his death: "He paused and a sop of

[24] *JMN*, 1:265; *JMN*, 1:235; *JMN*, 1:294–95.

[25] *JMN*, 1:337, n.109, differs, believing that "this ⟨I AM NO IAME CRAVEN.⟩ appears to be an unsuccessful anagram of the letters, written on the facing page, 'on a n a m e i r a n'—possibly from ἄμειραν, to rob some one of his share, or portion." However, introducing the Greek term does not resolve the anagram, while the concept of robbery is not relevant to Emerson's tale. "On an American" may be a neater solution, since it introduces no new data and would be an appropriate title for the tale that follows.

[26] *JMN*, 1:338; *L*, 1:197.

honey was offered him, which his parched and discoloured lips seemed to require. But he refused to taste mortal food and turned again to the priest."[27]

Emerson not only wrote but acted out such scenes as an undergraduate. Devoted to Scott (as the allusions in the preceding passages suggest), Emerson declaimed the part of Rob Roy's wife in the scene in which she condemned the spy, Morris, to death. " 'You shall die, base dog!' " he cried, so effectively that sixty years later his classmate W. B. Hill still remembered the "sensation" Emerson had made among his audience.[28]

There are lamentations over the death of genius and of fallen knights, references to funerals and funerary customs, to regicides, parricides, and cannibalism, to pits of snakes—the list is very long. One even finds, though rarely, humor: a strange bit of doggerel, possibly connected with the death of Emerson's own father ten years earlier in May 1811, described the death of a hog, "the grandson of Magog," and the ten-year decline and eventual death of his nine little pigs, his "little sons":

> O cruel March that thus didst blow
> And cruel clouds to storm
> The old hog's ghost & nine little ghosts
> Are seen in spectre form.

In the same vein, Emerson followed the description of King Richard's last delerious moments with the remark, "His hair stood up negligently, like forks."[29]

This merely samples such material, for Waldo not only invented his own fictions but copied out passages about death from a wide variety of writers. Unquestionably, he was involved in an obsessive process of repetition.

The temptation for the literary scholar to account for all this as mere literary romanticism or Byronism is clear, but should be resisted as reductive. Emerson's involvement with death was deeper, more irrational, and more important than that. One pattern stands out: death in this writing is not essentially a punishment for sin, or in general the effect of any cause at all. It is not really even an ending so much as a focal point, potentially generative. He does not give us Manfreds or Cains, weary of carnal knowledge and deserving the

[27] *JMN*, 1:266.

[28] W. B. Hill, "Emerson's College Days," *The Literary World* 11 (May 22, 1880): 180–81.

[29] *JMN*, 1:246, 358, 324, and passim; *JMN*, 1:275; *JMN*, 1:339.

fate they seek. On the contrary, Emerson's protagonists seem almost to die in order to gain experience and knowledge, so that death and mourning sometimes seem virtually first causes, glamorous and seductive. To cross into death is in some sense to grow sophisticated. And that knowledge and experience, as one may see again and again, seem to have been engrossed by patriarchial figures who—like Emerson's own father—are unable or unwilling to share it.

A sketch jotted into a random page of his journal in 1820 expressed perhaps better than words the links Emerson perceived between himself, magic, death, and the patriarchal past. On the left appears a robed figure, hooded, bearded, and wrapped in something like a shroud, who holds on a stick a small placard that bears tiny characters in an alphabet resembling Aramaic or some Eastern language. His eyes, which stare out blackly and strikingly, seem unfocused. A younger male figure, somewhat larger in size, approaches him, but although the youth's hand is outstretched in greeting or supplication, the older man does not see him. Near this seerlike head, Emerson has written, "A Magician of Might from the Dead Sea-shore." On closer inspection, the message is meaningless, the characters without shape. Almost a palimpsest as it makes its appearance from among random notes and jottings, this picture represents in all its crudeness the searching and bafflement then characteristic of Emerson's depressive and withdrawn fantasy life.[30]

Death had swallowed up his father when Emerson was so young that to lose a parent was to lose some yet unformed part of himself. As his writing hovers so obsessively at the threshhold of death, one senses that it is probing, that it represents an urge to return to the point of loss and *feel* there, so to speak, in a deeply unconscious and yet almost literal way for what was missing. Emerson's remark, quoted earlier, is apposite: "Prophecying is putting out an arm into the unseen world, and when some have done it they have felt the reaching and beckoning of somewhat unearthly." Derrida, quoting Torok and Nicolas, asserts that in uncompleted mourning, "the introjected object" becomes a "cryptic text."[31] Is not the shrouded "object" here William, and does he not visibly bear a "cryptic text"— that sign which teases but cannot be read? This graphic fantasy suggests not only the "reaching" Waldo wrote of to Mary, but also a fantasied response. Small wonder, if so, that he gave little attention to the work of the real world around him.

[30] *JMN*, 1:230.
[31] See chap. 1, n. 60.

No better illustration can be found of this desire to probe the secrets of the otherworld than in a prose fiction known in the family as "Uilsa," which Emerson began to compose during the months following his graduation from Harvard. Interspersed in the journals, the tale was written in four sections between August 1821 and February 1822. Though virtually unknown and seemingly disjointed, its abrupt stops and starts suggesting a kind of stammering, in fact the story is complete, coherent, and powerful. It is told by a young, nameless narrator who knows of Uilsa, the eponymous witch, because "she would come to the neighboring village and while a family were warmly seated about their evening fire they encountered her bright eye and frightful face at the window." Uilsa sees herself as a despised outcast: "If pursued she would be found perhaps squatted on the heath near her hut twisting a string out of the dead grass and muttering to herself. . . . this uncouth rhyme. . . . Your leaves are dead and your stalks are dry / Wrinkled hated—so am I."[32]

The narrator, fascinated, becomes a voyeur like the witch herself: "I watched her often in the town and secretly hid myself behind the brushwood to observe her motions." At length he sits down near a pile of leaves, for Uilsa is associated with "majestic" trees that cover her with their red leaves in autumn.

He is soon "shocked—to see a long bare arm outstretched" and to hear Uilsa "screaming to the woods and sky," evidently out of the leaf pile. Though she insults him by associating him with the local rustics, he perseveres and asks, " 'Can she not tell the young man how to guide his steps in life?' " Uilsa replies that although she is despised by the crowd as a "decrepit worm" and has "lived in a land which is hateful I did not come from the vulgar dust—Uilsa is highly and proudly descended from an hundred weird women, fatal and feared daughters of Odin." As the youth mentally acknowledges her claim of having "supernatural light" she stands up, glaring at him and looking north as if for a sign. Suddenly the narrative breaks off—the first of several such breaks. In the second brief fragment the narrator, named Wilfred, is seen crossing a northern waste at night; it ends as he hears an unnatural cry, neither human nor animal.[33]

The tone if not the setting of that section is echoed in part 3, which continues in midsentence from part 1, as Uilsa describes her history to the narrator. Speaking like a "Spirit of Prophecy, . . . a voice from the sepulchres and caves," she stands in her native forest

[32] *JMN*, 1:266–67.
[33] *JMN*, 1:268; *JMN*, 1:273–74.

while wolves run about her, lightning flashes, and the prose heightens until it virtually breaks into fragments.

In earlier years, she relates, she had borne a son (no father is mentioned—social legitimacy is beyond her ken) who was seized from her by a "gold caravan with galloping horses and tasseled elephants from Birmah." In reply to her screams, "Odin knew me and thundered." Her violent language emphasizes the capacity for tearing and eating alive possessed by Odin's wolves, who defend her and in some sense are identified with her: "A thousand wolves ran down by the mountain scared by the hideous lightning and baring the tooth to kill . . . " They mangled the flesh and crushed in the sand the bones of her captors. Thereafter she and the wolves had lived as equals together in their cave, sharing their food and the suckling of her son: a female had "nourished [Uilsa's son] from her dugs. I made my bed in the cavern, my feast with the whelp of a wolf. . . ."

The distinction between Uilsa and the wolves who both defend and betray her has faded: a wolf suckles Uilsa's son while Uilsa feasts with a wolf whelp in a cavern. The sadistic, almost cannibalistic elements of the tale expand further, for the boy grew up to reject and hate her:

My son commanded the snows of the pole. Who is he now but Vahn, the Master of Magicians? But the proud magician forgot the mother that bore him, and the circle of enchantments which he drew was a ring of fiend-dogs to bay at me,—to scare me over the snow-drift in the cold starless night.[34]

Hereafter Uilsa speaks no more; only her willed death lies ahead, while Vahn never appears at all. A "barbarian," her animality in sex and eating (linked taboos for Emerson) associate her with wild, dangerous terrain. An outlaw, her connection with extremes of setting is metaphoric of her moral extremity: to be as Uilsa is to be the Other, not human.

After a slight hiatus, the narrator, who now speaks like a gentleman in comparison to the "peasants" from whom he gathers information, seeks Uilsa out because he has learned she has become suicidal. Like a Romantic litterateur, he feels "elevated" by nature and its "fine shades" as he crosses the Kindlecoal woods—in contrast to Uilsa who lives in a cave and erupts from the woods, an autochthonous figure, seemingly born of the earth itself. The landscape grows in symbolic significance as, guided by a strangely prescient child

who suddenly appears, the narrator pursues Uilsa through a broken terrain of unfathomed chasms.[35]

After another narrative break, the child disappears unnoticed, but the seeker moves on, now accompanied by a villager who wants to warn Uilsa that a large *"ottar-snake"* lies among the rocks. They glimpse her rapidly moving toward the precipices, ignoring their shouts. Running around a rock they lose sight of her, suddenly see her again, and then discern the "immense folds" of the serpent, curled beside the chasm, while Uilsa, with "majestic gait," advances consciously toward the monster, looking north toward the dark clouds.

> She came within a few yards of the snake, and, stopping abruptly, raising both arms to the sky[,] stood like a giantess and cried aloud 'Art thou come, Minister!' The next moment that terrible animal was wound around her, tightening his terrific folds while his victim seemed struggling with superhuman strength and her hand grappled with the head of her destroyer. Suddenly they sunk and I rushed to the mouth of the abyss and listened, as there murmured up from its depths a loud cry to Odin from the suffocating gripe of the Serpent. THE END[36]

Clearly, magic and death are here again closely related issues, as supernatural insight is sought—and bequeathed to Vahn, master of magicians—but denied to the narrator, who learns only of Uilsa's self-destruction.

Interestingly, Uilsa bears many resemblances to Mary Moody Emerson. Mary and the rest of the family knew and were given to disseminating the tale. They also apparently associated her with that "weird woman"—to Mary's rueful amusement, if not disgust, for references to it have the earmarks of a family joke that will not die. Thus, Mary wrote Waldo in 1822, a few months after the completion of "Uilsa," "My young [ ] was so glad to read something new that the sorry tale of the old hag amused her and I promised something better. The Magician I said nothing off [sic]."[37] Her rueful tone about the "sorry tale" suggests her ambivalence about her role in a story she is at once publicizing and deprecating. No doubt she recognized the references to herself, described as a "weird woman" by Emerson both in the tale and in his letters.[38]

[35] *JMN*, 1:286.
[36] *JMN*, 1:302–3.
[37] MME to CCE/RWE, 1822, HMS.
[38] That the phrase took root in family parlance is evident from a letter Mary wrote

The family's interest is understandable, for "Uilsa" is a memorable and rich fantasy, open to many interpretations. But it obviously expresses the anxieties of a youth who is deeply ambivalent about death, finding it seductive and frightening at the same time. The tale presumes the existence of a supernatural world where power resides but whose sight will paralyze human observers.

Moreover, the power associated with both Uilsa and Odin is clearly that of the uncivilized aspects of existence, the libido, to which the narrator is a stranger. Animality, aggression, sexuality, eating, and her exceedingly intimate relations with nature—all these are part of the other world that the narrator visits, but only as an outsider. He comes from a village—she peeps into the windows of family homes at night, dwells in caves, shelters under leaves, and shouts that she is mistress of the woods and has "scared the eagle" in her flight. He admires the trees like a literary gentleman for their "fine shades"; she squats on the earth, twisting grass between her fingers and crooning a magic rhyme, and our first glimpse of her is when her long naked arm thrusts itself out of a pile of leaves. Not only is she defended by Odin's wolves, she essentially becomes one of them, eating and dwelling among these devourers of human flesh. The narrator is solicitous of her well-being, but anger and aggression are her ingrained modes of feeling.

The narrator is neither heroic nor cowardly. His vision makes clear that to live as Uilsa does, a kind of *daimon* mediating nature and the supernatural, is to risk too much, for her nonconformity, courage, and power lead her not to that meaning of life he seeks, but to the edge of the abyss and over it. While she does not answer directly the narrator's question of how to guide his steps in life, she does so by her deeds, which lead him literally to the brink of death.

The evocation of the "Minister" at the end of the tale is not irrelevant to its effect; on the contrary, it is one of the most striking elements of the tale and gives the impression of coming, as it were, straight from the unconscious. On the one hand, Uilsa calls upon the very identity—that of "Minister"—that Emerson sought for himself and knew as his father's. At the same time, the "Minister" is God,

---

Charles four years later: "Pardon the whim, if such it be, to ask you not to compare me to any wierd woman. I who live so as to try never to offend by one singular word—whose whole life is devoted to one and the same object, pray you spare my age and vocation." But the story lived on in Charles's memory, as evident from his request of 1827 to Waldo that he be allowed to print "Uilsa or some of your innumerable fandago effusions" should he become an editor of *The Harvard Register*. (The story did not appear there.) MME to CCE, 1826, CCE to RWE, 1827, HMS.

Odin, and the abyss. But the evocation is ambiguous: is the call a despairing one to a power that will not answer? Or is it to the monster-snake itself, the god of her weird rites? Is she abandoned or received when she commits herself to the pit? Certainly the ambiguity is deliberate, for she herself phrases it as a question, "Art thou come, Minister?" The sexual implications of the verb as slang were current long before the 1820s and are also relevant, if one understands that sexuality was one more terrifying alternative. At a deep level this may also be a reenactment of the primal scene, as the two voyeuristic watchers perceive a female giant in congress with a threatening but not completely unwelcome male force.

At any rate, Uilsa does not know: the meaning of the opportunity is not intellectually clear to her. Guided by instinct, or reference to her father in the north, she experiences a Fall, but it is not from an innocent Eden that she steps into the abyss.[39]

The affectless narrator, meanwhile, is safe but unenlightened. I have suggested elsewhere that only when Uilsa—who resembles aunt-mother-woman in gender—had ceased to terrify would Emerson be able to cross the chasm, accept sexuality and his own identity, and put into perspective the meaning of evil and death. These, however, were his moratorium years, to use Erikson's phrase, and until he reached their end he never felt at home in nature as Mary had done—as a letter to his friend John B. Hill explicitly says.[40]

As a whole, the events in this tale dichotomize paralysis of will and ambivalence in the face of action and life, and suggest a longing for a confrontation, however shattering, with the Father in all his love and supernatural terror. Perhaps in his daily strategies Emerson was learning the patience to nurture his private sense of self against all premature disclosures, but in his fiction he dramatized the strain and near impossibility of seeking to live when the calls of adulthood with its burdens of sexuality and aggression made life itself seem too full of pitfalls to be safely crossed.[41]

[39] See Packer, pp. x, 13. "Emerson is trying to replace the old division of the world and the psyche—according to which good things were above and wicked things were below—with a new division of his own, according to which good things come from within, wicked things from without." This seems relevant, but it is not entirely clear that even in his youth the two spheres were unambiguously distinct. See also the Epilogue.

[40] *Emersonian Gothic: The Misprision of an Aunt*, Bunting Institute Working Paper (Cambridge, Mass.: Bunting Institute, 1979); and Barish, "Magician."

[41] "Uilsa" provides an actual text strikingly close to Cheyfitz's theory that *Nature* contains a narrative subtext in which a child-hero "cannot hold its own in the conflict" with the "hero/ine." This is a "motherly hermaphrodite" who "subverts the hero of metaphor by involving it in the conflicts of her shadowy figure." She is at once a "beautiful mother"

The second of Emerson's two surviving fictions was actually published in *The Offering for 1829*, edited by Andrews Norton, as "Unpublished Travels in the East," but the tale has not been collected since. Written at age nineteen and much shorter than "Uilsa," like the latter it appears in Emerson's journals virtually without correction, written with energy and flow. In it a "bearded islander" from the Pacific Ocean tells the tale of the Siphars, a "vast musical apparatus" that proved "fatal to us." The siphars were trees consisting of "vast trunks perforated by a multitude of natural tubes without . . . external verdure. When the roots of these were connected with the waters of the river the water was instantly sucked up by some of the tubes and discharged by others and when properly echoed the operation [was] attended by the most beautiful musical sounds in the world."[42]

The islanders were worshipers of the "Great Zoa"—the plural form for the Greek word for animal, as Emerson knew. Determining to build their churches to the Great Zoa around these objects, the islanders gathered many of these siphars together (collectively called "the Organ") and thereby caused their own downfall. The music produced one night by the Organ was so ravishing that it made all the "hearers mad . . . with delight" and they began to dance, not noting the "unusual swell" in the river:

> Owing to [that] and to some unaccountable irregularity in the ducts[,] the pipes began to discharge their contents within the chapel . . . the water rose in spouts from the top of the larger ducts and fell upon the multitudes within. . . . The faster poured the water, the sweeter grew the music, and the floor being covered with the torrent the people began to float upon it with intolerable extacies.

Finally, "many hundreds were immediately drowned" but since the music only grew more and more perfect, "the ear could no longer bear it, and they who escaped the drowning died of the exquisite music." "Thenceforward," Emerson's narrator notes severely, "there was no more use of the Siphar trees in the Pacific islands."[43]

---

and a savage figure who tempts the child to leap into an "endless or FATHERless abyss," a "perpetual fall of uncertainty" (pp. 148, 167).

[42] "An Extract From Unpublished Travels in the East," *The Offering for 1829* [ed. Andrews Norton] (Cambridge, Mass.: Hilliard & Brown, 1829), pp. 8–10; *JMN*, 2:29–30.

[43] *JMN*, 2:30–31; for an alternative interpretation of this tale—as an expression of Emerson's interest in water pressure—see Kenneth W. Cameron, "Emerson and Hydro-

The sexual quality of the imagery needs hardly to be pointed out, so innocently overt are these gushing torrents, upright organs, and ecstacies of musical pleasure. What should be noted, however, is the swift and total punishment that falls without warning on these pagans: to worship the life force, for the nineteen-year-old Emerson, was a certain path to death. "Life only avails," he was to write much later, "not the having lived"—but that understanding came to him only after he knew what it was to have been stopped in his tracks by a deeply internalized vision of life as something whose pleasures and responsibilities he was not permitted to assume. In a passage titled "Preface to Travels in the Land of Not," which appears immediately after the tale of the Siphars, Emerson's persona acknowledges some sense of its latent content, for he raises the question of auctorial "modesty," calls the material not "subtle & delicate . . . but . . . enormous and gross to the last degree," and justifies publication of it by analogy with *The Arabian Nights*, which he hopes thereby to supplement. "It is now nineteen years since I left the land of Not," says the islander elegiacally, but he cannot return to that paradise, for "no man who leaves the limits of the country shall ever be permitted to set foot within it again."[44]

One might be born into the pleasure of this Eden—as the coincidence of Emerson's own age and the narrator's period of exile suggest—but, as in "Uilsa," to yield to the Great Zoa, or to one's animal nature, was to yield to death itself. Whether by a monstrous male snake named "Minister" grasping its female consort in a sexual but deadly embrace, or by a bearded islander's narrow escape and interdiction, the way was barred. In the second tale, the Great Zoa—the life or animal spirit—is itself the peril. One cannot be born without recourse to it, yet its "use" was forbidden by the story's end.

So to perceive life is indeed to be stranded on an island—isolated—just as Emerson was cut off by the failure to connect with his heritage or to build bridges across his sense of alienation from other people. Even the fantasy that witchcraft or magic might provide the key to survival and success was self-evidently fallacious, for in the repetitive pattern of these tales and images, magical properties adhere not to the seeking youth but to the older figures who, coming from or on the brink of death, ignore or reject the supplicant youth.

---

statics: The Siphars," *Emerson Society Quarterly*, 48, no. 3 (1967): 93–99; also F. Y. St. Clair, "Emerson Among the Siphars," *American Literature* 19 (March 1947): 73–77.

[44] *JMN*, 2:31–33.

THE PROTAGONIST'S sense of isolation in these tales is central also to an actual episode of abortive friendship that occupied Waldo's feelings for a couple of years. Recognized by Rusk as an "infatuation," the relationship deserves more notice than the brief references Emerson scholars have accorded it. The evidence for this attachment may be found throughout Emerson's journals from 1820 to 1822, by which time he thought his feelings for his contemporary Martin Gay had subsided; the editors of the *JMN*, however, point out numerous entries that they believe are references to this attachment.[45]

Martin Gay was a well-to-do member of the class of 1823, the son of a lawyer, and, although a year younger than Waldo, considerably more free and aggressive in his manner. The chronic student discontent with Harvard's food and governance broke out in the fall of 1820 in a large-scale rebellion, the so-called "bread riot," and Gay was one of the three leaders who were sent down. Three years later he and thirty-five others again rebelled and were expelled in May 1823. He never took his degree in person, but entered medical school directly, earning his M.D. in 1826. He received his B.A. in 1841 "out of course" when Harvard had apparently decided to close the books on the issue. In 1850 at the age of forty-six, a respected man in his profession, he died suddenly of a disease that the autopsy could not explain to the medical science of the day.[46]

The striking feature of this relationship, if it may be called that, is that Emerson and his contemporary exchanged only a few words during college and did not meet afterwards, so far as we know. They merely passed each other as undergraduates, and sometimes their eyes met. It was, in short, an ordinary enough "crush," but to Emerson it appears to have been as threatening as it was unexpected and intense. The first contact between the two occurred when Waldo, a junior turning seventeen in the spring of 1820, noticed the other, then a freshman, and realized that he wished to know this person, whose features suggested that he "should be a fast friend or a bitter . . . enemy." The penultimate word is so heavily cancelled that the editors could not recover it. This was typical of Emerson's treatment of his references to Gay, which tend either to be cancelled or to omit the object's name. In one case Waldo substituted meaningless letters where a name should have been.[47]

[45] Rusk, p. 85; Allen, pp. 52–54; *JMN*, 1:22, 38, 40, 52–53, and passim.

[46] Harvard College Papers, vol. 10, 2d ser.; "Records of the Immediate Government of Harvard College," vol. 10, 1822–29, 1828; C. G. Putnam, "The Late Martin Gay, M.D.," *The Boston Medical and Surgical Journal* 61 (Jan. 23, 1850), 506–7; *Boston Post*, Jan. 14, 1850; *Boston Daily Advertiser*, Jan. 28, 1850.

[47] *JMN*, 1:22; *JMN*, 1:53n.

By the fall of 1820, however, Gay had been suspended and his silent friend recorded the news that Gay was "proverbially idle." At the same time Waldo wrote his first poem to him, some eight lines in which he acknowledged that "thy lot in life is higher" but the writer "in grief or hope" would claim the other's heart and "fulfill a loyal part." He also drew a sketch of Gay—a somewhat snub-nosed, inexpressive profile—and tipped it into the page.[48] By the end of the academic year Gay had evidently returned from his rustication, and Waldo noted that he was "dissolute." By now he was puzzled at his own and Gay's behavior: he felt fascinated by the other's "cold blue eyes," but had spoken only a dozen words to him. Moreover, he had twice walked where they might meet but inexplicably at the last moment had deliberately and visibly turned aside. Any hope for friendship was thus aborted. Emerson was graduated in the summer of 1821, and they do not appear to have met again except in passing.[49]

Two more short poems, one fragmentary, and some three references written in the late winter and spring of 1822 show that Emerson, however, continued to think about Gay. One journal entry in Latin avowed that he had met both a man and another person, a woman (no trace of whom appears elsewhere in this document), and learned to know the beginnings of love "both[,] if it pleases God, will make a part of life, a part of me." The other entries reflected his disappointment with himself, nine months after graduation: "Now I'm a hopeless Schoolmaster just entering upon years of trade to which no distinct limit is placed." Interestingly, however, he perceived that his feelings for Gay had served a purpose. "There was pride being a collegian, & a poet, & somewhat romantic in my queer acquaintance with Gay; and poverty presented nothing mortifying. . . . But when one becomes a droning schoolmaster, and the other is advancing his footing in good company & fashionable friends, the cast of countenance on meeting is somewhat altered."

He added with an unconscious pun, "Hope . . . still hangs out . . . her gay banners," but she had been a cheat. A week later he was blaming himself for lacking "the kind affections of a pigeon. Ungenerous & selfish, cautious & cold, I yet wish to be romantic. Have not sufficient feeling to speak a natural hearty welcome to a friend or stranger and yet send abroad wishes and fancies of an ⟨alliance⟩ friendship with a man I never knew."[50]

Like other of Emerson's strictures on his own supposedly "cold"

---

[48] *JMN*, 1:39, 40, and *J*, 1:facing p. 70.

[49] *JMN*, 1:53; *JMN*, 1:39; *JMN*, 1:54.

[50] *JMN*, 1:94–95; *JMN*, 1:130; *JMN*, 1:134. Hereafter, angle brackets enclose rejected variants.

temperament, this remark has been taken out of context by some observers as revealing the truth about himself, though little could be more misleading. Although shy, he was far from cold; what he did feel was a profound inhibition in his capacity to express love or gain it, a recognition that he sometimes admitted with great pain. These self-accusations generally followed experiences not of his own emotional coldness but of scarring rejection through the loss of some beloved person, such as his father, a hoped-for friend, or, in later years his son. Confused and miserable at what he thinks he sees, he notes that in a score of years perhaps "these will appear frightful confessions," but they are certainly a "true picture of a barren & desolate soul."[51]

The last of his overt entries on the subject was written in late November 1822. "The ardour of my college friendship for [Gay] is nearly extinct" but "to this day, our glance at meeting, is not that of indifferent persons, and were he not so thoroughly buried in his martial cares, I might still entertain the hope of departed hours." Presumably, Waldo still ran into Gay occasionally, and the latter may have been involved in the militia. But the young teacher believed it was better so, for the inevitable "late discovery of insurmountable barriers to friendship" would have been reason enough to avoid it. Significantly he added that "from the first, I preferred to preserve the terms which kept alive so much sentiment rather than a more familiar intercourse which I feared would end in indifference."

The two little poems that the editors suggest are addressed to Gay follow the same line as the first, which swore humble fealty: the second avows love ("Malcolm I love thee more than women love / And pure and warm and equal is the feeling / Which binds us and our destinies forever"), and the third together with its epigraph deserves quotation in full, for it suggests the genuineness of the feeling:

This song to one whose unimproved talents and unattained friendship have interested the writer in his character & fate.

> By the unacknowledged tie
> Which binds us to each other
> By the pride of feeling high
> Which friendship's name can smother
>
> By the cold encountering eyes
> Whose language deeply thrilling
> Rebelled against the prompt surmise
> ⟨Confessed⟩ Which told the heart was willing;

By all which you have felt and feel
My eager gaze returning
I offer to this silent zeal
On youthful altars burning,

All the classic hours which ⟨come⟩ fill
This little urn of honour;
Minerva guide & pay the pen
Your hand conferred upon her. [R.W.E.][52]

The effect of this abortive encounter on Emerson's development
was not good, for he seems to have drawn from it self-punitive and
even paradoxical inferences about his own incapacity for love and
doubts—although these dissipated in a relatively short period of
time—as to his masculinity. Sensitive, literary, intellectually very sophisticated, he was probably also at this time sexually inexperienced.
He had neither the knowledge and defenses that common street life
might have given him, nor the sense of freedom to experiment that
more permissive cultures grant. His brother Charles was to write
Waldo when he himself reached a similar age that he desired to ex-
pound on the "disgust" and "nausea" a "pure boy" felt on discover-
ing the wickedness of the real world.[53] Some combination of influences in their lives—no doubt including the ridigity of their early
training—had failed to teach them the pragmatic tolerance that recognizes human beings, themselves included, as morally mixed, not
simple or pure. He could not know that to be inhibited was not necessarily to be cold, or that to love a person of his own sex was not
necessarily to be perverse.

Gripped, however, by his inexperience and tendency to go to extremes, Waldo began to wonder if his attraction to Gay did not reflect homosexual tendencies. What he had earlier perceived more accurately as a product of his own romanticism he began to question
more seriously when at twenty-one he began to prepare for the ministry, a step whose implications in regard to his sense of identity
were most serious, arousing once again the deep anxieties that had
been unquiet ever since his father's death. That such attractions are
common at some stage in the growth of the adolescent is now accepted, and even in Emerson's own day the ordinary man or woman
probably wisely ignored or forgot their juvenile passions when they
had grown beyond them.

[52] *JMN*, 2:59; *JMN*, 1:291–92; the editors note that "the song seems almost certainly
addressed to Martin Gay" (*JMN*, 1:321–22).
[53] CCE to RWE, 1827, HMS.

Waldo, however, could not do this. "All human pleasures have their dregs," he wrote, "& even Friendship itself hath the bitter lees. Who is he that thought he might clasp his friend in embraces so tight, in daily intercourse so familiar, that they two should be one?" He could not dismiss it, but rather expanded on the loss of mutual respect that would have ensued has two such intimate friends "trusted to each other the last secret of their bosoms . . . even its secret sensuality . . . [and] regret and fear remained . . . the consequences . . . of their violent love." It was curious, he reflected, that the object of attraction is "a stranger of whom Nothing is known, & nothing will come, whose eye, hair, or coat takes the fancy." Citing James I, whom he knew from his reading of Hume to have been actively homosexual, he took the lesson, "Misery to himself & seed grew out of his intemperate fondness for Robert Carre, and George Villiers."[54]

A month and a half later, in the course of writing a long, painful self-analysis as he considered his fitness for the ministry, Emerson overtly described his anxieties:

> In my frequent humiliation, even before women & children I am compelled to remember the poor boy who cried, "I told you, Father, they would find me out." Even those feelings which are counted noble and generous, take in me the taint of frailty. For my strong propensity to friendship, instead of working out its manly ends, degenerates to a fondness for particular casts of feature perchance not unlike the doting of old King James.[55]

Emerson, it seemed, could do nothing right.

The "poor boy" who feels humiliated before both his "Father" and the world was shortly to appear again in the youth Isaac, protagonist of the poem "William Rufus and the Jew," which he wrote a few months later. Before this punitive and internalized judge, no life-affirming or risk-taking commitment could stand. His only defense was further repression: "Stateliness & silence hang very like the Mokannah's suspicious silver veil only concealing what is best not shewn. What is called a warm heart, I have not."[56] What is most relevant about the episode is that Waldo was not able or did not dare to take the opportunity of making a friend of Gay. Another youth in his position might at least have attempted to channel and control his emotions enough to have some contact with this interesting, more

54 *JMN*, 2:227–28.
55 *JMN*, 2:240–41.
56 *JMN*, 2:241.

confident, and worldly person from whom he might have learned much. Instead, Emerson accepted the judgment of others that Gay was "dissolute," and he "preferred . . . [the] sentiment" of what was "romantic" to the attempt of making a real friendship with its attendant possibilities of "indifference" and rejection.[57]

Years later Emerson was to write, "I ate whatever was set before me. I touched ivy & dogwood. I kept company with every man in the road for I knew that my evil & my good did not come from these but from the spirit whose servant I was, for I could not stoop to be a circumstance as they did who put their life into their fortune & their company."[58]

But this was far from the reality in his youth, when his "wish to be romantic" took precedence over engaging with real life. Malcolm/Martin was important essentially not as an object of mature love but as a step toward metamorphosis, a player in the private scenario by which Emerson was seeking to transform himself. In that project he did not need as a companion another youth like himself. He needed a hero; if none was available he would invent one, or at least keep far enough away from an attractive peer to permit a burgeoning sense of his own romantic potential. The price was a delayed sense of worldly competence.

THE DEEPER MEANING of Emerson's loss, then, only gradually became apparent in the years following his father's death. "Few men have ever suffered more genuine misery than I have suffered," he wrote at twenty-three, referring not only to his physical disability of the time, but to his emotional state as well.[59] Readers can now better understand the sources of some of that misery. Knowing the father for Emerson was crucial to knowing the self, but it would be difficult to know himself and find his place in the world while he was so estranged from such knowledge and, by extension, from all authority and paternal surrogates. With that core uncertainty, even friendship with his peers was routinely unsatisfying and could be dangerous.

Useful light is shed on this problem by the studies of the bereaved child cited earlier.[60] Analysts from Freud to Bowlby have shown than Emerson's fantasies and behavior as a child present a classical

57 *JMN*, 1:53, 130, 2:59.
58 *JMN*, 9:116.
59 *JMN*, 3:13.
60 See chap. 1, n. 53.

reaction to the unmourned loss of a parent. Fantasies involving violence and animality, obsessions about death, suicide and reunion
with the missing person are all common. Depression with its concomitant withdrawal is the most frequent symptom, along with anxiety, guilt, and anger at the missing parent. Disturbed object relations are also common.

Equally important is the light this clinical material sheds on
Emerson's repeated self-criticism for his failure to feel deeply enough
when new losses struck him, such as the death of his son. His actual
behavior might display the reality of intense depression, but the kind
of self-blame expressed in his remark, uttered when in pain, that he
lacked "the kind affections of a pigeon" has led some scholars to believe it and discredit him.[61] Research supports intuitive recognition
that Emerson's response, on the contrary, matches that of others in
his situation, whose apparently "dull and apathetic reactions" to new
losses, or "no reactions to the loss of individuals" are misleading, the
results of prior scarring. The "painful affect continues to flourish,"
in the words of Helene Deutsch, but the emotional energies will take
a distorted form—a fact that should be remembered in considering,
for example, his opening of his first wife's grave, or his denial in his
essay "Experience" of any emotion beyond regret for the loss of "an
estate" following the death of his first son. Far from being indifferent
to wife and son, Emerson probably loved no other two people as
much; it was precisely the extremity of his loss that led to such inappropriate and clearly neurotic reactions.

It is important to understand that Emerson's profoundly inhibited
expression of grief, or his asserted inability to feel it "appropriately,"
do not reflect the true feelings of a cold man, however much he accused himself. At the deepest level, love to him meant pain, but he
went on loving. Trust meant loss, and the fear and anger that accompany such loss; he therefore made the relearning of trust his project
and syllabus. That it was not easy critics of his language have been
demonstrating as they tease apart his "unstable antitheses." But his
readers would not have found him useful if what was so hard for
themselves had been easy for him. One does not become a "doctor-
of-the-soul" by leading a charmed life.[62]

[61] E.g., James M. Cox, "R. W. Emerson: The Circles of the Eye," *Emerson: Prophecy,
Metamorphosis, and Influence*, ed. David Levin (New York: Columbia University Press:
1975), pp. 71–80: "Emerson literally feeds off the death of those around him." Cited
hereafter as Cox.

[62] Bishop, pp. 145–48, discusses the intensity of many who responded to Emerson in
his own day; Bloom, *Poetry and Repression*, p. 239.

The insights and research of this century, however, were not available to Emerson. Caught by feelings of sometimes blind suffering, he could at times answer only by repetition and repression. For a considerable period his fantasies evoked not enlightenment but only new rehearsal of the loss. The magician looked away; King Richard died; the islander survived only by turning his back forever on beauty. From this perspective, death had a certain glamor, for if it could swallow up life it might on an unconscious level in some way be the same thing as, or perhaps better than, life.

The dilemma is well expressed in a poetic fragment he wrote at age seventeen. It begins the story of Ariel, an Inca prince who was instructed by the priesthood in the mysteries of space and time. Their "mighty visions" told him how "their swift star from the far centre hurled" might "cross the bright orbit of another world." Such teaching elevated yet alienated his spirit, "till Ariel wept to think himself a man."[63]

As well he might. For what could manhood be worth to Ariel if insight and wisdom were qualities estranged from his own nature? The same complex of questions about death, gender, and identification with the father was posed in the poetic fragment in which the speaker boldly asserted that he sought to die in order to quit one identity and take on another. It was a man's act, he insisted:

> I stand amid the wilderness. Disdain
> Hath marked her victim; Hunger, Cold,
> Misfortune shake their shrivelled hands at me
> And gird me in their hideous company.
> I have conversed too long with life, and fed
> The appetites of dull mortality
> With nectar from the paradise of God.
> Unchastened, I have put my hand upon
> The wheels of the revolving Universe
> To pluck another nature thence than mine.
> Amid the deafening battle of the clouds
>   . . . and the cry
> Of ⟨alarmed⟩ Nature I have lifted up
> No woman voice to hush the awful roar.
>
> . . . .
> Come! scatter ashes on my fragrant couch
> I will shake hands with Death and hug Despair.[64]

[63] *JMN*, 1:37.
[64] *JMN*, 1:82.

The language was inflated, but the feelings real. If the model of manhood lay beyond the grave, separated by fantasy and long-buried guilt and anger, how to lift a man's and not a "woman voice" was not easy to resolve.

While turning nineteen, a despairing Emerson determined that like Jacob, "I will yet a little while entertain the Angel."[65] In his maturity Emerson appealed to wide audiences when he recognized that he must speak to them out of his own deepest fears and desires. That ability to draw on such knowledge may have grown from periods like this one when, for years and with strange lucidity, Emerson defended his right to reach out to the universe and pluck from its "revolving wheels" a self grander and finer than his own insignificant being.

For a while, then, magic was the key. Associated with death, magic might mediate a needed vision of the self, bringing finally into focus the message from the "Dead Sea-shore." But neither the female Uilsa nor any of the other prophets or supplicants in Emerson's fictions ever speaks clearly: Ariel weeps, the young man or nameless narrator watches in mute horror as Odin's or God's language ends with the dying protagonist. The father, lost in romance, never returned. Emerson's real growth only began in the next few years, when he renounced the struggle to find him, and turned from romance to history.

[65] *JMN*, 1:134.

Chapter 5

HUME

"Next comes the Scotch Goliath"

—RWE to MME, 1823

THE ANTIDOTE to romance would be the hard subjects leading to masculine and professional spheres: philosophy and
history, then at the cutting edge of intellectual endeavor.
And the way would be through study of David Hume, a great mind
who had worked in both fields. Though dead some forty years,
Hume was still anathema to the leading Protestant theologians; de-
voting extended study to him suggests how much it was already
characteristic of Emerson to rely on private judgment. The first evidence of this self-directed course came when Emerson set himself
to compete for the Bowdoin Prize, offered by Harvard on such subjects as the "Character of Socrates" and the "Present State of Ethical
Philosophy."

In the course of writing his essay for the second of these competi-
tions Emerson, still only seventeen, made his aunt a silent but not
unwitting contributor to his effort by placing near the beginning of
his essay some twenty-nine words of Madame de Staël, whose au-
thorship he acknowledged, and some sixty-four of his aunt—whom
he did not cite. Both quotations, in fact, had their source in one of
Mary's letters. Together their words won him a second prize.[1]

This intrafamilial plagiarism apparently did not bother her,
though she noticed it, for she was proud to help shape his thoughts.
He had apparently sent her a draft copy of his essay, which asserted
that it was a historical study. She responded, "Of that MS I find nothing in the nature of history—highly metaphi[sical] and boldly interspersed with my objections and queries." She then went on to discuss de Staël in the passage he would eventually incorporate. That
an early draft already contained her ideas, and that the final version
(the only one extant) included yet further material he had learned

[1] This borrowing was first noticed by Prof. Eleanor Tilton; *JMN*, 1:335n.

99

from her—the de Staël quotation—suggest how intimately and securely he drew on her intellectual "treasuries" at this period.[2]

He probably felt he needed all the help he could get. The essay was highly ambitious, for it took aim at the skeptical philosopher David Hume, whom no professional theologian had been able to refute. Edward Everett Hale, Emerson's friend and commentator, thought that it must have "surprised and sometimes annoyed the sort of men" who judged it and were the reigning powers at Harvard. Hale was not explicit, but the essay is important in understanding Emerson's development, for it reveals that Emerson was involved with skepticism from the very beginning of his intellectual career.[3]

The opening shows Mary's influence—which soon dropped away—most clearly. His aunt's letter and his essay both assert in identical language that in contemplating the possibility of the mysterious connections between humans and nature, "we recognize with a scientific delight, these attractions; they are material, still they are the agency of Deity, and we value them as subservient to the great relations we seek and pant after, in moral affinities and intellectual attractions, from [God's] moral influence."[4] In short, the analogies or "correspondences" between the material and unseen worlds that Mary, following an earlier tradition, loved to meditate upon—"panted after"—were here also celebrated by her nephew, and in her very language. Her words were especially apt in this instance because her insistence on innate ideas was so consciously opposed to the Humean skepticism his essay was to duel with.[5]

Moral science, they held, was "the beautiful and eternal offspring of other worlds"—a conventional reference to its source in revelation, but couched in language whose poetic quality rings with his aunt's diction. It had been revealed "to this frail and fleeting order of beings," Emerson wrote. His aunt, in another unnoted parallel, had

---

[2] MME to RWE, 1821, HMS. At least one other passage in the essay shows a clear parallel in their writings. For an example of the difficulty editors have had in distinguishing their styles, see chap. 8.

[3] Edward Everett Hale, ed., *Two Unpublished Essays: The Character of Socrates: The Present State of Ethical Philosophy. By Ralph Waldo Emerson* (Boston: Lamson, Wolffe & Co., 1906), p. 4. The judges were President Kirkland, John Davis, Dr. William Prescott, and Dr. Eliphalet Porter, with Gov. Gore assisting in 1820.

[4] Ralph Waldo Emerson, "The Present State of Ethical Philosophy: An Early Essay of Emerson," in *Ralph Waldo Emerson: Together with Two Early Essays of Emerson*, ed. Edward Everett Hale (Boston: American Unitarian Association, 1902), p. 100; cited hereafter as "EP."

[5] See "EP," pp. 100–101, MME to RWE, 1821, HMS.

written in her same letter of January 8, 1821, that "to the order so frail, so afflicted, and so hazardous as man, the 'rewards of grace' a magnificent plan has been laid for him."

Ethics, of primeval origin, had descended in undeveloped form first to various ancient peoples and then to the Greeks, all of whom had seen connections existing between humans and nature. (This veiled reference to early polytheism was treading on shaky ground. It had been a vexed subject ever since David Hume had asserted in *The Natural History of Religion* that polytheism, not monotheism, was the natural, universal and earliest form of worship.[6])

After dwelling at some length on Socrates and adverting favorably to Aristotle, Zeno, and especially the Epicureans, Emerson quickly passed to the early Church fathers. Upon these and their successors he showed himself an orthodox inheritor of the Puritan tradition, freely casting aspersions upon their "parade," "disputations," "obscurity," and all the ills of popery, even comparing certain Hindoo practices favorably with those of the unreformed Church.

This "historical survey" that he had announced, however, took less than a third of his space. His essay began to focus when discussing the seventeenth century and sharpened quickly on the eighteenth, so that after a few references to Cudworth and Bacon and some swipes at Hobbes, he settled into his fundamental argument, that "the truths of morality must in all ages be the same."[7] As Mary's letter had put it more succinctly, in a phrase he often quoted, "Morals [are] coeval with existence."[8] Here, however, he cited not Mary but Samuel Clarke, Richard Price, and Bishop Joseph Butler, as well as other theologians like Dugald Stewart and William Paley, as having settled the issue.[9]

---

[6] David Hume, *The Natural History of Religion*, vol. 2 of *Essays and Treatises on Several Subjects* (Edinburgh: Bell & Bradfute, 1804), 2: 402ff, cited hereafter as Hume, *NHR*; *Encyclopaedia Britannica*, 1911.

[7] "EP," p. 111.

[8] *JMN*, 2:49, 149; MME to RWE, 1821, HMS.

[9] "EP," p. 112. He erred in one point here, for Paley, as Todd has shown, was a follower of John Locke on the important question of innate knowledge and could not have held such a view of moral knowledge. See Edgeley Woodman Todd, "Philosophical Ideas at Harvard College, 1817–1837," *New England Quarterly* 16 (March 1943): 77–78.

The intricate question of Emerson's mixed debt to the Scottish Common-Sense philosophers has been attacked repeatedly over generations. See Merrell R. Davis, "Emerson's 'Reason' and the Scottish Philosophers," *NEQ* 17 (June 1944): 209–28; and J. Edward Schamberger, "The Influence of Dugald Stewart and Richard Price on Emerson's Concept of the 'Reason': A Reassessment,"*Emerson Society Quarterly* 18, no. 3 (1972): 179–83. Schamberger (p. 181) points out that it was Mary who suggested while Emerson was preparing his dissertation that he should read Price on morals, and that he took her sug-

Having demonstrated his acquaintance with orthodox ideas, Waldo then turned to David Hume. In doing so he entered uncharted waters. Hume was the focus of the attacks of the Scottish Common-Sense philosophers who were the mainstay of Harvard's curriculum; in fact, Hume's arguments had called them into existence.

Emerson's approach was somewhat ambivalent. He argued that Hume's attacks on faith were wrong, but even if he were right, "mankind will be content to be deceived; if the system of morals which we hold to be true be a dream, it is the dream of a god reposing in Elysium; and who would desire to be awaked from the sublime deception?" Harvard's government undoubtedly did not want to hear from a young whippersnapper that Christian revelation *might* be a "sublime deception" (a Humean locution), any more than they wished to accept his invitation to dispose of their doubts by accepting that they were dreaming in Lotosland.[10] To grant the enemy so much ground, even in the subjunctive mood, was a tactical error and may have looked like a breach in the dike. The aim of these readers, after all, was to train ministers and thinkers to battle more hardheadedly than this.

Waldo went on to say that the "reasonings" of the liberal establishment he had just cited as his authorities in doctrine "as yet want the neatness and conclusiveness of a system, and have not been made with such complete success as to remove the terror which attached to the name of Hume." In so doing he probably prejudiced his jury against him. "Terror" was not what the still-established church wished to feel, especially before an infidel whom Waldo immediately next termed a "great man"—another offense. Hume's opponents, he added—turning on them the very phrase that had been cast at Hume—foolishly attempted to demolish him by "that irresistible weapon, a *sneer*."[11]

This was provocative, but whether the rather naive seventeen-year-old understood that is not certain. On a democratic note that eulogized the moral potential of periodical literature, condemned slavery, and reaffirmed morality as "the rule by which the world must stand," Emerson ended his highminded, well written, but unpolitic discourse on ethics.[12]

---

gestion in March 1821; see *JMN*, 1:51. None of these sources, however, discusses the irritating stimulus of Hume.

[10] "EP," p. 122.
[11] "EP," pp. 122–23.
[12] "EP," pp. 126–27, 133.

The essay presented other problems also. While he was orthodox in much, crucial sections of it swerved from received opinion. First, nowhere did Emerson refer to what Mary later objected to as missing from an early sermon: the "saving power of the Saviour." Nor did he mention Christ's superiority to all other revelations as a source of ethical doctrine. Protestantism recognized several revelatory sources, among them the covenant with Noah, the Old Testament itself, biblical miracles, and nature, but Christian revelation was paramount.

Second, by not stressing that monotheism was morally superior, and by insisting that morality was eternal and independent of specific agents of revelation, Waldo again was moving through the door that Hume had opened. Next one might infer (as Waldo in fact did a few years later) that morality might be independent of religion itself.

Third, and important, Emerson never mentioned Locke. Locke's contribution to the history of nonconforming theology was significant, though not undisputed, and he was a set text in the Harvard syllabus, the most important modern philosopher studied. To be thus silent on Locke's work can only have indicated Emerson's sense of the irrelevance of an epistemology that rejected the notion he cherished of inherent ideas and held instead that the mind was instead at birth a tabula rasa.

In view of these crucial silences in Waldo's argument, one can better understand President Kirkland's criticism of Emerson's previous essay, made in a remark to Sarah Alden Bradford Ripley, Waldo's other learned aunt. "She told me," Mary wrote her nephew, "that when the President read your Socrates he asked why not a better Locke, Stuart [Stewart], and Pally [Paley] Scholar?"[13] In short, Emerson was reading the wrong people. But though he received the message, he did not heed it.

The distance between the youth and his teachers, however, was not one merely of doctrine or fact, but of intellectual method. Waldo thought that humans were born with the same sort of moral knowledge that they had had two thousand years earlier, and he therefore felt free to omit from his study even a reference to the author of a different theory, no matter how powerful and influential that theory had proved. His judges, on the other hand, presumed that the aim of the exercise was to demonstrate scholarship—objective, positive knowledge—albeit in the service of foregone conclusions. What Em-

[13] MME to RWE, 1821, HMS.

erson was giving them was one-sided and close to enthusiasm. Years later Emerson was to speak of the "corpse-cold Unitarianism of Brattle Street" and Harvard College. Nurtured in the heart of that culture, yet not of it, Emerson already by the age of seventeen had felt and rejected the strictures it imposed upon his native bent.

The four pages Emerson devoted to Hume instead of Locke were surely misjudged, had Emerson's main goal been to please his examiners. But in following his own inquiries, he encountered one of the major minds of his era, and one that was to shape his thought significantly. Hume (1711–1776) had been dead for over forty years when Emerson entered Harvard, but he was still known as the "Great Infidel," the skeptical enemy whose impeccably logical doubts about the necessary connection of cause and effect and whose devastating attacks on the common sense inferences of natural religion had never fully been answered.

Born a Scottish Presbyterian (and like Emerson fascinated in youth by romance—he devoted his first adolescent treatise to a discussion of chivalry), Hume had studied as a young man in France and come with a newly rigorous epistemology to uncomfortable conclusions about how little necessary connection there was between any given cause and its apparent effect. Much of contemporary theology based itself on the argument from design—the idea that just as one can infer the existence of a basketmaker from perceiving the product, the basket, so one can infer the existence of God from observing the wonderful work of his hands, the universe. Hume joined in lyric praise of that work—the human hand itself was his metaphor of such beauty—but ultimately denied that one can actually know more than that the basket or the world exists, and that we think it proceeds from a maker. When a billiard ball strikes another, he suggested, the movement of the second is obvious, but the idea that the seeming effect is necessarily connected to the motion of the first ball is only an inference. It comes from experience, but it is not the same thing as knowledge.

Hume developed this argument and other equally unsettling lines of thought in *Treatise of Human Nature* (1739–40), *Philosophical Essays* (1748), *Dialogues Concerning Natural Religion* (1779), and *The Natural History of Religion* (1757). When he had finished his philosophical work, he turned to history, and his six-volume *History of England* (1754–61) summed up in lapidary, mature, and ironic style the world view that lay behind and had been shaped by his philosophic inquiries.[14]

[14] The major biographers are Ernest Mossner, *The Life of David Hume* (Austin: Uni-

Known as "*le bon David*" and living on intimate terms among the French philosophes of the eighteenth century, Hume was a master stylist, whose enormous intellectual lucidity and power are permeated by a humane and tolerant, but imperturbable irony. Here, for example, is what he had to say in his devastating essay "Of Miracles," dealing with the events that had for so long been offered as the Bible's proof of the revelations of Christianity:

> Reason will expose the Christian religion as founded on Faith, not on Reason. To examine its miraculous accounts would be a sure method of exposing it, to put it to such a trial as it is, by no means fitted to endure. The Christian religion, not only was at first attended with miracles, but even at this day can not be believed by any reasonable person without one. Mere reason is insufficient to convince us of its veracity.[15]

Hume's stance was to avoid aggressive contradiction, but to change the terms of the argument, redefining with a shrug and a laugh and irreversibly altering the status of the object discussed from thing to epiphenomenon.

"The intellectual age was Hume's," Mossner wrote, but he met concerted and ongoing opposition from contemporary Scots and English theologians. Hume was equally unwelcome at Harvard, which was deeply influenced by the same Scottish Common-Sense philosophers who had sprung up partly in an attempt to refute their free-thinking countryman. Thus, while there may have been an informal tradition among intelligent undergraduates of reading Hume on one's own, as Channing seems to have done, the skeptic was omitted from the syllabus entirely.[16]

Instead stress was placed on Butler, Locke, Stewart, and Paley as understood by professors Levi Frisbie and Levi Hedge. (Although there is no direct evidence for it, it is possible that Andrews Norton's

---

versity of Texas Press, 1954), cited hereafter as Mossner, and *The Forgotten Hume: Le Bon David* (New York: Columbia University Press, 1943), cited hereafter as Mossner. See also David Hume, "My Own Life," in *History of England* (London: A. Millar, 1754, 1756), 1: vii–xviii; cited hereafter as Hume, *History*. The best general survey of Hume's effect on English philosophy is still Leslie Stephen, *History of English Thought in the Eighteenth Century*, 2 vols. (New York: G. Putnam, 1876), 1:309–78, on Hume, and 1:379–415 on his opponents; cited hereafter as Stephen. In the last couple of decades there has been a resurgence of interest in Hume's logic. For the present discussion, however, see James Collins, *The Emergence of Philosophy of Religion* (New Haven, Conn: Yale University Press, 1967), pp. 3–88.

[15] "Of Miracles," in *An Inquiry Concerning Human Understanding*, vol. 2 of *Essays and Treatises*, 2 vols. (Edinburgh, 1804), 2:136–38.

[16] Mossner, p. 210.

later ferocity toward Emerson's "latest form of infidelity" may have sprung in part from the old man's early acquaintance with Waldo's leanings. When he wrote in 1822, "the good suspect me," he may have had in mind the doubts that would have been aroused in the small world of Harvard's faculty and Boston's ministers as they observed the tendency of thought in this son of their late colleague.[17])

Emerson was not exaggerating when he spoke of "terror." Organized religion in general feared Hume and preferred to ignore him. Sixty years later Leslie Stephen wrote that eighteenth-century theology had been "paralyzed" by Hume and that under his attacks "the religion of nature had expired of inanition." "Hume's keen skepticism had pierced its vitals," the Victorian wrote, attributing much of the stagnation of English nineteenth-century philosophical thought to its incapacity to come to terms with Hume. The age had chosen, Stephen wrote, to "avert its eyes" from the problems Hume posed, and intellectual barrenness and hypocrisy had been the result. On the other hand, when Hume was not ignored but attacked, serious damage to the questioner's position might result. The issue of miracles in particular became a crux.[18]

John Henry Newman, for example, whose career in some ways was a mirror image of Emerson's (and who later wrote that he had "bragged" of reading Hume at age fourteen), believed Hume's attack on miracles so central to Christian faith that in 1826 he tried to defend their existence by developing the ideas of probability and "certitude" as justifying belief. His *Essay on Ecclesiastical Miracles* was part of the more general debate initiated by Hume. Nevertheless, even the closely reasoning Newman was so dissatisfied with his own arguments that ultimately he rewrote the essay in 1842. Within another three years he converted to Catholicism, where he could base his search for certitude in the tangible evidence of Catholic tradition, rather than in the ambiguities of a Bible whose history was increasingly unclear. That he led others to Rome with him added to the insult.[19]

Such evidence of uncertainty among the leadership tended to weaken the capacity of consensual institutions to enforce their sanctions. Doubts had to be kept to oneself. Newman was seen by the Anglicans as an awful example of what might be called a kind of dynamic cognitive dissonance. As he moved to new positions with

[17] *JMN*, 1:130.
[18] Stephen 1:313–16, 372–85,
[19] Newman, pp. 15–16, 29–30.

ever increasing drama and publicity, his career epitomized a lack of balance and subversion of all authority.

The lid had to be kept on. When Thomas Arnold was preparing for ordination as a young man at Oxford in 1818, he became aware of doubting the Trinity. He appealed for help to the revered prelate John Keble. Keble told him to "suppress" his doubts, devote himself to holy living, and go on with the ministry. Arnold did so, but the Unitarian leader James Martineau later focused on that as an act of bad faith that had muddied all Arnold's doctrine thereafter and made his proselytizing of "Broad Church" Anglicanism merely expedient and doctrinally empty.[20] Under similar circumstances, Waldo's brother William was counseled in 1825 by Goethe to do the same. Cynicism existed among the esoteric on a fairly widespread basis. Later in the century Walter Bagehot was quoted to the effect that no educated man ever but entertained fundamental doubts, and no intelligent man ever publicly admitted them. When much later the then-famous Emerson was asked by young men, apostates in spite of themselves like James Anthony Froude and Arthur Hugh Clough, to come to Oxford and address their dilemmas, he must have recognized in them the same conflicts that had torn and changed the lives of himself and his brothers, taking as victims not the dull or self-serving, but some of the best, the most promising, and the most concerned minds of their generation.[21]

Undoubtedly the necessity for privacy, even secrecy, made such battles excruciating, and this need for confidentiality was part of the reason, though only a part, that Emerson wrote so freely to Mary, on whom he could rely both for protection and determined opposition to his developing views. Even as late as 1829, the problem of Hume remained a touchy one. Only months after his ordination, Emerson cancelled from his sermon "Cultivating the Mind," intended to help the "poor man and woman" toward self-education, a suggestion that among other texts they should read Hume's *History*. (This, in fact, had been the first work he listed.) A second thought must have told him that it was too early on so minor a matter to court the criticism that would have ensued if, as a newly ordained minis-

[20] Arthur Penrhyn Stanley, *The Life and Correspondence of Thomas Arnold, D.D.*, 2 vols. (London: B. Fellowes, 1844), 1:20, 22–23; James Martineau, *Essays, Reviews and Addresses*, cited by Frances J. Woodward, *The Doctor's Disciples: A Study of Four Pupils of Arnold of Rugby* (London: Oxford University Press, 1954), p. 2.

[21] Evelyn Barish Greenberger, *Arthur Hugh Clough: Growth of a Poet's Mind* (Cambridge, Mass.: Harvard University Press, 1970), pp. 104–8 and passim; cited hereafter as Evelyn Barish Greenberger, *Clough*.

ter, he had recommended the study of this heretic and enemy of faith.[22]

MARY OBJECTED to her nephew's "Humism," pointing out that it had imbued his style with a skeptical, epicurean tone. But although her criticism is not unknown, scholars in general have not taken it seriously or considered the implications for his intellectual development.[23]

This is due in part to the general obscurity in which their relationship and correspondence have remained, and to the absence of an edition of either the journals or the letters in which their interchanges would be fully recorded. Emerson's skepticism during his formative years, 1821–26, is hard to perceive except in this interaction, but Hume was still a touchy subject when the early biographies of Emerson were written, and the subject was not dwelt upon. By the twentieth century, Mary's role in her nephew's life seemed less interesting to Emerson's new biographers and editors than it had been to his son, Edward Emerson, who at the turn of the century prepared the first edition of the *Journals*; thus material that Edward Emerson had included was omitted from the *Letters* and the *JMN*. To reconstruct both the subject and the relationship, therefore, requires careful reading of the different editions of these works, as well as of the manuscripts and Hume's own writings.

What by now has become clear is that Mary was right, and that Emerson was indeed "imbued" with Humism from at least his seventeenth year—swept off his feet, in fact, might be a better way to put it. He summed it up in 1824, three years after writing his second attempt at the Bowdoin prize, when he asked Mary for her answers to the questions Hume posed:

> Next comes the Scotch Goliath, David Hume; but where is the accomplished stripling who can cut off his most metaphysical head? Who is he that can stand up before him and prove the existence of the Universe and of its Founder? He hath an

[22] RWE, Sermons, HMS; there are several manuscript examples of Emerson canceling his desire to quote Hume publicly. In the sermon mentioned above, however, he left in a recommendation to read Robertson, whom Stephen named along with Hume and Gibbon as one of the "great triumvirate" of rationalistic historians of their day (Stephen, 1:57).

[23] Whicher is an exception. His discussion of Emerson's early thinking is generally dismissive (finding in it "helplessness," "impotence," and "sophomoric" reasoning), but he rightly perceives that skepticism underlay much of Emerson's later faith (pp. 3–26, especially 5–6 and 12–13).

adroiter wit than all his forefathers in philosophy if he will con-
found this Uncircumcised. The long and dull procession of Rea-
soners that have followed since, have challenged the awful shade
to duel, and struck the air with their puissant arguments. But
as each new comer blazons "Mr. Humes objections" on his
pages, it is plain they are not satisfied the victory is gained. Now
though every one is daily referred to his own feelings as a tri-
umphant confutation of the glozed lies of this Deciever, yet, it
assuredly would make us feel safer and prouder, to have our
victorious answer set down in impregnable propositions.[24]

By 1818, at age fifteen, Emerson had read the *History of England*.
By 1821 one finds references to the *Essays*, and from then through
1825 to the other major works—*Dialogues Concerning Natural Religion* and *The Natural History of Religion*.[25]
Most probably he had read all these productions before these stray
references. As he wrote to John B. Hill in 1823: "Hume, in a single
page, will often give a more distinct and perfect account of a course
of events, than Sully will, of the same, in a whole voluminous chapter." And to his brother William in the same year, "I am an idolater
of David Hume save when he meddles with law and prophets." That
saving proviso, however, represented wishful thinking rather than
fact. Law and prophets—that is, the fundamentals of belief—were
exactly what were most shaken by "Humism." Emerson's admiration of the "perfect," seemingly casual concision of Hume's ironic
style was a sign of his influence, which was not limited to style.[26]
As time went on Emerson in fact was to become more and more
responsive to—almost a prisoner of—both Hume's ideas and his own
stance as a David contending against Goliath. But if Hume was Goliath, he was also the giant-killer, the model opponent of all the Fathers and their works. There was much to learn from the mingled
suavity and power of his mind and style. Emerson was to be deeply
distressed by Hume, but with an unerring instinct for what was central, he learned much from the finesse and apparent simplicity with
which Hume framed his anti-authoritarian arguments. That stance
had brought him honor and affection from the best minds of his day.
"Sublimity of motive must precede sublimity of style"—this phrase
of Mary's Emerson was already repeating. It followed that a sublime
style portended a sublime motive. No one could write as lucidly,

[24] *L*, 1:138.
[25] *L*, 1:131n; *JMN* 1:343; *JMN*, 2:8, 414, and passim.
[26] *L*, 1:131; *L*, 1:135.

humanely, and on the whole benignly, if not hopefully, as Hume and be a bad man. Emerson was prepared to resist Hume's errors while studying his methods.

In fact, however, both Emerson's style and substance were affected. At an early date he had accepted Hume's proof that there was no necessary connection between the Christian miracles—if indeed they had taken place—and God's existence. Since post-Enlightenment belief among liberal thinkers now rested heavily on the argument from analogy and on belief in miracles, to give up the latter was a crucial step. Hume's argument was not so much that these had not taken place—though he cast doubts upon that. Rather he argued that even if they had occurred, they would not prove God's existence. In fact, nothing could prove it.

By October 1823, when he was only twenty, Emerson had begun to accept this reasoning, although he found it intensely and painfully alienating. The more he read, the more clearly he saw that the advances of humane letters, and of higher criticism and philosophy in general, might not reveal the history of the Church—or therefore the Church itself—to be anything more than a list of massacres and deceptions. "Mr. Hume's Essay upon Necessary Connexion proves that Events are conjoined, and not connected; that, we have no knowledge but from Experience. We have no Experience of a Creator and there[fore] know of none." The distressing effect of this recognition on "every humane design" was powerful. "The melancholy truth is that there are ten thousand abortive to one successful accomplishment." Only hope could save humankind; "Remove hope, and the world becomes a blank and rotteness. . . . If the past were presented to our hearts in all its dark reality relieved by no contrasted Hope for the future, men would instinctively rebel in spirit against the Providence which placed them here."[27]

This proof that "we have no Experience of a Creator and therefore know of none" could only inflame the problem of theodicy that even an ambivalent believer could find excruciating. At about the same time, and in the same letter in which he described himself as David contending against an uncircumcised Goliath, Emerson wrote to Mary asking the kind of unanswerable questions he later called a "confession of sin." Why, he asked her, were God's "moral operations . . . irregular," so that faith "sometimes passes away like the morning cloud before the queries of the sceptic?" Why did millions live and die in "squalid and desperate ignorance" throughout the

[27] *JMN* 2:161, 163, 164.

globe? Echoing the Epicureans, he suggested that life might be less than real, "a smoke, a dream, a bubble."[28]

Waldo's phrase about God's "inexplicable enigma" clearly echoes Hume, who had concluded his *Natural History of Religion* with the assertion that "the whole is a riddle, an enigma, an inexplicable mystery." Emerson protested that the universe could not proceed from the operations of "mountebank." Hume had argued in parallel fashion that "in the popular religions of the world how is the Deity disfigured in our representation of him! What caprice, absurdity, and immorality are attributed to him! How much is he degraded even below the character, which we should naturally, in common life, ascribe to a man of sense and virtue." Doubt, "suspense of judgment," and "escape into the obscure, though calm, regions of philosophy" were all that Hume had to offer in the face of these enigmas.[29]

Waldo wanted something more, for Hume, the Goliath, threatened to triumph. He begged his aunt, whom he called "the pen of a living witness and faithful lover of these mysteries," to strain her prophetic vision into that obscurity on his behalf. Then, using language close to Hume's, he asked:

> Now what is the good end answered in making these mysteries to puzzle all analysis? What is the ordinary effect of an inexplicable enigma? Is it not to create opposition, ridicule and bigoted scepticism? Does the Universe great and glorious in its operation aim at the slight of a mountebank who produces a wonder among the ignorant by concealing the causes of unexpected effects? . . . So please tell me what reply your active meditations have forged in metaphysical armoury to What is the Origin of Evil?[30]

Emerson was beginning to feel a kind of disgust at the world's being overpopulated by masses living in spiritual and physical meaninglessness. Even this theme echoes Hume. In 1823 Emerson asked how "a Benevolent Spirit persists in introducing onto the Stage of existence millions of new beings, in incessant series, to pursue the same wrong road and consummate the same tremendous fate?" Similarly, three years later in June 1826 in the grip of serious depression and hastening illness, he spoke with sharper language of "this fulsome generation, this redundant prodigality of being,

[28] "Over-Soul," *CW*, 2:284; *L*, 1:139.
[29] Hume, *NHR*, pp. 469, 468.
[30] *L*, 1:137.

whereby they are cast out, clean and unclean, heroes and underlings by millions." Mind, "as she sits serene in her firmament," is nevertheless a female married to the body, her "gross mate, who, because he hungers and thirsts, makes her forsake her celestial musings to find out where he may go to be fat and where to be warm."[31]

In a parallel passage from *Dialogues Concerning Natural Religion*, the skeptic Philo first used the metaphor Emerson adopted to express his inability to see in the world any replica of the divine being:

> Look round this universe. What an immense profusion of beings, animated and organized, sensible and active. You admire this prodigious variety and fecundity. But inspect a little more narrowly these living existences . . . How hostile and destructive to each other! How insufficient all of them for their own happiness: How contemptible or odious to the spectator! The whole presents nothing but the idea of a blind Nature, impregnated by a great vivifying principle, and pouring forth from her lap, without discernment or parental care, her maimed and abortive chldren.[32]

Clearly, the powerful image of nature as a contemptibly fecund mother, unable to control her reproduction and spewing out defective offspring, was borrowed from Hume.

By May 1824, around the time of his twenty-first birthday, issues that had appeared as questions in 1821 and as problems in 1823 were now firm positions; it is fair to say that by 1824 he was closer to skepticism than deism. He undertook to put his ideas together in a kind of essay he called "Letter to Plato" that went unpublished until it appeared in the second edition of his journals in 1961. He probably showed it to no one but Mary. That she received it one may infer from her own answering "Letter from Plato," still unpublished.[33]

An old issue among protestant theologians was the nature, number, and priority of God's revelations to the world. Traditionally the Bible and Christ's life and miracles constituted these, but in the nineteenth century intellectuals, seeking to broaden the authority of

---

[31] *L*, 1:138; *J*, 2:102.

[32] Hume, *Dialogues Concerning Natural Religion*, book 3 of *Treatise of Human Nature*, *The Philosophical Works of David Hume*, 4 vols. (Boston & Edinburgh: Little, Brown & A. C. Black, 1854), 2:518; cited hereafter as Hume, *Dialogues*.

[33] MME to RWE, 1824, HMS.

science and humanistic studies, argued for additional sources of revelation.[34]

By 1824 Emerson asserted that biblical revelation "has not for me
the same exclusive and extraordinary claims it has for many. I hold
Reason to be a prior Revelation. . . ." He went further. The creator
would not "mock" humanity by extorting from it an assent made by
"fear and superstition." That would make "a ruin of the mind" and
would please "none but a cruel and malicious divinity." To believe
in a God of such "sublime depravity [would be] absurd." And since
God could not be thus wicked (as Hume had also argued) Emerson
found here his grounds for the rejection of miracles: "What we do
not apprehend we first admire and then ridicule. Therefore I scout
all those parts of the book which are reckoned mysteries."[35]

That was a broad rejection, much more than enough to make him
uneasy, as he was to be, two years later when he had to attend Andrews Norton's classes on biblical interpretation. Again following
Hume, he also questioned the activities of "the priesthood," which
found "riddles in their vocation hard to solve." Emerson pointed out
that Plato himself had not been blameless in "inculcat[ing] the vulgar Superstitions of the day." He accused him: "You Plato did not
know if there were many gods or but One," and he asked the subtle
question, which again showed his close study of Hume, how if a
society actually rested entirely on its purported religion it could in
fact be workable: "How could those parts of the social machine
whose consistency and just action depend entirely upon the morality
and religion sown and grown in the community, how could these be
kept in safe and efficient arrangement under a system which besides
being frivolous was the butt of vulgar ridicule?"[36]

The inevitable inference was that sane people everywhere had always, like himself, "scouted" the "mysteries" of religion. Hume had
challenged the supposedly revealed origin of religion. Now Emerson
suggested the same thing, saying that generally people acted not as
their often "frivolous" religions required, but out of understanding
their own interests. They merely liked to think their motives came
"from religious motives and a powerful bias to Virtue." The reli-

[34] Broadening the several sources and loci of revelation was the project of liberal and
unorthodox theologians like Thomas Arnold (who named history as a source of sacred
light) and Friedrich von Schlegel, who considered the Eastern religions to have been
inspired by God before the Judeo-Christian era. See Evelyn Barish Greenberger, *Clough*,
pp. 38–39.

[35] *JMN*, 2:250–51.

[36] *JMN*, 2:248.

gions of the priesthood, in short, were often irrelevant to actual life—
and always had been.[37]

THE IDEAS of Hume continued to prey on Emerson's mind until at
least 1826. Intellectually, at least, he was by the age of twenty-one a
somewhat ambivalent skeptic, perhaps not even a deist, if by deism
one understands belief in God as the maker of a world whose perfec-
tion proves his existence. Since Emerson believed that Hume had
proved there was no necessary connection between an orderly universe and an originating orderer, at least theoretically he must have
entertained doubts of the existence of any kind of maker. Undoubtedly it was in that spirit that he at times saw the world as a mere
chaos and regarded hope as the only means he possessed to secure a
sense of meaning. His study of history, which he carried on simultaneously with his philosophical inquiries, was to be equally frustrating.

Nevertheless, in the long run Emerson came to believe that
Hume's influence was essentially positive, not only upon himself but
on philosophy in general. In January 1826, after almost a year away
from Cambridge, he wrote to Mary an important statement, sum-
marizing thinking that enabled him at twenty-three to lay down this
particular burden. "The name of Hume, I fancy," he pointed out in
the style at once dispassionate and subtle that marks his clearest and
deepest formulations:

> has hardly gathered all its fame. His Essays are now found all
> over Europe and will take place doubtless in all Pyrrhonian bos-
> oms of all other freethinkers of England or France. German the-
> ology will prop itself on him, and suggest to its lovers a sort of
> apology and consolation in his mild and plausible epicureanism.
> He is one of those great limitary angels to whom power is given
> for a season over the minds and history of men, not so much to
> mislead as to cast another weight into the *contrary scale* in that
> vast and complex adjustment of good and evil to which our un-
> derstandings are accommodated and through which they are to
> escape by the fine clue of moral perception.[38]

To name Hume a "limitary angel" was a significant remark. The
drama of the image stems in part from the same myth-making ten-

[37] *JMN*, 2:246–52.
[38] *J*, 2:77.

dency that earlier had made him a "Goliath." But Hume is also "limitary" perhaps in the sense that the angel with his flaming sword was
to Adam as he left Eden. Both told humanity where it could no
longer and where it must in future go. It could not seek for clear,
rationally comprehensible connections to a creator. It must instead
be content to find its way out of—to "escape" from—a labyrinth by
pursuing "the fine clue of moral perception." The image, of course,
also alludes to Theseus,who is taught by his lover Ariadne to escape
the labyrinth by following the thread or clue she has left for him. In
the same way Emerson was coming to see that the soul, which he
perceived as his more feminine persona, would alone be a reliable
guide to religious knowledge.

If Hume was "limitary," then, he was also liberating. The "fine
clue of moral perception" that Emerson came to value so highly led
to his later emphasis on an entirely intuitive mode of religious
knowledge. This was not Hume's intention of course, but Emerson's
eventual induction. But following that clue freed him in another way
also.

By attacking trust in a meaningful universe in which one had a
foreordained function and place, Hume essentially forced Emerson
to confront his own isolation, a condition that for him was no metaphor but had a biting, personal reality as well as a more abstract
philosophical meaning. In doing so, Emerson moved beyond a
merely wishful or blind belief in divine purpose. Before he was
twenty-one he had recognized that he lived in a universe whose explanations, when pressed by the rational mind, seemed merely chaotic. And when, therefore, Emerson finally did begin to name "sentiment"—"blushing, changing, shining Sentiment" he called it with
ironic self-awareness—as the source of his ongoing belief in God, it
was clear to him that the origin of his knowledge lay in human feeling. He was not led there by reason, and he knew it.

He was not yet ready to manage the massive difficulties of this
position. Much of the delays he was to suffer in entering his profession came from the debilitating and bewildering effects of these
ideas—the "tangling vines" of which he later spoke.

Chapter 6

HISTORY

"But Isaac my son to idols hathe gone over
And no man I can find my firstborn to recover."

A T THE END of the summer of 1823, the twenty-year-old
Emerson took a fortnight's solitary walk through Massachusetts and Connecticut. He had by then been teaching
full-time for two years, but he was about to enter a new stage in his
life, and he went alone. The journal he kept, designed to be shown
to his family, was deliberately outward-looking and unreflective in
tone with one exception, a brief Hawthornian tale of "the subterranean man," a lead miner Emerson met who in perfect solitude had
been digging a tunnel through stone for twelve years. He had not
yet found any lead. Employed by an absent "Boston gentleman," the
unnamed miner had "advanced 975 feet," Waldo reported, "and
spends his days, winter and summer, alone in this damp and silent
tomb." He had found only "some excellent granite" and learned that
"the place [was] excellent for meditation." A year earlier he had
written of a giant named Californ, waiting passively in a womblike
cave for "the Hand" to bring him to birth and light. But this miner—
or Emerson's capacity to see him—was more advanced, for he was
"a brawny personage and discreet withal, has a wife, and lives near
the hole."[1]

This "subterranean man" endlessly tunneling through an existence whose only reward was consciousness, its "excellen[ce] for
meditation," is an analogue resonant with broader meaning. A few
weeks after returning from his journey, Emerson in his journal described man as a slave who glances upward at freedom and then
returns to the hammering of his chains. Freedom and slavery were
much on Waldo's mind, but consciousness, the first step toward freedom, was not readily achieved; waking up was not easy.

He had for some time been painfully aware that more fortunate,

[1] *JMN*, 2:181, 179; *JMN*, 2:184–85.

better placed men like Gay were passing him by. "There was pride," as he wrote a year after graduating, "in being a collegian, and a poet, and somewhat romantic in my queer acquaintance with ⟨Gay⟩, and poverty presented nothing mortifying in the meeting of two young men whom their common relation and character as scholars equalised. But when one becomes a droning schoolmaster, and the other is advancing his footing in good company and fashionable friends, the cast of countenance on meeting is somewhat altered."[2]

He was aware of his needs as hunger. He reached out to friends in correspondence, but their meager replies left his appetite unsatisfied: "Here I sit in the barren-minded North, hungering and thirsting for something to think about and open my letters with greedy impatience for a morsel that shall last me a month—to chew the cud of thought—and, ye stars! my friends have sent milk for babes and kept their meat for strong men."[3]

Paradoxically, there is evidence that by deliberate fasting he was hoping to redirect sexual energy into more intellectual channels. He wrote with disdain of "vulgar appetite." The "masters of the moral world" were "temperate, unassuming men" who were great not because they saw differently but because they saw "*beyond* the . . . vulgar limit." Hunger might bring special vision: only "Mind" should "feed with unsated appetite," because it ate "immortal food."[4] This summer of 1823 was the period that Mary later called that of his "Roxbury fasts," blaming it and his school for the "defecion [*sic*] in health of optics" that afflicted him in 1825. Although he knew that "ascetic mortification" was likely to fail and therefore "merciless crucifixion of the lusts of the body" was "unwise," he was concerned with keeping his mind "perfectly pure" and triumphing over "bad habits," and it was probably against such "lusts" that he turned to this old monastic discipline. During this period, at any rate, he became concerned about his weight, recording it at 144 pounds, and actually weighed his daily intake of food, probably in order to control his consumption of it.[5]

What Emerson felt he needed to become one of those masters of the moral world was knowledge: positive, objective, and, as he perceived it, masculine, the opposite of his earlier, dreamy self. Those dreams he now believed he must root out of his character. In the fall of 1822, while awaiting the appearance of his first published essay

[2] *JMN*, 2:154; *JMN*, 1:130.
[3] *L*, 1:110.
[4] *JMN*, 2:100; *JMN*, 2:136.
[5] MME to RWE, 1825, HMS; *JMN*, 2:97.

on "The Religion of the Middle Ages," he wrote that he would never add a "straw" to the weight of theology until "my better judgment shall have at last triumphed over the daemon Imagination." But it was hard to change so greatly. He was still contending with that "daemon" in late 1824 when he projected an essay against the "evils of imagination"—one that would enlist the aid of Hume, among others. Even in 1826 he recorded that his younger brother Charles counseled him, "Let the fictions of Chivalry alone." Romance was all very well as an "ornament," but fictions could replace reality and do injury to truth. "Romance," as he wrote in late 1823, "is mother of Knowledge—this ungrateful son that eats up his parent." The violence of the cannibalistic image bespeaks the intensity of the attraction. Strong measures were needed to counteract his urge toward the fanciful, the poetic, and the morbid, all of which seemed to him weak and effeminate.[6]

In his new program knowledge, that hungry, even cannibalistic son of romance, was to thrive not on fiction but on history. History was an active, profitable, masculine study, whose central place in Enlightenment thought was by then well established. As the Bible, geology, and language itself had come under scholarly scrutiny, they had revealed their complexities through the evolving methods of historical analysis. History had assumed new importance as both the defenders and attackers of orthodoxy—the shapers of modern thought—turned to the past for evidence in their arguments. Emerson's lengthy preoccupation with the study of history deserves attention, therefore, for several reasons. It was chief among his concerns during this period and—hardly less important—as in an unrequited love affair the frustrations of this attachment eventually forced Emerson to go beyond its limits and enter new territory.

It also put him at the leading edge of his era's intellectual endeavors.[7] For history was "Philosophy teaching by Experience," Carlyle pointed out in 1830. Earlier, Hume had led the way, inferring from his own philosophical enquiries that "experience alone could decide questions of morality or politics." Hence the study of history was a practical necessity, and Hume's six-volume *History of England* was a testament in part to this belief.[8]

As with any deep attachment, however, Emerson's motives were complex and not a little ambivalent. On the one hand, the study of

---

[6] *JMN*, 2:34; *JMN*, 2:306–7; *JMN*, 3:19; *JMN*, 2:194.

[7] Peter Allan Dale, *The Victorian Critic and the Idea of History* (Cambridge, Mass.: Harvard University Press, 1977), pp. 1–2.

[8] Ibid., p. 3.

history promised positive intellectual progress, a worthy goal in itself. Moreover, it lay in the masculine sphere, and becoming a man,
especially difficult without the benefit of a mentor or male model,
was undoubtedly a part of Emerson's underlying program. Neither
his step-grandfather nor his maternal uncles had ever been close
enough to serve in this regard, and Mary was at this level of identity
only a potential source of confusion.

History was also—and not incidentally—constituted by information that could be converted by the imagination, its energies withdrawn from mere fantasy and fixed on outward reality into patterns
of meaning, notions about ideal behavior, useful visions of danger
and glory. To study it would be to internalize appropriate actions.
And, inevitably, history was deeply, inextricably concerned with
Emerson's own deepest level of fantasy. In it lay the dead past.
Across its threshold at some level there always lived for him magical
power, "the reaching and beckoning of somewhat unearthly," magicians of might, kings and prophets from the holy land, and even
their apostate sons.

With these multiple motives, Emerson made wide claims for this
favored study. Grandiloquently he wrote, "There are three things
chief which the human mind studies; itself, God, and the Universe.
I know not how these high pursuits can be better combined than in
that branch of art which is called History." History showed "the
hand of Providence most visibly." God's wisdom as well as humanity's was implicit in its study; in fact, "in a vague sense, history may
be said to comprise also all the store of Natural knowledge."⁹

To increase his share in that store, Emerson read a fairly wide
variety of historians and memoirists, including Mosheim, Gibbon,
Froissart, Hallam, Robertson, and Sully. All, however, were over-
shadowed by Hume, whom he compared to Sully, the French Protestant memoirist and statesman, saying that in a "single page" the
Scot could "give a more distinct and perfect account" of any event
than the other might in a "voluminous chapter."¹⁰

Emerson taught Hume's *History of England* not only in his classes
but as supplementary reading. Thus, when a graduate of his school
appealed to him for further direction of her reading, Waldo replied
by soberly casting up as six the maximum number of hours she
would have per day for "our best and chief employment," that is,
"devotion, study and thought." Then he began his program for her:

⁹ *JMN*, 2:242–43.
¹⁰ *L*, 1:131.

"One of these hours every day I would give to history so go get Hume . . . [and read] the reign of Elizabeth. . . . After finishing Hume from that reign you will find yourself sufficient [*sic*] interested in English Story to go back to Henry VIII." The prescription was Hume, to be followed by more Hume—with Shakespeare's history plays and another historian, Robertson, to add variety.[11]

So great was the sense of pressure he felt on the subject of history, and so great his sense of its centrality, that with his characteristic anxiety and tendency to go to extremes he sounded almost frantic a few years later. He experienced a lack of "order . . . in the mass of reading that occupies or impends over me. . . . What arrangement in priority of subjects? When shall I read Greek, when Roman, when Austrian, when Ecclesiastical, when American history? Whilst we deliberate, time escapes." He therefore decided on a daily morning chapter of the Greek testament, to be followed by the Swiss theologian LeClerc, and then William Mitford, author of *History of Greece*. "All history is ecclesiastical," he summed up, "and all reasonings go back to Greece."[12]

But despite the seriousness of his interest, he was also ambivalent about it. He wrote poetry to the Muse of history, but it had a rueful note:

> Who so alas is young
> And being young is wise
> And deaf to saws of gray Advice
> Hath listened when the Muses sung
> And heard with joy when on the wind the shell of Clio rung.
> Go hapless youth.[13]

Fifty men, he perceived, might in historical accounts be cited as supposed "representatives of a nation" and yet not speak for anyone but themselves. Again he noted more strongly, "We mistake the part for the whole. It is a vulgar obeisance to names and not philosophy which makes but one story of the Rome of Kings, the Rome of Consuls, the Rome of Emperors, the Rome of Ostrogoths. . . . And this is true, though not so obviously, of all histories. The union which is effected . . . is forced, artificial, contrived for obvious purposes of convenience but not founded in truth."[14]

There was evidently a strong emotional component in Emerson's

[11] *L*, 1:155–56.
[12] *JMN*, 2:300, n.64.
[13] *JMN*, 3:7.
[14] *JMN*, 2:250.

commitment to this new subject. Like his involvement with romance and death in the preceding period, his interest in history seems to have been somewhat obsessive, finding its way into the different roles he played, whether that of poetic lover, urgent teacher, or anxious student. What seems apparent, however, is that he was not seeking the sort of knowledge or adopting the methods a professional historian might amass or wish to follow. Thus he never tried to master a broad range of specific facts in a single area, or to inquire into or compare historical sources as a historian must soon learn to do. This was in keeping with his attitude toward the German and Hebrew languages, which would have been essential to serious historical—not to mention theological—study, but which he "hated."[15]

What he wanted instead from history was, on the one hand, the empirical evidence it offered about human nature and, on the other, insights, the same insights perhaps—though now on a more sophisticated level—that the questing youth had wished for from the "Magician of Might from the Dead-Sea-shore." He sought teleogical explanations, the locus of wisdom and a source of authority, but his repeated frustration in the pursuit resulted from the inevitable recognition that no broad and incontrovertible truth was to be found. Grasping this, one understands better how Emerson could have turned so quickly from his involvement with the notions of romance and death to history. History was a respectable, intellectual, and manly pursuit, purged of the merely personal or magical. Yet since by definition it was constituted by the dead past, it was also the repository of all the experience that had perished with its protagonists. To recapture and vivify them was potentially at one level to erase the borderline, to cross the threshhold of "the unseen world."

Ultimately, however, this fantasy too would be disappointed by reality. Searching for teleological explanations that would not come, frustrated at understanding that there could be no historical view prior to a philosophical one, he put his disgust, as he had put his love, into verse:

> Old mouldy men and books and names and lands
> Disgust my reason and defile my hands
> I had as lief respect an ancient shoe
> As love Old things *for age* and hate the new
> I spurn the past, my mind disdains its nod
> Nor kneels in homage to so mean a god.

[15] *L*, 1:154.

Two years later, in an extended figure alluding to *Childe Harold*, he wrote that "in the order of recorded History, Chaos is the parent of things, then came paradise, and now is the degenerate world. . . . I represent to myself—the Opinion of men ever calling all the past, Chaos, at present walking through Hell to a retreating Paradise, 'the unreached Paradise of our despair.' "[16]

"Chaos is the parent of things." That was the rub: history was chaos, a parent that did not answer his despairing call. The relationship of parentage to disorder was uncomfortable, disquieting, and Emerson's language returns to this connection from time to time during this era, gnawing at it. There was all the more reason then why chaotic ignorance must give way to knowledge, the "law-giver" that "introduces order . . . even into the character of Deity." Knowledge was the third generation, for ignorance had first produced romance, "the curse of its own age, the ornament of those that follow." But in turn, "Romance is the mother of Knowledge—this ungrateful son that eats up its parent."[17] Conquest of the confusing past, even in fantasy, meant an eating up that was as criminal for the subject as it was dangerous for his object.

Reading Bossuet on history made Emerson evoke a figure around whom he was beginning to construct a myth, named the "Spirit of Humanity," seen as a youth for whom the "firmament is forever magnificient." In contrast to this figure's energy were "Asia, Africa, Europe, old, leprous and wicked." The youth here becomes identified with both America and Emerson himself—a connection that was to energize his later myth-making. By comparison with these humanized, worn-out continents, "a strong man has entered the race and is outstripping them all. Strong man! youth and glory are with thee. As thou wouldst prosper forget not the hope of mankind. Trample not upon thy competitors though unworthy. Europe is thy ⟨mother⟩ father ⟨support her Asia⟩ bear him on thy Atlantean shoulders. Asia, thy grandsire, regenerate him. Africa, their ancient abused ⟨slave⟩ bondman. Give him his freedom."[18]

There is here a consistent metaphoric pattern in which the relationship of son to parent—a tie fraught with hostility or competition—is the equivalent of the relationship of consciousness to the past, to history. Interestingly, in this passage the gender of the parent Asia, originally female and a mother, was adjusted by Emerson

[16] *JMN*, 2:244; *JMN*, 3:26.
[17] *JMN*, 2:193–94.
[18] *JMN*, 2:218.

to the male "father." This act was probably part of the ongoing process by which he was consciously reorienting himself into a masculine universe. The more he read, the more disordered the world seemed. Leslie Stephen was to point out what Emerson was now learning, that to study history without an underlying philosophical bias was to see the world either superficially or as mere "chaos."[19]

Emerson knew himself to be an original thinker, and he had realized, too, how little originality there was in the world. He might become one of the "masters" who "present the people . . . with all that moderate stock of conclusions" that they shared.[20] But he felt he had been "born in a time of *war*," and the war was within: "A chaos of doubts besets him from his outset. Shall he read or shall he think?" To read was to gather facts, but to "think" was dangerously close to letting the imagination have its way. "He cannot read all. . . . Must he read History & neglect Morals; or learn what *ought* to be, in ignorance of what *has been*?"[21]

Years later Emerson was to announce as if it were a settled question that "books are for the scholar's idle hours." But more than a decade earlier the "question of equal moment to each new Citizen of the world is this; shall I subdue my mind by discipline, or obey its native inclination? govern my imagination with rules or cherish its originality? Shall I cultivate Reason or Fancy . . . ?" His "native inclination" was original, fanciful, imaginative—but therein lay danger: a "chaos of doubts," the primeval disorder related to ignorance, disordered parentage, dependency, passivity, and indeterminate identity, sexual and otherwise. Chaos must be resolved, at whatever price.[22]

AT THE END of 1823 William went to Germany to study theology, subsidized as a rising young star and the son of William Emerson by various Cambridge men, as well as by his younger brother. Waldo helped William to prepare and wrote amusingly of his own supposed impracticality: "Why man, creditors double a bill if they know I am to pay it."[23] In fact, he was always a good manager of his business, not anxious but attentive to it. William's absence, however, affected

[19] Stephen, 1:57–58.
[20] *JMN*, 2:206.
[21] *JMN*, 2:219. This early passage foreshadows the famous lines from "Life and Letters in New England" that describe the young men born with "knives in the brain."
[22] *JMN*, 2:219.
[23] *L*, 1:136.

him with unexpected force and depth. He was now the real head of
the family, responsible for all or part of the support of four brothers
and their mother as well as himself (and though he did not know it,
he would continue in that role for the rest of his life). At first he
responded by silence. But within a week of his older brother's departure he burst forth in rebellion and self-assertion: "Who is he that
shall controul me," he demanded. "Why may not I act and speak and
write and think with entire freedom? What am I to the Universe, or,
the Universe, what is it to me? Who hath forged the chains of Wrong
and Right, of Opinion and Custom? And must I wear them?" The
slave, one might say, had seen his freedom and not looked away; the
lead miner was downing tools. "Is society my annointed King? Or
is there any mightier community or any man or more than man,
whose slave I am? I am solitary in the vast society of beings; I consort
with no species."

Nine months earlier he had preached to himself that "the great
illusion by which men suffer themselves to be mocked is the idea of
their independence" and concluded that "nothing can destroy or
abridge the claim of obedience which a Creator advances upon his
creatures—his *barely existing creatures*." No longer was Waldo ready
to repeat such terminal Calvinism. Intellectually it had been destroyed by Hume and rationalism; psychically it could not survive in
a universe whose paternal God was so indifferent.[24]

Raising his voice, he announced at once his unique loneliness, his
independence, and his sufficiency unto himself: "I see the world, human, brute and inanimate nature; I am in the midst of them, but not
of them; . . . the yell of their *grief* it touches no chord in me; . . . I
disclaim them all. I say to the Universe, Mighty one! thou art not
my mother; Return to chaos, if thou wilt, I shall still exist. I live. If I
owe my being it is to a destiny greater than thine. Star by Star,
world by world, system by system shall be crushed,—but I shall
live."[25] There is much inflation in the language, but there is also
anger and desperation. The indifferent parent (here for once a
mother) is sent back to chaos.

A few days later he took up the theme of independence. "By comparison with others he felt unworthy, but "I am an immortal being,
born to a destiny immeasurably high, deriving . . . from Almighty
God . . . his child . . . forever independent of the controul or will of

[24] *JMN*, 2:119, 122.
[25] *JMN*, 2:189–90.

my fellow children."[26] At this crisis, the concept of the fatherhood of God had a certain heuristic usefulness in rearranging his parentage. That which belongs to everyone belongs to no one, but to be God's child would have to do. To accept the indifference of the universe was crucial in breaking out of his long ambivalent waiting for it to take notice of him. He was ready, or thought he was, to take those steps that would define himself and to face the risks that his inevitable errors would bring.

HE DID NOT delude himself that he had resolved his intellectual dilemma. Three months after what might be termed this declaration of ontological independence, he was writing to Mary in March 1824 that the "hope" on which his faith must rest if it was not supported by experience was a slender and uncertain support. He was a skeptic *malgre lui*. Truth, as history was revealing it, was ugly indeed. In a repeated and painful metaphor, he described truth as an ugly drab, stripped by the impious and degraded by drunks and scoffers. The villainous attacker was "Science," meaning not merely the physical sciences but all modern, analytical, and systematic thought, history included.

"Why is the fruit of knowledge sorrow?" he asked, with ironic knowledge of his own irrationality:

> I think I could have helped the monks to belabour Galileo for saying the everlasting earth moved. . . . Every step Science has made—was it not the successive destruction of agreeable delusions which jointly made up no mean portion of human happiness? . . . What has reason done since Plato's day . . . How are we the wiser? . . . How has Faith fared? Why, the reformer's axe has hewed down idol after idol . . . until Faith is bare and very cold. And they have not done stripping yet, but must reach the bone. The old fable said Truth was by gods or men made naked. I wish the gods would help her to a garment or make her fairer.[27]

He had summed it up well a month earlier. "If knowledge be power, it is also pain." But with knowledge, however painful, came the strength to move forward. Together with irony came lucidity. In the middle of April, approaching his twenty-first birthday, he

[26] *JMN*, 2:192.
[27] *J*, 1:359.

made a crucial decision aimed at getting on with life. He entered in his journal a long, painful self-analysis in the course of which he formally dedicated himself to the Church. There, despite his defects, he could "hope to thrive."[28]

Self-consciously he listed his deficits: lack of self-confidence, unpolished manners, and especially a sense of shame, a nameless anxiety. When he compared himself to his age mates he found a "signal defect of character" that "neutralize[d] the just influence [his] talents ought to have." He could not name the defect precisely, but it expressed itself in lack of "*address*" or "*good forms*," which, exaggerating, he termed "an absence of common *sympathies*." He was afraid of offending and afraid of being offended, "unable to lead and unwilling to follow." As a social being he was not able to project "that good humored independence and self esteem which should mark the gentleman."

Self-reliance, in short, was the last quality he could have attributed to himself at this state of his life, but precisely the one he knew he most needed. Interestingly this list of failings was suddenly punctuated by a seemingly irrelevant anecdote that ejaculates an appeal to the absent father. "In my frequent humiliation, even before women and children I am compelled to remember the poor boy who cried, 'I told you Father, they would find me out.' " Even in this allusion to a fantasy, the role played by "Father" is at best neutral; evidently he is no defense against the internalized attacks of "they," the Other.[29]

So much self-doubt inevitably reawakened in the inexperienced young man uncertainty about sexual identity and probably the old conflict about Martin Gay. His "strong propensity for friendship" (admitted even while he criticized his "absence of common *sympathies*") now became part of his potential for wrongdoing. It was "perchance not unlike the doting of old King James"—that is, homosexual: "Stateliness and silence hang like [a] veil . . . only concealing what is best now shewn. What is called a warm heart, I have not."[30]

Nevertheless, he knew that he was gifted with eloquence and was very confident indeed in that. "Entire success in [public preaching] is the lot of few, but this I am encouraged to expect." He knew too that his imagination and poetic talent would be helpful in this profession. He would never be a logician or philosopher like Locke,

[28] *JMN*, 2:222; *JMN*, 2:237–42.
[29] *JMN*, 2:240–41.
[30] *JMN*, 2:227–28.

Clarke, or Hume, but Dr. Channing's career proved that in divinity "moral imagination" could bring success.

He would rely on his talents and sheer will. He knew he was young, and sinful, and—probably most important—"I already discern the deep dye of elementary errors," an allusion probably to his religious skepticism. But "I judge that if I devote my nights and days *in form*, to the service of God and the War against Sin,—I shall soon be prepared to do the same *in substance*."[31]

He would go forward by acting the part he would then come to believe. This, of course, was one of the oldest remedies for ambivalence, and it was what Keble in England and Goethe in Germany were telling his contemporaries. By the 1820s, however, a man of Emerson's culture and sensibility could no longer give up fealty to truth as the highest doctrine, for by now both rationalism and the liberal wing of Protestantism claimed authority derived from their pursuit of truth. Yet rationalism was constantly said to lead both to atheism and despair (a theme Mary harped on), while strict adherence to orthodoxy, even of the sort taught at the liberal Harvard Divinity College, was nonsense—it was the end of thought itself. He was caught in the dilemma that was to wreck many careers in that century. This was the "war" he later described between "intellect and affection." What he did not then say was the extent to which in his early manhood he had been a casualty of that internal conflict.[32]

A VIVID but little-known expression both of this "war" and of the penetrating influence of Hume on Emerson's creative thought came during the summer following this self-dedication when around July 1824 he wrote a poem titled "William Rufus and the Jew." Although it was published in 1829 by Andrews Norton in his collection *The Offering*, it has been generally ignored, for it was not collected by Emerson himself or by subsequent editors. Although written in a deliberately unpolished style, it is nevertheless important for what it reveals of Emerson's state of mind at a turning point of his life.[33]

Based on an antireligious and antimonarchical story Emerson

---

[31] *JMN*, 2:241.

[32] See Evelyn Barish Greenberger, *Clough*. Clough's experience was an example of the shambles that scruples could make of a career. He became one of Emerson's protégés, their friendship owing much to Emerson's identification with the struggles of Clough and his friends at Oxford in the late 1840s.

[33] *JMN*, 2:267.

found in Hume, it focuses in one burning lens several painful inferences: that history does not teach moral progress; that religion may
be a cloak for greed and hypocrisy; that blood may be thinner than
water and the tie of father to son suspect and loaded with threat; that
apostasy and silence may be the only responses to bad faith.

One cannot condense the laconic understatement of Hume's language as it demonstrates the "irreligion" of William Rufus, son of
William the Conqueror, a man of violent and greedy character who

> once accepted of 60 marks from a jew, whose son had been con-
> verted to Christianity, and who engaged him by that present to
> assist him in bringing back the youth to judaism. William em-
> ployed both menaces and persuasion for that purpose; but find-
> ing the convert obstinate in his faith, he sent for the father, and
> told him that as he had not succeeded, it was not just that he
> should keep the present; but as he had done his utmost it was
> but equitable that he should be paid for his pains; and he would
> therefore retain only 30 marks of the money.[34]

The differences between the two treatments of the story are revealing. Hume focuses entirely on the king, whom he regards as "violent," "perfidious," and "encroaching," an infidel who played the
role of shady businessman out of both sport and greed, a cynic who
cheated his associate and demeaned the kingship for the pleasure of
mocking the Church. Consequently, Hume's lapidary style does not
bother to name the Jew, who was no partner and could not expect
equity from this ruthless monarch.

Emerson's version by contrast is emotional in language, melodra-
matic in construction, and laden with biblical typology. Its prominent features—the four-stress line, the focus on a crucial event in a
dramatic narrative, and the historical subject—mark it as a literary
ballad in the romantic style he had learned from Scott and Byron,
while the mixed diction of the father's language suggests elements
of Shylock. The twenty-three irregular lines, mostly end-stopped
rhyming couplets, can best be scanned by giving them four feet, but
the number of syllables varies greatly, producing the effect of a dis-
organized pulse, as weak and antinomian perhaps as the event itself.

Time is conflated in Emerson's reverse typology: the king becomes a Nazarite, or type of Christ, the son becomes Isaac, and the
father is associated with Abraham:

[34] Hume, *History* 1:266–67.

May it please my lorde there's a Jewe at the doore.
Bring him in, sayde the King, what waites he for?
I wot sir you came from Abraham's loins,
Eat no porke, love no Christ, doe no good with your Coins.

Abraham, of course, was the biblical figure most exemplary of religious faith to both the ancient Jews and the New England Puritans
who felt themselves their spiritual offspring. Driving home that typology, Emerson has the Jew name the king "Magog," or Satan,
while William cheerfully describes himself as the "fittest Pharisee,"
a byword for hypocrite.

Emerson is less interested than Hume, however, in the king,
whom he reduces to a coarsely jesting bully, and more interested in
the Jew and his son, whom he names Isaac and brings onstage,
while giving most of the dialogue to the father:

My lord the king I doe as Moses bids
Eschewing all badness I shut my coffer lids.
From the law of the Mountain, God forbid I should swerve
The uncircumsized Nazarite my race cannot serve
But Isaac my son to idols hathe gone over
And no man I can find my first born to recover[.]

Emerson's use of typology, however, deliberately travesties the
tale of Abraham and Isaac. Far from instilling reverence for God's
covenant with his chosen people, the two speakers attempt to buy
and sell religious allegiance like a commodity, while the silent anti-
hero is a morally ambiguous apostate:

The King filled his mouth with arguments and gibes
To turn the lad's head to the faith of the tribes
But the young Isrealite [sic] was so hard and stiffnecked
That by no means could the King come to any effect.
So he paid back the old Jew 30 merkes of his gains
Quoth he I'll keep the other 30 for the payment of my pains[.]

Neither love nor religion is part of the moral universe of the poem;
Isaac is silent, but money talks. Lacking other evidence, one may
conclude that he has sold out, while the father, who hypocritically
has said that he has "shut his coffer lids," in his next breath offers
payment for Isaac's return. Cash, as Carlyle put it in describing the
contemporary world, is the sole nexus. The king hires himself out as
a kind of deprogrammer who will "turn the lad's head" as a cattle

driver would. He fails, not because Isaac is a passionate convert, but because the head is "hard and stiffnecked." Isaac has joined the majority, and his motives are obscure. They may be as avaricious and worldly as those of his father and the king, but as Emerson's misspelling (Isrealite) suggests, the son's silence may be more honest than their speech.

This Hebrew father, associated with "phylactered Rabbins, far, far oversea" may remind one of the magician from the "Dead-Sea-shore," but the roles are here reversed, for it is now the son who refuses to communicate. Intensifying the parody is the fact that this seed of Abraham treats not with God but with his worldly surrogate, a king, and one who uses his power not to bestow a privileged position on his followers, but to cheat them. His name, William, happens to be that of Emerson's own father.

The strikingly awkward meter is consistent with the diction, tone, and materialistic imagery throughout. The poem is, at least superficially, a well-realized if unpleasant dramatization of a subject not normally associated with Emerson. It focuses on the interaction of religion and worldly interests, the complexities of bad faith and apostasy. Some time later Mary told Waldo she regretted that he "prefer[red] society to the solitude of an Abdiel." In later years he was better able to articulate his love of her Miltonic model. But in 1824 Waldo's imagination was haunted by another story, and there was no Miltonic certainty to his vision of the youth who stood alone. He would have to think his way beyond this conception of a tongue-tied rebel before he could act or write with freedom.

The moral ambiguity of this poem may also suggest how difficult and guilt-ridden aggression on his own behalf still seemed. Asserting one's own religious identity could appear a shameful betrayal of father and heritage both, an act—or "task," as Nietzsche was to call it—to which one had no moral right. The unsympathetic, even hostile conception of the father meanwhile reflects Emerson's own unresolved anger. For at the deepest level William, the king-father, and the Jew who comes from Abraham's loins and is the religious father, both merge into one figure of paternal authority seeking to control the thought and negate the free will of the subject-son. Such internalized fathers may exert a more effective brake on self-realization than any external authority ever could. One does not see beyond Isaac's mute and blocked rebellion into his motives because Emerson himself could not. Every step he took, therefore, toward entering the ministry—his father's profession—only exacerbated his conflicts. The actual intellectual content of these conflicts was in emotional

terms the least important issue. He was in a classic double bind, for while identification with authority was impossible, challenging it was a task he could not imagine being permitted to win.

"William Rufus and the Jew" is not an appealing poem. It sheds valuable light, however, on the crisis Emerson was to experience as soon as he encountered the professional training at Harvard Divinity School.

Chapter 7

THE ANGEL OF MIDNIGHT

"We are not pans and barrows, nor even porters of the fire and torch-bearers, but children of the fire, made of it."

—RWE, "The Poet"

W HEN HE WAS seventeen and seeking to differentiate him-self from ordinary persons—people who were merely eccentric, lacked common sense, "did jobs," or possessed "gaunt lantern countenances—who have at one time and another shocked my nerves and nauseated my taste by their hideous as-pect"—Emerson determined that the crucial factor was the capacity for fancy and "sublime contemplation." To the mind with such a gift, he wrote, it is "given to command the disappearance of land and sea, and mankind and things, and they vanish. Then," he went on, "comes the Enchanter, illuminating the glorious visions from heaven, granting thoughts of other worlds."[1] All his life Emerson at some level wanted to be that Enchanter, the seer whose power over reality was complete. The desire was related to his fascination with death and the supernatural, and later was the seedbed from which sprang the Merlins, the Saddis, Sphinxes, and Bacchuses of some of his best poems.

In his aim to envision them, his model had from the beginning been Mary. The significance of the Bowdoin Prize episode is prob-ably not that Emerson appropriated her language, for she knew of the borrowing and did not object. She wrote in fact that one of her deepest wishes was "to find [him] in the same paths" and to have a part in forming his mind. At some level they no doubt both knew that she encouraged his use of her material. More significant is the extent to which, at this stage of his life, what might be called both Emerson's langue and parole flowed from this familial source.[2]

Contact between aunt and nephew by this time was almost en-

[1] *JMN*, 1:33–34.
[2] MME to RWE, 1821, HMS. For a more detailed discussion of Emerson's linguistic debt to his aunt, see my essay, "The Angel of Midnight."

tirely literary. Once Waldo had been established as a fourteen year-old freshman at Harvard and William had begun to earn his living as a teacher, Mary had given up residence in Boston. She lived for the most part at "Elm Vale," the farm she shared with her sister and her family in Waterford, Maine, from which she made frequent journeys to visit relatives and clergymen in nearby Massachusetts. Her withdrawal did not mean that she ceased to be interested in the family. On the contrary, she was very conscious of them and especially of their health, warning Ruth for example with some prescience against the excessive stress she saw Ruth permitting young Edward to endure.[3]

But Mary knew herself to be unsociable and sometimes quarrelsome. She had loved Ruth, but she came to disapprove of her "coldness and pride" and her tolerance of worldliness. Moreover, Mary feared seeming to compete with Ruth as a mother. Withdrawal to her own ground was best.[4]

None of this mattered to Waldo, who profited from his aunt's geographical removal by extending his correspondence. They probably grew closer, in fact, through their writing, for the written word was the easiest mode of communication for both of them. "I want the long letter you mention," she wrote him after a contretemps in 1826:

Indeed *we* can only commune by pen. You are more sensitive than ever—that dolefull shake of head and grim look I had when you interested me thursday in parlour disgusts you so that you wont talk—all the way going you said nothing that you might. That destiny of which the freedom of our wills seems but an obedient member, forbids me to enter fine society at the peril of constant and hopeless disgrace from the ebullition of confidence w'h lies so [dead] in solitude—Therefore write I say if you can and I will write to remember that I have self existence of some sort.[5]

By then, writing to him was clearly a necessity to her "self existence" as well as to his own, perhaps. Yet as early as 1821 she had

[3] When he was thirteen, she wrote to Ruth, "I heard with some attention what Aunt Sarah stated in her lamentation—that as [Edward] was so liable to excitement it would be the most hazardous thing in the world to trust him from home." Again, the next summer she cautioned that Edward ought to leave Waltham and go to Medford for the good air, adding that the light work he would do there "would not wear out his nervous system." MME to RE, 1818 [?], HMS.

[4] MME to RWE, 1821, HMS.

[5] MME to RWE, 1826, HMS.

told him that while she hoped they might meet in heaven, "I am too much beguiled by you and your imagination to wish to see you much—Other ways demand one—Oh sd I be so blest as to find you in the same paths. And there you will one day be, after the truths which God has sent down."[6]

He studied her writing closely. Often he entered in his journal both his letters to her and her replies, a record of interaction he kept with no other person. He also sent to her the journals themselves for her comments, while keeping up a steady barrage of demands for her own "almanacks," requests to which she ultimately acceded, but often coyly and only after much teasing and flattery. At age twenty-five he told her that "all your letters are valuable to me; those most so I think which you esteem the least. I grow more avaricious of this kind of property like other misers with age, and like expecting heirs would be glad to put my fingers into the chest of 'old almanacks' before they are a legacy."[7] Four years earlier he wrote that he had despondently been seeking more than a "spider thread of intellect" in the accepted gospels of learning, but finding only "meagreness" concealed by ornament. Therefore he turned to her. "I am therefore curious to know what living wit (not perverted by the vulgar rage of writing a book) has suggested or concluded upon the dark sayings and sphinx riddles of philosophy and life; I do beseech your charity not to withhold your pen."[8]

He saw her, that is, as someone who wrote and thought not out of ambition, but out of pure natural talent and energy. She had threatened to destroy her writings, but he insisted she must preserve them, comparing her favorably with de Staël, who had sought mere vulgar fame. Mary's motives would be disinterested philanthropy and friendship. He flattered her, as they both knew, but only to reach through the armor of defenses she had grown about herself.

His fascination with her style endured throughout his life. After she died Emerson, then in his sixties, spent many hours with the help of his son transcribing selections from her letters and almanacs into four fresh volumes. The cover of one volume is decorated in Emerson's style with a curious pen-and-ink silhouette of what appears to be a river—possibly the Styx—with a wrought iron fence, a gate, a ferryman, and a ferry lying nearby on the water, which the mottled blue paper of the cover itself suggests. Mary had twitted

⁶ MME to RWE, HMS.
⁷ L, 1:208.
⁸ J, 1:357–58.

him that he was "somewhat morbid as to [his] decorations," referring probably to his manuscripts, as these are covered with sketches
of dragons, an occasional corpse, and the like. Perhaps this untitled
sketch was Lethe, and the design a last joke between them.

WHAT WERE the sources of her fascination for him? He thought her
an inspired writer, capable of hitting off phrases and ideas that no
one else could have produced, and since their shared concern was
religion, what she said and how she said it were of great importance
to him. According to a contemporary, Emerson regarded his aunt as
"the best writer of her day in Massachusetts"—that is, in his culture—"not even excepting Dr. Channing or Daniel Webster." Elsewhere he compared her style to Dante's, saying that it was "inimitable, unattainable by talent, as if caught from some dream," and that
reading Dante had reminded him of her "eloquent theology."9

Emerson regarded his father's style as ordinary, Mary's as extraor-
dinary.10 Regardless of Emerson's objectivity about his father, there
is no question that Mary's language, even after a century and a half,
is vital and original where her brother's is merely correct, her ideas
bold where his are timid. Nor can there be any question of her influence on her nephew's style. Their styles at times are so similar that
even Emerson's editors have occasionally had difficulty distinguishing her language, copied by him into his journals, from his own.

But her faith and her personal style were very different from Waldo's; she was passionate, baroquely complex, impatient, and though
a maverick, yet a great believer in traditional faith—so long as it did
not constrain her own speculations. When as a girl she had heard
about the differences in the synoptic Gospels, she had set about "col-
lecting the harmonies"—repairing the rending of the fabric of which
Waldo was to complain.11 Her mission as a believer was to explore
her talent for mystical vision through private meditation pursued
deep in nature. Since she expressed these experiences largely in her
almanacs, the audience provided by Waldo was actually of great
value. To her, the world was emblematic of God's favor, and faith

9 Sanborn, *Sixty Years*, p. 48; "MME," *CW*, 10:404.

10 He thought of William Emerson's work on *The Monthly Anthology* and of the whole
Federal period, indeed, as mediocre, a "*Month-of March*" in quality (*L*, 4:179); cited by
Lewis P. Simpson, *The Federalist Literary Mind: Selections from the Monthly Anthology
and Boston Review 1803–1811* ([Baton Rouge]: Louisiana State University Press, 1962),
p. 5, cited hereafter as Simpson.

11 MME to RWE, 1826, HMS.

and poetry were inextricable. "We love poetry," she wrote after an evening walk, "as we do the flowers of the field—because they supply not the necessaries, but the luxuries of life and give presentiments to the soul so rich, of an existence where all cares and labours cease."[12]

Or she might watch a cloud, then think about "éclat of name—of fame" and the relation of these to the movement of the cloud "as it . . . climbs the sides of the mountain over bog and brake and tree and suddenly disappears at the instant of arriving at its summit." Just as "shadows add to the beauty of fleeting scenes," so does "the aspirant of other mounts to the interest of life." She did not have to add that the "éclat of name" that she envisioned was Waldo's. His future was to mount, as fleetingly as the clouds and all human wishes, up the peaks of human renown and disappear into eternity. "This richly laden season," she went on that fine September day, "when every leaf begins its own mystic story, which soothes the soul and dwells upon the soul and blends itself into the soul, derives a zest . . . from prophecy of those who are rising into honor."[13]

There were many other ties between them. To write to Mary was to communicate with both parentage and history, for Waldo associated her with the past. This was true not only because of her fascination with death, but because she was the conduit for his relationship to his ancestors. It was his "humor," he wrote in 1825, "to despise pedigree," but "I was educated to prize it. The kind Aunt whose cares instructed my youth (and whom may God reward) told me oft the virtues of her and mine ancestors. They have been clergymen for many generations and the piety of all and the eloquence of many is yet praised in the Churches. But the dead sleep in their moonless night; my business is with the living."[14]

And in 1837 he recalled the stories she had told him about their legendary piety—stories mixed with the supernatural:

> I cannot hear the young men whose theological instruction is exclusively owed to Cambridge and to public institution, without feeling how much happier was my star which rained on me influences of ancestral religion. The depth of the religious sentiment which I knew in my Aunt Mary imbuing all her genius and derived to her from such hoarded family traditions, from so many godly lives and godly deaths of sainted kindred . . . was

[12] MME to RWE, 1824, HMS.
[13] MME to RWE, 1824, HMS.
[14] *JMN*, 2:316.

itself a culture, an education. I heard with awe her tales of the pale stranger who at the time her grandfather lay on his death bed tapped at the window & asked to come in. The dying man said, 'Open the door;' but the timid family did not; and immediately he breathed his last, and they said one to another It was the angel of death.[15]

Beyond her other attractions, however, Mary seemed to him in some ways closer to the supernatural world, the world of pure spirit than he; he sensed that through her relation with nature she had special insight into what he called "the old eld." He could be humorous about his project of gaining her visionary stance, as in a letter he wrote at twenty-one to his friend John B. Hill, but his aim was very serious. He felt himself still short of the mark that Mary had, he imagined, set him:

> I am seeking to put myself on a footing of old acquaintance with nature, as a poet should. . . . I confess I cannot find myself quite as perfectly at home on the rock and in the wood, as my ancient, & I may say, infant aspirations led me to expect. My aunt, (of whom I think you have heard before & who is alone among women,) has spent a great part of her life in the country, is an idolater of Nature, & counts but a small number who merit the privilege of dwelling among the mountains.[16]

Nature had not inspired him as it had his aunt: "The coarse thrifty cit profanes the grove by his presence—& she was anxious that her nephew might hold high and reverential notions regarding it (as) the temple where God & the Mind are to be studied & adored & where the fiery soul can begin a premature communication with other worlds."

The last phrase is an amusing description of Mary's obsessive passion, but in fact he had clearly been trying to live it out: "When I took my book therefore to the woods—I found Nature not half poetical, not half visionary enough. There was nothing which . . . phantasy could deceive me one instant into the belief of more than met the eye. In short I found that I had only transported into the new place my entire personal identity, & was grievously disappointed."[17]

In short, Mary—who had already named him "Magician of Na-

[15] *JMN*, 5:323.
[16] *L*, 1:133.
[17] Ibid.

ture and art"—was central to the formation of his fantasied but powerful sense that he could get a glimpse of the Enchanter's world; their frequent play on this theme forms a prelude to his more self-consciously serious years after 1823. He was convinced that only from such a vision would the poetic gift flow, and the end of his important letter of July 1823 to Hill indicates how closely he associated the ideas of insight, blindness, and the penetrating powers of the great poets: "Parti-coloured Nature makes a man love his eyes. I thought tonight when I watched in the West 'Parting day die like a dolphin' what a mutilated mind & existence belongs to the blind. The history of poetry, however, seems to say,—Pluck out his eyes before he meddles with the harp."[18]

Insight had come only with blindness to Maeonides, Thamyris, and Ossian, Waldo said. Oddly, the history of his own life was soon to show that he was willing or required to pay the same price himself.

Mary did not, however, indulge his lapses from her standard. When after a long walk with William he reported to her that nature had fed his senses rather than his mind, and that he had filled his journal with jokes, she replied, "You should have gone separately." Finding his own "stream of thought" was more important than enjoying brotherhood.[19]

Waldo complained that his Muse was become " 'faint and mean.' " Mary returned to her strong theme: "Oh would the Muse forever leave you, till you had prepared for her a celestial abode. . . . You flag—your Muse is mean because the breath of fashion has not puffed her. You are not inspired in heart, with a gift for immortality, because you are the nursling of surrounding circumstances—You become yourself a part of the events which make up ordinary life."

He was not yet, in short, self-reliant, and therefore not yet either a poet or seer. She ended the letter, however, by prophesying a fame for him "like Cicero['s] perhaps[,] [when] your poetry will not be valued because your prose is so much better." At the bottom he wrote, "This letter is a most beautiful monument of kindness and highminded but partial affection. Would I were worthy of it. Reread Dec. 1828 RWE."[20]

Mary advocated solitude and closeness to nature because they

[18] L, 1:134.
[19] L, 1:115; MME to RWE, 1822, HMS.
[20] MME to RWE, 1822, HMS.

would lead to autonomy and inner power while feeding the soul and the poetic gift. Social intercourse should be avoided, for it opened one to falsity.

> Byron and Wordsworth have there [in solitude] best and only intensely burnished their pens. Would to Providence your un-foldings might be there—that it were not a wild and fruitless wish, that you could be disunited from travelling with the souls of other men, of living and breathing, reading and writing with one vital time fated idea[,] their opinions.[21]

"The images," she wrote, "the sweet immortal images are within us—born there, our native right, and sometimes one kind of sound-ing word or syllable wakens the instrument of our souls and some-times another. But we are not slaves to sense any more than to po-tential Usurpers, but by fashion and imbecility."[22]
   The vitality of her faith and language made her particularly useful to her nephew when he struggled with the problems of theodicy and skepticism. When he echoed Hume in complaining that the world seemed a cruel enigma, she replied, "The ordinary effect of an inex-plicable enigma can do no hurt, for while it remains inexplicable it tells no bad tales . . . of nature. . . . Were not the laws Newton dis-covered inexplicable before his day? And did *he* ever complain that he remained as ignorant as the vulgar?"[23]
   Referring to Hume, she added, "Of that old scotsman you surely feign respect." She took whatever opportunity she could find for ver-bal swipes at a thinker she felt had had far too much influence on her nephew. "Old Hume was a morbid hermit in the nest of being," she wrote him testily in 1827. (This was an allusion, typical of their verbal interaction, to one of Waldo's own phrases, for he had previ-ously written to her that Shakespeare was "so singularly grand as to be a hermit in the fields of thought where he travels."[24])
   When in 1828 she thought Waldo in a sermon seemed to take too much new notice of "prudential considerations," that is, of worldly interest, she blamed it on "mean fears of want and dependance." She related these to skeptical doubts and urged him, "Above all quit the doubts of epecurian theology," which would lead him not to fear hell or to hope for heaven.

[21] MME to RWE, 1824, HMS.
[22] MME to RWE, 1822, HMS.
[23] MME to RWE, [1823], HMS.
[24] *J*, 1:101.

Your reading Hume when young has rendered you, I cannot but think, so imbued with his manner of thinking, that you cannot shake him off. There seems, or I am stupid, so much of his *manner* tho' *better* in this letter that I feel as I do when reading him. But to *my old* frame his arguments, if such they can called, make no more impression than the spray of a child's squirt.[25]

Skepticism never seemed real to her. It was not a temptation or logical inference to be resisted, but only a sign, probably, of insufficient response to the abundance of life. The only "enigma" that she found in existence was the mixture of good and evil in human nature. That there could be persons who owned slaves, for example, suggested the puzzle of "manichism," that "this soul can adore the Creator, while it finds much to hate in itself and something in every body."[26]

Like Dante, she was most puzzled by the lukewarm, and she criticized those who could be "calm" and rational in contemplating God.[27] To one whose faith was so total, passionate, and without ambivalence, Hume could not be taken seriously. "I am reading Hume's essays—never was more disappointed—expected to find new mental excitement and many moments of inspired thought. You must tell me whether there are any direct answers to his epicurean argument about the universe being a 'singular effect.'" She was irritated that "this Outlaw should cast such a mist . . . that we cant get hold of his sofistry." At best Hume was a "use[ful]" warning, she concluded, that in this disordered world, only conscience could be a guide. (A conclusion not so different from Emerson's ultimate resolution to rest belief on intuition.) "How far is he exceeded and put down by the letters of Voltaire," she concluded.[28]

Moved by obsessive zeal to see God face to face, she pursued her vision in the high romantic mode with a lack of self-conciousness that was both her strength and weakness. (A lover of Byron, she imagined that had he been religious, he would have been a Calvinist—Unitarianism would have been too tame.) Her favored tropes included not only death and the grave, but stars, ascent into space, and lights, especially strange lights. She uses this language for a covertly autobiographical description:

[25] MME to RWE, 1828, HMS.
[26] MME to RWE, 1823, HMS.
[27] MME to RWE, 1823, HMS.
[28] MME to RWE, 1824, HMS.

So close was this conformation, that a certain pilgrim lived for some months in an eclipse so monotonous as nearly to discern the disk of her own particular star. Could a mind return to its first fortunate submission when it opened with its own peculiar coulers and spread them out on its own rhymy palette with its own added stock and spread them beneath the Cross, what a mercy to the age.[29]

Such language suggests the influence of the Hopkintonians or New Lights. These mysterious months of blessed eclipse and meditation are perhaps also the subject of another comment, made in response to one of her nephew's requests for her writings: "I send you an almanack?—Catch me! Soberly, I will not till you return the others. They are my *home*; the only proof of having existed; and the Andover life was to be remembered."[30]

She liked to imagine that she sought the grave, for there one was closest to God. Consequently she could conclude a high-flying letter on the beauties of self-sacrifice ("the humblest example of meekness will shine in light when the meteors are gone") with both a pun on her own name and the cry, "Good night. Oh for that 'long and moonless night' to shadow my dust, tho' I have nothing to leave but my carcase to fatten the earth—it is for my own sake I long to go. When you pray, remember ME."[31]

She could remark after teasing references to playing his Muse, "I will no more stop for apples. Before I knew you, I did not ask even a dirge. I invoked nature with rapture to sweep over my grave with her roughest elements; for there [in the grave] would be the voice of a strange spirit, and there might be a strange light to guide the icy worm to his riot."[32]

Her often baroque, sometimes bizarre use of language undoubtedly reveals her as the true eccentric Emerson's late essay showed her to be. During her later period in Concord, for example, she rode about in her shroud, and that not once, but so frequently that it wore out and had to be replaced several times. And she indulged as well in such tricks as sleeping in a bed she had made in the shape of a coffin. This lent credence to the story, which came down in a Concord family that she had visited, that she "astonished the neighbor-

[29] MME to RWE, 1824, HMS.
[30] MME to RWE, HMS.
[31] MME to RWE, 1821, HMS.
[32] MME to RWE, c. 1821, HMS.

hood by crawling out on the roof . . . and sitting in her ascension robes to be ready for her translation."[33]

But although she always had a strong strain of theatricality in her, she was entirely focused and serious in preaching total commitment and sincerity on significant matters. She feared as well as desired success for Waldo, perhaps foreseeing the kind of life her brother William had embraced.

In an early letter (characteristically dated "Space and time") she predicted such success while snuffing out the heresies he had not yet committed. And she could turn sharp: "My sister was good enough to tell me your intentions of professing publicly your faith in xianity. In less liberal days, it was the right of the meanest member to inquire the motives of the Noviciate. If I doubted yours, I would not use this absolute privlege. Yet I may ask, *what mean you by this rite?*"

His public statement could be sincere, but "if the rite means nothing more than many teach, why pass so many hours to a vague purpose, unless it be the *key* to a profession?"[34]

She feared that his motive might be careerism. Yet when he uncharacteristically suggested that " 'instead of intellectual excellence [he] hoped to be a good man' " she replied that this was a "most abhorred thought," for she felt no such division herself, and always attacked her nephew when he returned to what became one of his themes.[35]

Her most extended response to his skepticism was in a letter "from Plato," responding to his own "Letter to Plato" that she had read in his journal.[36] Waldo had asserted that moral behavior since Plato had not improved and that behavior was evidently independent of religion. Mary answered by insisting on the primacy of Platonic or innate ideas and asserting that Hume's influence would pass, like that of his predecessors. She did not attempt to account for the relationship of religion and morality, but rather dramatized Plato as witness to eschatology, describing him emerging from "a rainbow pavillion, where he had been holding converse" with other martyrs.

Mary's Plato rebukes the "familiar style" of Waldo's letter, but answers at length. "Your vaunted revelation," Plato tells the young American, is of a "nature untold," and some Christian laws were

---

33 *CW*, 10:428–29; Blanche E. Wheeler Williams, *Mary C. Wheeler: Leader in Art and Education* (Boston: Marshall Jones Co., 1934), p. 39.

34 MME to RWE, 1822, HMS.

35 MME to RWE, 1822, HMS.

36 *L*, 1:160. He delightedly wrote William that he and Charles had "gone on a pilgrimage to our lady at Waterford—who has written me a prodigiously fine letter 'from Plato.' "

more miserable than any of Greece. But Hume, "the scotsman, so eminent" will be found to have added nothing: "What *did* he know or *prove* to vanquish my universals, my innate ideas independent [of] perception?" Hume's epistemology was based on sense perception; Plato insists his system is superior, for his ideas were

> forms existing originally in the divine mind. . . . In my "formation of the universe" was nothing to blush at even here. Surrounded with nature, which I was capable of studying and loving; yet it was filled with phenomena, with mystery, with some that spoke of terror and pain. My Demiorgus—the stars inhabited by Genius—could *you then* have imagined better? in my theology, was there not the unity, the absolute perfection of the first Cause? . . . In my Republick, apart from the woman kind [i.e., the subjection of women] and the neglect of the ignorant, what can you object?[37]

The long letter concludes with a remarkable Dantesque vision of the last things that Plato saw after taking "the wings of light":

> That spherical figure [the earth] . . . here a measureless dial— its dread gnomis [pointer as on a sundial] pointing to dreader numbers—and not all of these alike veiled in countless waves of light—and some of these which were marked with human destinies were covered with blackness—interminable—the wheels within wheels which gave motion, if it were motion, to this terrific circle appeared to be impelled by living beings—others whirled beyond the ken of these selected seraphim devoted to knowledge.

It was for visions such as these, the diction "inimitable . . . as if caught from some dream," as well as her harsh and biting wit, that Waldo cherished her letters.

But for all its visionary splendor, Mary's response did not address the central problems: that history did not reveal moral progress and that religion and morality, whether pagan or Christian, might have no necessary connection. It was becoming increasingly clear that objections so unimportant to Mary as to be virtually invisible engaged Waldo more and more. His solutions, when they came at last, were to her worse than the doubts. Gradually in the next few years he would resign entirely his search for external proof of God's immanence and begin to speak of it as residing only within the individual,

[37] MME to RWE, 1824, HMS.

mediated by "Sentiment" perhaps, but nothing more tangible than that. By the time his ideas had more fully developed, she was both disgusted and scornful.

By 1825 the era of their close communion was drawing to a close. In the short run, Emerson was to move in a different direction. As he began that year he commented on her "love of pedigree" and rejected it: "But the dead sleep in their moonless night; my business is with the living." Undoubtedly, his struggle to turn away from his own juvenile morbidity would have to implicate one who had shared some of his obsessions and fostered them. But in the long run, though a heretic in her view, his thought returned to her emphasis on the primacy of intuitive religious thought, on the capacity of the individual to "see God face to face." Perhaps it was from her "fiery spirit" also that he learned to insist, as he did in "The Poet," that "we are not pans and barrows, nor even porters of the fire and torch-bearers, but children of the fire, made of it, and only the same divinity transmuted and at two or three removes, when we know least about it."[38] He had first seen Mary claim that power of direct communion, and it was through her mediation that he came to believe he shared it. But although he rejected part of her doctrine, in the long run the sense that he was "made of" the fire, so fundamental to his vision of himself as poet and mythmaker, was her legacy.

[38] "The Poet," *CW*, 3:4.

Chapter 8

HARVARD DIVINITY SCHOOL

"From the views I have already expressed, you will infer the
sad conviction, which I share I believe, with numbers, of
the universal decay and now almost death of faith in society.
The soul is not preached. The Church seems to totter to its
fall, almost all life extinct. On this occasion, any
complaisance would be criminal which told you, whose
hope and commission it is to preach the faith of Christ, that
the faith of Christ is preached."

> —RWE, "An Address Delivered Before the
> Senior Class in Divinity College,
> Cambridge, Sunday Evening, July 15,
> 1838."

I N 1838 Emerson, already known as an iconoclast, deeply offended the Unitarian establishment and effectively broke with
it when—at the request of the students, not the professors—he
delivered a commencement address to the Harvard Divinity School.
In that famous speech he referred to Christian doctrines as "cultus"
and "mythus." He told his audience that the church around them
was dying—this he asserted was common knowledge. But "the old
is for slaves"—let it go. So much for eighteen centuries of doctrine.
"The man who aims to speak as synods use, as the fashion guides,
and as interest commands, babbles. Let him hush." So much for the
work of the college and its professors. He urged the graduates not to
wreck their faith in God and usefulness to their people by attempting to teach or interpret traditional doctrines repugnant to their hon-
esty. They must speak only from their own lives and "refuse the
good models," even the sacred ones.

What he feared on their behalf—and painted for them so that they
could not miss its threat—provides a clue as to why this man of normally superfine manners was indeed so very rude. "I once heard a
preacher," he said,

145

who sorely tempted me to say I would go to church no more.
Men go, thought I, where they are wont to go, else had no soul
entered the temple in the afternoon. A snow-storm was falling
around us. The snow-storm was real, the preacher merely spectral, and the eye felt the sad contrast in looking at him, and then
out of the window behind him into the beautiful meteor of the
snow. He had lived in vain. He had no one word intimating that
he had laughed or wept, was married or in love, had been com-
mended, or cheated, or chagrined. If he had ever lived and
acted, we were none the wiser for it.[1]

The enemy was death. Emerson's object was to save not their immortal but their mortal souls from the death-in-life for which he felt
their pallid creed was preparing them. "Deal out to the people your
life," he urged them, "life passed through the fire of thought."

Andrews Norton, who was present, took the speech as a "personal
insult," and in a sense he was right. Neither convention nor the
"highly respectable officers of the Institution" expected Emerson to
speak of these things—to address the innate fear in young adults of
the death they daily see around them in their elders and their urgent
need to reach out consciously instead toward life. Emerson's empa-
thy for the novices and the intensity of his wish to warn them of what
lay ahead must have been impelling forces. For to return to Harvard
Divinity School was for him to revisit the scene of the near wreck of
his life. As he wrote his speech, he must have relived his own experience there, when the only triumph open to him was escape.

PARADOXICALLY, Emerson had gone to great lengths to secure the
very training he later condemned. After three years of teaching and
saving while supporting his mother and younger brothers, he had
formed a plan for going "*by* the rogue" Penury if he could not con-
quer him face to face. Edward was now graduated and keeping
school. There would be some money from the Haskins family's sale
of real estate, and Waldo had been studying with Dr. Channing privately. With Channing's backing, he would enter the divinity school
as a second-year student and save a year's expenses.[2]

Dr. Channing was a prominent Unitarian minister who had begun as a Hopkintonian and whose sermons asserting the priority of
reason over revelation Emerson sometimes thought "sublime." "I

[1] *CW*, 1:144, 135, 137–38.
[2] *L*, 1:146–52.

take a hebdomadal walk to Mr. C[unningham] or Dr. C.[hanning] for the sake of saying I am studying divinity," he wrote to William, but although he deeply respected Channing, he found no mentor in him, any more than in any other older man. "Dr. Channing received him kindly," Edward Emerson wrote, recounting his father's story of the interview, "gave him a list of books to read, and was ready to talk with him from time to time, but would not undertake the direction of his studies; indeed, seemed to be hardly capable, Emerson said, of taking another person's point of view, or of communicating himself freely in private conversation. Neither of them was particularly gifted in this respect, and they never really came together." Since Emerson probably wanted less rather than more direction from others, this distance did not discourage him; Channing's purely formal sponsorship would have been enough to ensure his admission on his own terms at the divinity college.[3]

William, however, was not impressed by the idea, calling it "a rather bold plan," and he wrote to Waldo that he was "rushing to jail" for two or three years without any certain "means of bread."[4] That William, writing from Göttingen, should have used this phrase is relevant, for there was a vast difference in the perspectives from which theology was studied in Germany and at Cambridge. For a variety of reasons—including his dislike of the language and his desire to make tangible progress—Waldo did not wish to go to Germany, but he understood well that that country had long been the home of speculative philosophy and especially of the study of the Bible on historical principles. While traditional thinkers both in England and America regarded Germany as an infectious source of irreligion, the more intellectual—if not necessarily more liberal—minds in the church had made it their business to come to terms with the new findings about the probable composition of the Bible and its internal discrepancies—studies that came to be known in their different branches as the higher and lower criticisms. In England the Anglican liberals who took these issues seriously were known pejoratively as the Noetics—the Knowers—and were centered in Oriel College, Oxford. Led by such intellectually aggressive theologians as Richard Whately and Thomas Arnold, the movement in turn produced its own counterreaction in figures like Hurrell Froude and John Henry Newman, who eventually converted to Catholicism.[5]

[3] L, 1:138; L, 1:146; EIC, p. 102.
[4] L, 1:149–54; L, 1:158–59.
[5] The most detailed discussion of the group is the Rev. William Tuckwell's Pre-Trac-

The fight, bitter and divisive, lasted generations, for gradually it became clear that at stake was the beginning of what later was called modernism. Freedom of thought and the right to speculate beckoned on the one hand; loss of moral authority, alienation, anomie, and any sense of personal connection with God's will threatened on the other. Everywhere the basic issues were the same. How literally must one interpret the Bible? What priority, if any, did faith have over reason? Was truth an absolute value, attached immutably to specific creeds and formulas, or was it relative to its era, changing in its specifics as knowledge advanced, as Arnold among others held? What was the meaning of particular mysteries of doctrine, such as the Trinity or Atonement? To reinterpret or demystify them typically could give rise to responses like Newman's famous question on hearing of one of Arnold's positions, "But is *he* a Christian?"[6]

The status of revelation was crucial. The Bible was God's revelation to man, but so were the miracles described therein, and so also was nature itself. Which had priority? If nature and reason took precedence, tradition, dogma, and the Bible itself were at some risk. What credence must one give miracles?[7]

The question of how much risk to permit oneself each scholar and preacher had continually to answer. Protestants, uninstructed by a dogmatic central church, were especially open to the puzzles presented to reason by the ongoing contradictions that science had been posing to the Bible at least since Galileo. The Unitarian reverence for Newton was based in part on his status as a man of science who was yet deeply religious, but by the beginning of the early nineteenth century the new scientific arguments offered by geology had become crucial. Fossil evidence that the world had long preexisted the biblically described period was hard for the orthodox to accept but impossible to ignore.

Few in America were qualified to join the dialogue, which had begun to turn on analysis of the Bible as a text, some of which was clearly corrupt and must therefore be purged so that the saving remnant might continue to be worshipped as the undefiled word. This

tarian Oxford: A Reminiscence of the Oriel Noetics (London, 1909). For a summary of the issues involved, see Greenberger, *Clough*, pp. 17–18.

[6] Newman, p. 39.

[7] For the English battles over rationalism, see Alfred William Benn, *The History of English Rationalism in the Nineteenth Century* (London, 1906), chaps. 2, 8, and 9; Francis Cornish Warre, *The English Church in the Nineteenth Century* (London: Macmillian, 1909), 1:186–90; L. E. Elliott-Binns, *Religion in the Victorian Era* (London: Lutterworth Press, 1936), pp. 181ff.

was a highly technical process, and the reason for Moses Stuart's eminence. Although situated in remote Andover, as an orthodox opponent of the liberals, self-taught, and not unheroically, Stuart had made himself an authority on the Greek and Hebrew grammars that would be the fundamental disciplines of these polemics. He had gone so far as to import from Europe the type fonts necessary to print his Hebrew grammars—thereby becoming the only owner of such fonts then in this country.[8] Andrews Norton was Stuart's major opponent. Between them, essentially, the great debate found its American representatives, or rather, its American echo.[9]

Waldo from the beginning had a preternaturally sharp sense of style, of what the important issues were, and of where—if not how—he was likely to come out on them (a talent already at work when at twelve he had thought, Dr. Johnson notwithstanding, that Donne was a poet worth looking into). At nineteen he quickly sensed the moral weaknesses betrayed by these polemics, writing to William Withington, then a seminarian at Andover, "Here was a *Christian Disciple* come out with its meek motto—'Speaking the truth in love'—and a most bitter christian sarcasm, and terrible christian contempt launched out against poor Dr. Mason for his equally apostolic exhortation." The *Christian Disciple* was a Unitarian journal that his father had helped found. It was now edited by the same Henry Ware, Jr., whose pulpit Emerson was later to assume at the Second Church, and the publication was to print Waldo's first article some seven months later. The intimacy of Unitarian circles and the welcome he received among them, however, did not lead him to identify with their cause. The crude hostility of both parties offended not ony his instinctive suavity, but sharpened his insight into the sterility of such conflict.[10]

[8] Hebrew as a subject was traditionally unpopular; the illegibility of Stuart's fonts caused seminarians to complain of damage to their eyesight, while Sidney Willard, the single Hebrew scholar at the Harvard Divinity College, taught only part time. Even the first professor of Hebrew, Judah Monis, had languished for want of willing students (Morison, pp. 57–58); George H. Williams, *The Harvard Divinity School: Its Place in Harvard University and in American Culture* (Boston: Beacon Press, 1954), p. 23.

[9] Robbins, the most pillaged source of information on Stuart and Andover, wrote of a Dickensian father. A rigid, dyspeptic, and demanding man, Stuart had fathered ten children, but "his home life was only an incident in his scholarly career." Liable to bad nights, he was given to making "loud wailing prayers in his study alone morning and night. . . . Often he might be met gliding around the house seeking for rest but finding none" (pp. 163, 185).

[10] *L*, 1:109–10, prints this letter in part; see also manuscript courtesy of Prof. Tilton.

IT WAS to escape the pettiness and provinciality of these disputes, as well as to study at a great university, that scholars who could afford it, such as George Ticknor and the brothers Edward and Alexander Everett, had traveled to Europe and especially to Göttingen in the second decade of the century. Its library held two hundred thousand volumes, and it was staffed by forty-one professors and their assistants; learning was abundantly available there. William had not personally been able to afford it, but he had been willing to borrow money and risk much to gain the opportunity to study there. The dreaded "rationalizing" process, however, which men like Stuart and Leonard Woods thundered against, in fact took its toll. Edward Everett, one of the great preachers and teachers at Harvard and an idol of Waldo, gave up his pulpit some time after he returned from Göttingen and entered politics; Alexander was never ordained.[11]

By contrast with Göttingen or even Andover, the Harvard Divinity School that William warned against barely existed when his younger brother matriculated there in February 1825. Begun in 1819, it was extremely small and remained so for a long period. The class of 1824 had only five members; that of 1838, the year Emerson addressed the senior class, numbered only seven. By comparison with that of the orthodox, the school seemed rationalistic, while its association with Harvard made it seem elite and suspect, as Conrad Wright has shown, in democratic eyes. The Boston *Patriot* attacked it in 1819 because of its "alleged aristocracy and atheism," and demanded a "people's university." The seminary at Andover, on the other hand, flourished. It had nineteen class members in 1819, and eighty-one in 1836. Waldo, in fact, actually thought in passing about enrolling there, but decided not to, scrupling that it would not be appropriate to learn from the orthodox the use of "the weapons which I intended to wield, certainly not *for*, and perhaps against them."[12]

Methodism and Baptism were increasingly the popular religions. Congregationalism, although rooted earlier in the nation's history, had been influenced by the mercantile and liberal pressures of Boston life and had often evolved into Unitarianism; as such, it was widely resented. Although its members were by then the minority, it was still a state-supported religion in Massachusetts, and the populace was taxed to support its ministers. The bitterness these issues aroused is illustrated by the career of Emerson's uncle by marriage,

[11] Tyack, pp. 53–54.
[12] Wright, pp. 60, 155, 23, 27, 13.

the Reverend Lincoln Ripley. He together with his wife and sister-in-law, Mary Moody Emerson, had helped to found the village of Waterford, Maine in 1799, but when Maine gained statehood and the Baptists held a bare majority, he was dismissed from the pulpit he had held for twenty-two years and forced to resettle in Greenfield, Massachusetts. Visiting Greenfield in 1827 as a "missionary," Waldo Emerson reported, perhaps with special family satisfaction, that "I do not find orthodoxy so strongly rooted as I had imagined. At elections in the County Unitarians almost always get majorities. Intelligent men are of opinion that the majority of this County is unitarian."(Emerson used "intelligent men" in the same sense as his father had done in his *History of the First Church*, to denote as better-educated the opponents of the evangelicals.)[13]

HARVARD DIVINITY SCHOOL (known only officially as Harvard Divinity College) had been created in 1819 in this highly politicized atmosphere specifically to meet the growing threat to upper-class power such upheavals represented. It intended to rival Andover, which was producing a spate of more aggressive, evangelical ministers, missionary-minded men ready to lead such flocks as those in Maine.

Dominating the new graduate college was Andrews Norton. He only later became Emerson's overt opponent, but Waldo already knew him directly or indirectly, for Norton instructed undergraduates and seminarians alike. Young Emerson had written in 1822, probably alluding to him, "Of Prof. N. Shakespeare long ago wrote the good and bad character: 'O tis excellent / To have a giant's strength but it is tyrannous / To use it like a giant." He referred to the same tyranny in 1838 when he wrote in his journal that Norton was "the old tyrant of the Cambridge Parnassus."[14] Although an "arch heretic" to the so-called orthodox Christians at Andover, in Boston Harvard's Professor of Sacred Literature was an integral part of the intellectual and social establishment. But he was at least as intolerant of disagreement as his opponents. A biblical editor, Norton engaged himself not with the broader philosophical issues of the

[13] Henry, William, and Samuel Warren, *The History of Waterford, Oxford County, Maine: Comprising the Historical Address, Record of Families: Centennial Proceedings* (Portland, Me.: Hoyt, Fogg, & Donham, 1879), pp. 144–48, 153, 255–56. See also Thomas H. Gage, Jr., *Notes on the History of Waterford, Maine* (Worcester, Mass.: n.p., 1913); *L*, 1:213.

[14] *JMN*, 2:57n.; *J*, 5:34.

Enlightenment struggle, but with the task of separating the authentic from the corrupt portions of the sacred text. Having made his judgment, he gave himself to that saving remnant with rigid and exclusive veneration. "It was more than belief: it was knowledge," Andrew Peabody, himself a famous nineteenth-century clergyman and educator, wrote of his former professor's attitude. "He was so sure of his beliefs that he could hardly imagine those who differed essentially from him could be both honest and wise."[15]

The other instruction Emerson received, although perhaps less overbearing in tone, was probably also less modern. Sidney Willard taught the Hebrew that Emerson wished not to study, and old Henry Ware, Sr., filled many roles, instructing in ecclesiastical history (meagerly and for one term only), church doctrine, and pastoral care. The authorities he used and the formulation of his thinking were long out-dated.[16]

The curriculum, moreover, reflected Norton's hegemony, for his teaching of textual criticism and interpretation of the Bible formed two of the four or five courses students carried each term. There were three terms per year, and three years of training.[17] Thus when Waldo matriculated he faced the prospect of formally confronting, twice a week at least, in a group of not more than four or five peers, a man whom he already regarded as a "tyrant" and who judged those differing from him to be either dishonest or foolish. To recognize this would have been dismaying to any student; to one so uneasy with figures of authority as Emerson, the prospect must have been deeply disquieting.

Clearly, he was in a double bind. Protest under these circumstances would have been self-destructive. But leaving was impossible; he had no choice if he was to be licensed to preach. Moreover, he had no models in dealing with such ambiguities. It is easy to forget when reading his precocious journals and essays that he was still only twenty-one, a young man who had learned a good deal from books, but almost nothing from people. (He was, to put it differently, the antithesis of the "American Scholar.") Apart from his aunt—who was no practical guide to managing a career—and perhaps Edward Everett, whose lectures he revered but whom he did not otherwise know, Waldo had evidently not been exposed to anyone he could admire. Unlike an English youth just graduated from

[15] Peabody, p. 76.
[16] Wright, p. 40.
[17] Ibid., p. 58.

Oxford, he had taken no tour, been instructed by no cultivated tutor, and attended no court or salon. He had heard little, even at second hand, of how the great and influential minds of the day arrived at or disseminated their ideas; all he had for such instruction were months-old copies of the *Edinburgh Review* and its ilk. In short, he was part of the still very thin New England culture of its day that had permitted his father, having left the village of Harvard and his farm three years earlier, to become editor of America's first literary journal and his aunt—when not herself farming or keeping house— to write occasional anonymous pieces for the same publication.

Emerson tried to convince himself that accepting his environment would be easy, that his was a "meek and quiet temper," and that his sense of conflict and depression of the summer and fall were unimportant. He wished to conform: "Altho' it did once require heroism to be virtuous it has now, praised be God, ceased to do so. . . . A meek and quiet temper, a due conformity of life to the relations which you were created to bear to the Universe is not now the laughing stock of the world." It was undoubtedly this sort of thinking that prompted from Mary occasional impatient excoriations on Waldo's deference to society. But the bone-deep nature of his own nonconformity was something he could learn only through experience.[18]

That he was entering the profession of his father probably did not seem to him connected to anxiety or anger. He was probably not aware of any related residue of resentment at his loss—or guilt about that anger—when sometime during this period, perhaps in October 1824, he took or was given one of his father's old notebooks and tore out its contents, leaving only William Emerson's handwritten indexes on its end leaves. Waldo used the covers and spine for his own fifteenth journal.[19]

More than once the figure of Saturn, the god who turned on his children and ate them, appears in Emerson's journals. The symbolic reversal of Saturn's act, with all the unconscious guilt that it implies, thus to eat up the words of his father, cannot escape attention. What could not truly be joined—the father and the paternal heritage of religious faith—must be resisted.[20]

As the time for matriculation grew closer, a depression that he perceived rather as sobriety and gravity grew more heavy, and anxiety was often expressed with odd prescience through the imagery

[18] *JMN*, 2:291.
[19] See chap. 1.
[20] *JMN*, 2:272.

of light and seeing and their possible loss. In December 1824 he closed his school and wrote of "the crisis which is but a little way before when a month will determine the dark or bright dye [my years] must assume forever." He contemplated his next step. "I turn now to my lamp and my tomes. I have nothing to do with society. My unpleasing boyhood is past, my youth wanes into the age of man, and what . . . is youth to me?" Still longing for a high fate, he wished both to be seen and to be invisible.[21]

Even if cold and graceless, he might yet add dignity to his folly; "great argument" could stir his soul and enable him to "fill the eye of great expectation . . . I will not quite despair nor quench my flambeau in the dust of Easy live & quiet die."[22] He thought of friendship and marriage, but he thought more of being alone, and he protested too much that he was only moderately withdrawn: "I commend no absurd sacrifices. I praise no wolfish misanthropy that retreats to thickets from cheerful towns and scrapes the ground for roots and acorns either out of grovelling soul or a hunger for glory that has mistaken grimace for philosophy. It is not the solitude of place but the solitude of soul which is inestimable to us. . . ." He wrote simply and painfully, "It is not that you should avoid men, but that you should not be hurt by them."[23]

The closer drew the date, the more he examined himself, and the less satisfied he was with the results. On February 8, 1825, he wrote that "I go to my College Chamber tomorrow a little changed for better or worse since I left it in 1821." Stoically he noted that he had learned the "bottomless depths" of his ignorance, paid his debts, "obligated my neighbors [supported his family], and learned how shallow men are and how the mind is its own place." His cardinal vice was "intellectual dissipation—sinful strolling from book to book." That malady, he concluded with a now rare flash of humor, "belongs to the chapter of Incurables."[24] He was twenty-one, and what conscious will could achieve, he had tried. He was not at ease, but ease was not his aim. He was to matriculate next day. The world lay all before him—or at least all that portion of it bounded by Brattle Street and Harvard College, by Andrews Norton and Henry Ware, Sr.

[21] *JMN*, 2:309.
[22] *JMN*, 2:309–10.
[23] *JMN*, 2:326.
[24] *JMN*, 2:332.

BUT he could not make those grounds his own. Instead, almost as soon as he entered Divinity School, he left, with eyes suddenly so afflicted by an unspecified disease that he could not see to read. He was genuinely ill, and new information will clarify the nature of both this and the other sicknesses he suffered from during the ensuing period. Physiological causes, however, are only part of the explanation. It is important also to grasp his state of mind at the time his sight became impaired.

One can learn much from the draft of the sole essay he wrote there. Begun three weeks after matriculating, its unfinished state makes it a poignant symbol of his bafflement at this institution. The piece was another attempt to prove the unity of God and to explain the existence of evil in a God-created universe. It is a last-ditch attack on Hume, but most striking about it is the extent to which the structure of Emerson's argument itself was shaped by the patterns of Hume's thought.

Hume had argued in his last and most scandalous book, *Dialogues Concerning Natural Religion* (suppressed by Hume's executor, Adam Smith, and not published until ten years after its author's death), that there could be no explanation for evil.[25] Proposing instead to prove the unity of God, Waldo began in the old way by alluding to polytheism. Hume before him had made this a crucial point, arguing that polytheism had everywhere prevailed initially and that the unity of God was not a revealed truth but a natural inference, made gradually by men of different cultures for a wide variety of reasons.

Emerson began by insisting somewhat vaguely that God had been known to be One for a long time, but also by accepting Hume's dismissal of the weak a priori arguments for God's existence raised by Samuel Clarke and others. Then he fell back, as for a minor third point, on the testimony of the Bible itself as to its revealed origin. But he could not long avoid the central paradox posed by the existence of evil, and he quoted Hume's summary: "Epicurus's questions are yet unanswered. 'Is he willing to prevent evil, but unable; then is he impotent. Is he both able and willing? then is he malevolent.' "[26]

The Scotsman knew well how to end his book with his strongest argument, and he drew his *Dialogues* to a close after Philo, the skeptic, had made this final point. Emerson, however, tried to meet it with an early example of an argument from compensation, a theory

[25] Hume, *Dialogues*, p. 501.
[26] *JMN*, 2:419.

we associate closely with him. Interestingly, he used the example of his own failing eyesight to prove that good might come from evil: "The pain of the eyes in watching is to warn us of the mischief that will accrue to the organ if we persist in using it." The pain of a fall is to teach us discipline, which leads to virtue; thus evil is the "seed" of virtue.[27]

Even the idea of compensation, closely associated with Emerson, may have had for him its origin in the Scottish philosopher's language, for Hume had suggested at the end of *The Natural History of Religion* that a "universal compensation prevails in all conditions of being and existence. . . . The more exquisite any good is . . . the sharper is the evil allied to it and few exceptions are found to this uniform law of nature. The most sprightly wit borders on madness, the highest effusions of joy produce the deepest melancholy." Hume concluded stoically with the inference Emerson was also sometimes to draw, "happiness is not to be dreamed of. . . . A mediocrity and a kind of insensibility in every thing" should be one's goal.[28]

The old pattern thus was repeated one last time. Even in answering Hume, Emerson drew on him for arguments, formulations, and definitions of the issue. The youth's last paragraph only restated the paradox he had earlier quoted from his mentor: "Whether the soul that does a good action was created by the good principle or by the evil? If by the evil it follows that good may arise from the fountain of all evil. If it was created by the good principle, it follows that evil may arise from the fountain of all good." In effect, the last word was Hume's.[29]

THERE on March 1, 1825, he left it, the same "inexplicable enigma" he had described to Mary years earlier. He could write no more; the paradox was paralyzing. The essay hangs uncompleted on the page to this day, a thorn in the flesh—or rather, a needle in the eye. He wrote no more in his journal for almost a year. The pain in his eyes warned him not to persist. Emotional pain seems also to have been experienced as a lesson to go no further.

Three weeks later, at the second session of the Divinity School's newly organized Society for Extemporaneous Speaking, "Brother Emerson" was recorded as proposing for debate whether it was "expedient, in consideration of the spirit of the age, that a minister

[27] *JMN*, 2:413–20; *JMN*, 2:419–20.
[28] Hume, *NHR*, 467.
[29] *JMN*, 2:420.

should be a profound Theologian." But when Henry Ware showed up to respond to this despairing question, Brother Emerson was not present. Sometime around then, probably still in March, he went to Norton and was excused from recitation in class on the grounds that he could not take notes but would attend lectures. But before long he gave that up too, and left Cambridge, going to ground not in Concord at the home of his mother and Ezra Ripley, but in less familiar territory, on a farm in Newton that belonged to his Uncle Ladd, where he would not have to explain himself to the orthodox. Like Isaac, whom he had similarly projected as saying nothing while the arguments of father and king raged around him, Waldo was determined to be silent until the light, literal and figurative, should return.[30]

His illness was real. But it was also—as Mary at a later stage perceived—providential, partly induced by stresses that, having become intolerable, forced his withdrawal. To be unable for a while to see was probably the best temporary solution for a thinker who may at some level have felt himself being asked to live his intellectual life either in jail or a lead mine.

For in a certain sense, he had completed his essay after all. It does achieve closure if it is seen not as the attack on Hume it purported to be, but on Christian certainty, ending as it does on the unanswered and unanswerable challenge with which Hume had ended his book. From that point of view it might appear that Emerson had telescoped into three or four weeks all the training and struggle he might have experienced with no more profit over a much longer period of time. For what the very structure of the essay tells—more cogently perhaps than its language—is that Waldo was not at this point any longer Hume's opponent, but his student. Skepticism had carried the day, and its unanswerable arguments—and not the other, less difficult ones—are prominent in the essay because they dominated Waldo's mind.

A few years earlier, after watching the sunset die in its beauty, wishing for the Tiresian power to articulate what he felt, or wishing to feel it more deeply, he had exclaimed to his friend Hill, "Pluck out his eyes before he meddles with the harp."[31] Perhaps in fantasy he had been willing to pay with blindness for insight, for the chance to become what in "The American Scholar" he called "the world's eye . . . the world's heart"; now that rhetorical bargain was threatening to become a reality.

30 Wright, pp. 63–64; *EIC*, p. 31.
31 *L*, 1:134.

Chapter 9

THE MOONLESS NIGHT

"Sickness is the answer each time we are inclined to doubt
our right to *our* task."

—Nietzsche to Overbeck, 1877

T HE NEXT year and a half were full of so many reversals for
Emerson that only a very determined and resourceful man
could have persisted. He left Cambridge around March
1825, undoubtedly hoping that by turning away from books and
their associated stresses he would recover. His fragmentary autobiographical notes record that he had spent the summer on his Uncle
Ladd's farm in Newton. There he heard—and did not forget—the
words of a fellow farm laborer, a devout Methodist, who remarked
to him that men were "always praying," and that "their prayers were
always answered." In 1826 he took these words as the text for his
first sermon, improving them with his own, third part of the syllo-
gism: "We must beware, then, what we ask." Knowing what to ask
was everything.[1]

He was content to ask, at present, very little. But he was a man of
twenty-two and had to eat; in the fall he opened a school in Chelmsford even though he could still see only with impaired sight. That
village was situated some ten miles north of Concord in a pretty area
of widely rolling escarpments and broad horizons, but like Harvard,
the equally poor village not far away where his father had begun
professional life, it was thin in both cash and populace.

Some time during this period Waldo permitted a Dr. Reynolds,
not otherwise identified, to "operate" in some undefined and apparently experimental way on one of his eyes. Then, according to a letter written in January 1826 by Ruth to Mary, "Dr. R. said it would
not be a fair trial of the experiment unless he performed the operation on both eyes." The "experiment" was repeated the day after
Thanksgiving, 1825.

This helped somewhat. Waldo, however, must have been virtually

[1] Cabot, 1:111–12, quoting RWE autobiography, HMS.

blind before then, for Ruth reported that after a fortnight, or by mid-December, he had recovered only enough sight to "read a sentence or two," but "gradually [by January 1826] his sight has returned." The operations, however, although apparently not harmful, made only a temporary difference. By February Ruth added, "respecting Waldo's eyes, our fears have been excited, they have not been quite so well, he cannot well refrain from reading a few pages and this together with the use he makes of them in school is probably injurious . . . he probably uses them too much." Nothing more has been known about these mysterious operations until recently, for the Emerson family records are silent.[2]

MEANTIME, Emerson had pressed forward. If it were a question of survival, he could keep school and lead children through material he had been teaching for eight years without much use of the eyes. He continued at Chelmsford until the end of December, when he returned to Roxbury and reopened the school Edward had left behind. He could read only by further damaging his eyes, but based near the university he planned to return to Harvard Divinity College to qualify for his professional degree.

But by now a new malady had suddenly appeared. By December 20 he was writing to his brother of "that same lame hip of mine," as if William had already heard of it, and reporting that he was cosseting it, though "Dr. Dalton nicknames it rheumatism." More alarmed than Dr. Dalton—as well he might be in suffering "rheumatism" at the age of twenty-two—he adopted a light tone but insisted that that disease had "crippled its hundreds and slain its tens" and he would look after it. It is unlikely that Dr. Dalton connected it with his affliction of the eyes, but Waldo, who was suffering them simultaneously and whose general condition probably was weakened, may well have done so; in saying the doctor "nicknamed" it rheumatism, Waldo may have implied that he himself thought it was something else.[3]

Moreover, serious setbacks were also afflicting his brothers. Grave illness had broken out a third time in Edward, and he had set out for Europe for his health. And Bulkeley, who by then was a young adult and increasingly difficult to manage, "is perfectly de-

[2] RE to MME, 1826, HMS.
[3] L, 1:163.

ranged and has been ever since I have been here. I shall try to leave him [i.e. find a place to board him] here."[4]

To top it all off, Emerson soon became too crippled at times to walk. He had reentered Divinity School, but shortly thereafter he sent a note to the librarian, dated probably from the end of March, asking to renew his use of that institution without a personal appearance, "as I am confined by a lameness to my chamber." Library records show that Charles, then a student, drew out books on his brother's behalf on March 30, and he may have carried this note. Since he had closed his Roxbury school on March 28, Waldo may have taught just long enough to secure the funds necessary to return to the university and complete his degree.[5]

Whether he attended classes is not certain, for he got himself excused from examinations at the end of this, nominally his third and terminal year, on the grounds of his difficulty in reading. It was understood that his two years of technical residency and the real course of instruction he had pursued over many years would be sufficient. Completion of the course was important, however, for it was a preliminary to being licensed, or "approbated," to preach, as he expected in the fall. (This was an act of approval conferred by the local board of ministers, necessary for assuming a pulpit but not the same as ordination, which would occur on his actually taking on a parish.) Whatever may have been the degree of impairment of his sight at this time—and his handwriting attests to its weakness—it was also obviously in his interest not to confront teachers of such opposite opinions. Later he said, "If they had examined me, they probably would not have let me preach at all."[6]

On March 16 he wrote in his journal without explanation that "My external condition . . . may to many seem comfortable[,] to some enviable but I think that few men ever suffered ⟨in degree not in . . . amount⟩ more genuine misery than I have suffered."[7] The degree of his emotional suffering must have been great, then, for "externally" his condition could hardly have been worse. At twenty-three, after two operations, he was a scholar whose vision was sometimes so impaired that he could not see to read. Now he was suffering prematurely from a crippling disease. Ambitious, gifted with both eloquence and depth of thought, he was also at a professional disadvantage, for he was hobbled not only by poverty and illness but

4 *L*, 1:164.
5 *L*, 1:166–67 and n.
6 Cabot, 1:118.
7 *JMN*, 3:13.

by lack of that sponsorship which could have opened many doors, had his father lived. Even Ruth, whose health was usually good, was sick enough in the spring of 1826 to cause alarm.[8]

WHAT William had told Waldo in the preceding fall of 1825 had certainly contributed to that "misery." He had already been warning his younger brother, writing from Germany earlier in the year, that "every candid theologian after careful study will find himself wide from the traditionary opinions of the bulk of his parishioners. Have you yet settled the question, whether he shall sacrifice his influence or his conscience?"[9] On returning home, William went at once to Chelmsford and told his younger brother that during his two years of study for the ministry he in effect had lost his faith:[10] "He renounced the ministry; and had come home to begin the study of law."

More than that, it appeared that after about a year abroad, William—following in the footsteps of the Ticknors—had gone to visit the aged Goethe in Weimar, and he had confessed to him his growing doubts. That eminence, however, had advised the earnest young Unitarian to take up his ministerial calling but keep his opinions to himself. "Goethe unhesitatingly told him," Emerson's daughter wrote, "that he could preach to the people what they wanted; his personal belief was no business of theirs; he could be a good preacher and a good pastor and no one need ever know what he himself had for his own private views."

Emerson later told Ellen, "Your Uncle William never seemed to me so great as he did that day that he came to me at Chelmsford when he returned from Germany and told me this and that on the voyage home there was a great storm, and in that storm he felt that he could not go to the bottom in peace with the intention in his heart of following the advice that Goethe had given him. He renounced the ministry; and had come home to begin the study of law." Ellen's comment about her uncle unconsciously summed up a good deal of nineteenth-century post-Christian thought: "He still believed in goodness as much as ever."[11] But although from his own point of view William obviously felt he was obeying a higher morality, Moses

[8] MME to RWE, 1826, HMS.

[9] L, 1:352n.

[10] EBE to RWE, postscript by WEjr, 1825, HMS.

[11] "What," HMS, p. 16.

Stuart would not have been alone in thinking that German rationalism had once again taken its predictable toll.

The deeper implications of all this would not have been lost on Waldo. That cynicism and corruption were acceptable modes of thought within the upper levels of European intellectual life might well have been inferred from Goethe's "unhesitating" advice. It was, although not identical with, only a step or two away from Keble's advice to Arnold under similar circumstances. Paradoxically—and savingly—one thing William's example probably did not do for Waldo was intensify his intellectual doubts, for in these he had already gone as far as the most devoted rationalist could have wished. He was self-inoculated, through being self-educated in skepticism. Ideas that had come to William from external sources, as a sudden and stunning series of revelations culminating at sea in a seemingly providential deconversion experience, Waldo had long struggled with of his own volition. Gradually he had recognized the dimensions of the problem, and increasingly he had been depressed by it, but the strength necessary to live with ambiguity had grown with the pain of knowledge. A central core of faith in God's existence, however he was defined, remained.

While that endured, he would hold his position and not give up. If those who most set themselves up as moral guides were least to be respected—whether they ruled in Weimar or Cambridge—then one must remember that the church did not belong to them and should not be defined by them. Like the Oxford Noetics, Waldo had come to understand that if history taught anything, it was that particular doctrines changed as people and the times changed. It had also given him a perspective on the narrowness of a Unitarian circle whose best efforts, as exemplified perhaps by Norton's career, were now devoted— however pure and purifying the motivation—to a continual narrowing of the grounds of faith.

William's experience also may have reinforced for Waldo the central importance of private judgment. For William, precisely by consulting Goethe, had caused, even forced his intellectual environment to present him with a choice that in the circumstances was oversimplified: to be a cynic and a hypocrite, or to be a lawyer—which from the Emersonian standpoint was much the same thing. In an age in which apostasy was not rare, congregations needed not clergy whose doctrine might be acceptable to the small and ingrown inner circle of Unitarian leaders, but ministers willing to speak truly of their own faith. It was crucial, as Waldo was grasping, to "beware"—to be deeply aware—of what one asked, to choose carefully

the questions from which answers might eventually flow. William had asked the wrong question of Goethe by asking any. Authorities, whether named Goethe or Norton, could be deluded.

Still, William's news was depressing in its implications, for it could only mean that dealing with the world in its conscious and enlightened hypocrisy would be even more problematic than Emerson had yet foreseen. Moreover, it worsened his own financial position; instead of adding to the family income, as he had been expected to do, and to its status, as he certainly would have done, William would now sometimes be unable to support himself. Nor could he stay in Boston. The family never explained why he removed to New York, but it went without saying that given his failed expectations and new career, the latter could be better pursued in a larger, more anonymous city. These were serious reverses and not limited to his own life.

WILLIAM'S DECISION and its effect on Emerson constituted a turning point in the younger man's life. In deciding to continue with his proposed career against William's warnings, he was consciously taking on a burden of ambivalence that until then he might have preferred to ignore. The operations on his eyes following this important interview suggest that his sight worsened at this time, and as he pressed on toward his licensing his new complaint, lameness, emerged.

He appears to have suspected at least that this turmoil was implicated in the breakdown of his health. Early that year in "Fame" he wrote words strangely apposite to his condition. The opening stanzas of the four-stanza poem, in fact, suggest his knowledge that a bargain was being struck exactly of the sort Nietzsche later described when he said that "sickness is the answer each time we are inclined to doubt our right to *our* task." Emerson put it bluntly:

> Ah Fate! cannot a man
> Be wise without a beard?
> From east to west, from Beersheba to Dan,
> Pray was it never heard
> That wisdom might in youth be gotten
> Or wit be ripe before 'twas rotten?
>
> He pays too high a price
> For knowledge & for fame
> Who sells his sinews to be wise

His teeth & bones to buy a name
And crawls half-dead a paralytic
To earn the praise of bard & critick.[12]

Emerson ended the outburst with a reversal, asserting that it was *not* better "to dine and sleep thro' forty years / Be loved by few, be feared by none," that "Fate will not permit / The seed of gods to die," and that he would not hide his light beneath a measure. Nevertheless, he seems to have felt some connection between his ambition and disaster, between a grasping for success and the threatened retribution of disease. The poem is not general in reference, but particular and personal; it needs its baroque prosody and satiric distance to rescue it from unmediated confession, for only Emerson himself can be the reference for this man "fated" to be "wise without a beard," to sell "his sinews to be wise" and crawl "half-dead a paralytic / To earn the praise of bard & critick."

He was beginning to grasp that he must stand outside the mainstream, and imagery of a great flow, or fluid procession of men and ideas appeared in his writing. Alluding to the stoical vision of Epicurus, he figured humanity, living and dead, crowding forward in an "innumerable procession" to follow leaders who themselves had not known their destination. Christ had come, many had followed him, but Emerson makes clear that he himself had not yet chosen "our standard and our guide. Is there no venerable tradition whose genuineness and authority we can establish, or must we too hurry onward inglorious in ignorance and misery we know not whence, we know not whither?"[13]

The nature of his doubts was becoming more clear. He intended to be a minister, yet public prayer itself, the most fundamental of such a man's activities, now seemed a doubtful enterprise:

The trust in public prayer is rather the offspring of our notions of what *ought* to be than of what *is*. . . . It certainly is a question . . . whether a promiscuous assemblage such as is contained in houses of public worship, and collected by such motives, can unite with propriety and advantage in any petition such as is usually offered by one man.[14]

[12] "Fame," *JMN*, 3:11.
[13] *JMN*, 3:19.
[14] *JMN*, 3:23.

To speak of churchgoers assembled for prayer as a "promiscuous assemblage" might conceivably be accurate, but such a vision did not bespeak Emerson's readiness to embrace his calling.[15]

On the contrary, he was beginning to know that the condition of independence he had vaunted as his two years earlier was going to have to be his real and lasting stance. "I *feel* immortal," he wrote, "And the evidence of immortality comes better from consciousness than from reason." Such insight was "daring," he felt, but also "an evidence from my instincts of God's existence." This of course was Mary's position, as was his next sentence, a quotation from her: "Sublimity of character must proceed from sublimity of motive."[16] Feelings were truer than reason; action could not be wrong if feelings or motives were right.

At least part of the intervening summer months he spent working on his first sermons, but his few letters and the relatively skimpy entries in his journal indicated that his state of mind was increasingly inchoate and disturbed. While still involved with the college, he had been full of anger at "German faith" with its attacks on external evidence, criticizing it as an "eager appetite for novelty that rages among us undieted, uncloyed," filling "good men . . . [with] horrid anticipation" of what would follow. He would not suffer "every drunkard in his cups and every voluptuary in his brothel [to] loll out his tongue" at the history of Christianity: "It were base treason in his servants tamely to surrender. . . . If heaven gives me sight I will dedicate it to this cause."[17] But that had been written in February, and in fact, although his eyesight had held out, his limbs had not. The exaggerated anger could not be sustained, for it was not, as the clichés and inflated language show, his natural mode. He had "scouted" those very mysteries two years earlier in his "Letter to Plato" and had asserted his prior allegiance to reason.

The conflict was deep, for success in life was more likely to come from defense of the established thought than attack upon it. Moreover, to seem to join hands with cynics and "voluptuaries" disgusted him. It was not yet possible to imagine a stance in which total intellectual freedom could be linked to purely inner control. Yet angry defense of the past was sterile and merely confusing.

[15] Ibid.
[16] *JMN*, 3:25–26.
[17] *J*, 2:83–85, corrected by E. Tilton.

GRADUALLY, however, there began to dawn the first glimmerings of the idea that eventually was to lead him through these tangling vines. As the summer wore on, his tone became more open. Instead of rhetorical threats against German thought, he wrote to Mary that in the face of what now seemed this "queer life," his stance was "quiet astonishment. Others laugh, weep, sell, or proselyte. I admire." The stance is soft and undogmatic, bespeaking the quiet probing with which Emerson was walking, as it were, among the shards of belief. The issues he was touching on were the very grounds of belief, and the language he used was memorable as he evoked a feminine "Mind" at a culminating moment, turning her back on the past, ready with an awed love to respond to a "Presence" greater than she:

> There are ... in each man's history, insignificant passages which he feels to be to him not insignificant; little coincidences in little things, which touch all the springs of wonder, and startle the sleeping conscience in the deepest cell of his repose; the Mind standing forth in alarm with all her faculties, suspicious of a Presence which it behoves her deeply to respect—touch not more with awe than with curiosity, if perhaps some secret revelation is not about to be vouchsafed or doubtful if some moral epoch is not just now fulfilled in its history, and the tocsin just now struck that severs and tolls out an irreparable Past.[18]

The "Mind" here is that of a woman on the brink of a mystic marriage, and the tocsin that "severs" her from "an irreparable Past" is at once a marriage bell, promising a new bond, and a death knell, signaling that historical Christianity and biblical history are being forsaken in favor of this "Presence." The buried metaphor of religious belief as a marriage, present in much mystical language, is striking, as is the delicacy of the apprehension of "Mind"—alarmed, suspicious, curious, awed, and fulfilled, even while experiencing separation and renunciation. "These are not the State Reasons by which we can enforce the burdensome doctrine of a Deity on the world," Emerson summed up, "but make often, I apprehend, the body of evidence on which private conviction is built. In solitude and in silence, memory visits her inmost chambers to produce these treasured tokens of Connexion and immortality."

The importance of this passage to Emerson's intellectual development has been tacitly acknowledged by its being frequently

---

[18] L, 1:170.

quoted. The delicacy of the language rings true. Something had happened in Emerson's own mind—and it is of course his own that he is describing—that permitted this extraordinary and moving image to stand forth. It is powerful in its expression of resolution of conflict, for both sexes not only meet as one in a marriage that is specifically not a "burdensome" enforcement of male will as "duty" on female belief, but almost mingle in the same figure, as the "sleeper conscience," remote in "his . . . deepest cell," is moved out of his sleep into consciousness at last to become a feminine "Mind," *anima*, always the feminine principle since antiquity but particularly and virginally female here.

BURIED in these lines are allusions that suggest a significantly new turn of thought. Perhaps there was a way to mend what Hume had broken after all. "Connexion"— the fundamental concept that the universe was not intellectually and morally chaotic, that a moral agency did link itself to matter—might still be conceived to exist. Understanding would come, however, not from the "external evidence" offered so unsatisfyingly by theology, but from within human consciousness itself. Not quite yet did Emerson say or know that God was within, but that inference was now only a step away.

It seems apparent that Emerson that summer had at last gotten some help, and that it had come indirectly from Kant. This is suggested by several references in letters beginning in August that he sent to Mary and Charles. Dugald Stewart, one of Emerson's most revered sources, had pointed out that Kant had conceived that one might be "free" if one posited that mind, having no extension, existed neither in space nor in time. But though free, it must act, and on some principle—"practical reason," therefore, would lead it to be guided in part by feeling, or sentiment.[19]

Emerson took exactly this position when in September 1826 he wrote Mary an important letter. In it he cited not Kant but "modern philosophy" as having led him toward new solutions of old problems, new ideas that he, the novice, had overheard by eavesdropping: "I skulk into the lobbies that lead into the heaven of philosophy and listen when the door is open if perchance some fragment some word of power from the colloquy sublime may fall on mine

[19] Dugald Stewart, *Dissertation [on] the Progress of Metaphysical, Ethical, and Political Philosophy* vol. 6 of *The Works of Dugald Stewart*, 7 vols. (Cambridge, Mass.: Hilliard & Brown, 1829), 6:410, cited hereafter as Stewart.

ear—Such words purify poor humanity. They clear my perception for my duties."[20]

He did not cite the speakers in the colloquy, but he rephrased their "purifying words" as a rhetorical question: "Is it not true, that modern philosophy by a stout reaction has got to be very conversant with feelings? Bare reason, cold as cucumber, was all that was tolerated in aforetime, till men grew disgusted at the skeleton and have now given him in ward into the hands of his sister, blushing shining changing Sentiment."[21]

The term "Sentiment" and this line of reasoning were of course well calculated to please his correspondent, but Waldo was drawing on more than the tradition of illumination that Mary cherished. He continued: "It is one of the *feelings* of modern philosophy, that it is wrong to regard ourselves so much in a *historical* light as we do, putting Time between God and us; and that it were fitter to account every moment of the existence of the Universe as a new Creation, and all as a revelation proceeding each moment from the Divinity to the mind of the observer."

In December Waldo wrote more specifically to his brother Charles with approval of Kant's contribution, though as yet he thought its fruits not fully clear. Modern philosophy was the better for the

> painful speculations of Leibnitz and Kant. . . . The search after truth is always by approximation. The wise man begins a train of tho't whose farthest results he does not live to see, nor perhaps do his children's children. We have an instinctive perception of the value of certain ideas, which are the seeds of great conclusions, which all our efforts often are unable to unfold.[22]

It may well be that the "instinctive perception of the value of certain ideas" that he could not yet unfold refers here to his sense that Kant's teaching was to mean much to him—and that it had already proved valuable. For Kant had addressed himself precisely to the problem of time and history that Emerson had earlier alluded to in his letter to Mary. Kant had tried to resolve it, Stewart taught, along just such lines as Waldo sketched for her, although not adequately.

It is unlikely that Emerson had read Kant directly by this date. Nitsch's translation was available, but Cameron suggests that Em-

[20] *L*, 1:174.
[21] Ibid.
[22] *L*, 1:181.

erson did not read Kant until 1832.[23] Nevertheless in 1822 Waldo knew enough about the other's position to refer satirically to some "Folios" of Kant as examples, like Waldo's own "Travels in the Land of Not," of invented tales.[24] He certainly knew Kant through Dugald Stewart's *Dissertation [on] the Origins of Metaphysical, Ethical, and Political Philosophy*, for he quoted from it in both 1822 and 1823.[25]

From Stewart's work Emerson would have learned language very like that he used to Mary. Stewart had concluded that Kant's moral superstructure rested ultimately on the "conundrum that the human mind (considered as a nooumenon and not as phoenomenon) neither exists in space nor in time." Quoting Nitsch's redaction of Kant, Stewart expounded his thesis: "Man is not in time nor in space . . . if man exist not in time and space, he is not influenced by the laws of time and space, among which those of a cause and effect hold a distinguished rank; it is therefore no contradiction to conceive that, in such an order of things, man may be free."[26]

Stewart went on to suggest that Kant had inadvertently established a system of skepticism in attempting to "refute the doctrines of Hume" and that "he met with obstacles of which he was not aware. It was to remove these obstacles that he had recourse to practical reason [which] bears a manifest resemblance to what some philosophers call an appeal to sentiment, founding belief on the necessity of acting."

Stewart went on to quote another German commentator on Kant, M. Reinhold:

> "*Practical Reason* . . . bears a manifest resemblance to what some philosophers call an appeal to *sentiment*, founding belief on the necessity of acting . . . this manner of considering the subject is not unlike the disposition of those who, feeling their inability to obtain, by the exercise of their reason, a direct conviction of their religious creed, cling to it nevertheless with a

[23] Kenneth Walter Cameron, *Young Emerson's Transcendental Vision* (Hartford, Ct.: Transcendental Books, 1971), pp. 382ff. Henry A. Pochmann also recognized Emerson's debt to Kant, even perceiving it in Emerson's thought as early as 1823, but as Pochmann knew nothing of Stewart, he could not account for the approach: "Emerson in 1823 . . . was entirely innocent of any knowledge of Kant." *German Culture in America* (Madison: University of Wisconsin Press, 1957), pp. 158ff; cited hereafter as Pochmann.

[24] *JMN*, 2:32.

[25] *JMN*, 2:94n, 159n, and passim.

[26] Stewart, pp. 412, 410.

blind eagerness, as a support essential to their morals and happiness."[27]

Emerson in reading Stewart was learning of Kant, but very indirectly through the refracting lenses of yet two other critics. Grasping
this, one can understand better his irony when he wrote to Mary
that he had "skulked into the lobbies" of philosophy and eaves-
dropped on "the colloquoy sublime" about the "appeal to sentiment." Nevertheless, the arguments had value for him because they
clarified his position. He could not *know* the truth, but he could
know the nature of his doubts and the opposing urge to believe. And
he could know that greater scholars than he had already struggled
with the same subtleties and sophistries.

Although Dugald Stewart has been severely criticized in this century for his inadequacy as a commentator on Kant, his shortcomings
would not have affected Emerson.[28] Emerson too has with some justice been criticized for the indirectness and errors in his knowledge
of German philosophy, but it is only fair to recognize that he was
both very young and entirely isolated in his studies. Stewart himself
admitted to being baffled by Kant, and no one around Emerson
knew more than he.[29] To him, the direction of the ideas made them
useful.

Moreover, it was only natural that Emerson should have found
the formulation attributed to Kant to be helpful, for he would have
seen it as an antidote to Hume. As a modern student of Kant's
thought has pointed out, Kant was like other contemporary philosophers and theologians in focusing on the problem of history, for in
defining its status he articulated some of the key questions then agi-
tating Christian thought. He asked, "(1) How did evil arise (2) Why
does God tolerate evil (3) How will history end, and (4) Can evil be
overcome.—is there moral progress?"[30] Since these questions are
virtually the agenda or syllabus for Emerson's own inquiries, it is
not surprising that the young American's tentative formulation, as
he presented it to Mary in September 1826, should have embodied
the essence of what he could have learned from Kant through his
mentor, Stewart.

[27] Stewart, p. 413, quoting M. Reinhold, *Hist. Comparée*, 2:243, 244.

[28] Pochmann is especially severe, pp. 86–87 and notes on pp. 190, 192.

[29] Rene Wellek, "Emerson and German Philosophy," *New England Quarterly* 16
(March 1943): 41–62.

[30] Michel Despland, *Kant on History and Religion* (Montreal: McGill–Queens University Press, 1973), pp. 5–6; cited hereafter as Despland.

To be sure, Kant's resolution of the debate between reason—
which suggested that God's part in the world was at best that of the
indifferent watchmaker—and feeling, which insisted on God's personal presence—was not fully satisfactory. To Emerson himself it
smacked of sophistry, but it was to continue to help other minds in
similar fashion, among them Emerson's friend and, for a time, protégé, Arthur Hugh Clough. Contrary to any inference Emerson may
have drawn from Stewart, it was not Kant's intention to set humanity free of history—on the contrary, as Despland points out, Kant
saw man rather as living in "a world of his own [culture] defined by
historical and social . . . characteristics." But it was now possible for
Emerson, reflecting on his reading, to begin to find a theoretical
ground for seeing human development in other than purely a *historical* light."[31]

Emerson apparently saw that as history became less important, as
the authority of the past diminished, Christianity appeared, as he
wrote Mary, covered by "the dust of 16 or 18 centuries." It remained
"the Priest, the expounder of God's moral law," but its lengthy past
became not its grounds for claiming hegemony but its handicap, an
obstacle to clear sight. Emerson now wanted to judge Christian doctrine not on the "pretensions" of its origins but on "what it is and
what it saith to *us*." If humans did not exist, as Kant taught, in time,
then time and its witness history might screen the clear sight of
God.[32]

The new test, he told Mary in this important letter, was perceived
authenticity, and the perceiver was therefore of crucial importance.
He granted that there was some "sophistry" in the argument and
that the perceiving subject might after all be wrong in its judgment,
but he was willing to grant the subject's right to hold to its vision of
truth: mysticism, after all, which had always been the honored co-
hort of Christian faith, was equally subjective. At any rate, he concluded:

> We hold truth by a tenure so subtle that the most grave specu-
> lation carried many steps from our first principles, loses itself in
> irrecoverable cloud. "Despise nothing" was the old saw. and
> this ambiguous light in wh. we live is authority for the rule. To
> grow wise is to grow doubtful, and it ill becomes that man to
> pronounce an opinion absurd who feels in the consciousness of
> the changes his mind has already undergone, that before an-

[31] Greenberger, *Clough*, pp. 100–101; Despland, p. 6.
[32] *L*, 1:174.

other sun the truth of that exploded dogma may be dearest to his mind.

"How does Aunt Sarah?" he finished firmly, underlining practically the ambiguities of mind, "Mother sends . . . her best love."[33]

"This ambiguous light in which we live is authority." In a few years he had moved from being "God's child," to being only the child of chaos, from projecting an image of the unanswered supplicant, to being himself the denier of "16 or 18 centuries" of dusty church history that might now have but a relative claim to truth. What else, he may well have wondered at some deepest level, was he to deny before the cock crew?

The changes were enormous, and he had come to them without support, "in solitude and in silence," stumbling, as he was later to write, over the "nettles and tangling vines in the way of the self-relying and self-directed," and feeling intensely "the state of virtual hostility in which he seemed to stand to society, and especially to educated society." When he wrote these lines in "The American Scholar," he cannot but have been thinking of this period in his own life, when every advance toward truth must have seemed equally a letting go and a falling away: "Long must he stammer in his speech; often forego the living for the dead." That, of course, was just what, in his twenty-third year, Waldo had done and was to do even more literally.

How could Emerson tell the future audience of his sermons—or tell anyone but Mary—that the essence of the religious experience was known not through Reason but "his sister, blushing, shining changing Sentiment?" Change the language how he would, make acceptably masculine the pronouns by which the soul was metaphorically evoked, or eliminate all references to ambiguity as the intellectual rule of life—his doctrine still did not add up to the preachment of a crucified Christ, or of miraculous powers, perceptible to the senses, exercised by God's agency on earth, or sent by him as revelations of himself.

Emerson also objected that this mode of belief was passive, even emasculating. As usual in periods of intellectual stress, he turned to his aunt and confided that to be "a passive receiver or channel through which flows forever the stream of immortal thought" was wrong, for in such a posture, "we find ourselves emasculated by a description that leaves out our active faculties."[34]

The process of integrating such powerful new ideas was slow. It

[33] L, 1:174–75.
[34] J, 2:104.

took great courage to recognize that they drew on the feminine side of his nature, for the new stance they demanded of watchful waiting was not that of past heroes of the faith.[35] The new emphasis on consciousness they implied might well be a challenge to a youth whose earlier fantasies had admired bloodthirsty and aggressive combatants, and whose deep desire to "shine in the assemblies of men" was, as he saw within the year, a fundamental sticking point.

Although communication with his aunt stimulated him, Emerson could not shake off a grimness, a sense of alienation from mankind that had begun to oppress him. "I know that I exist, but the age and the Universe are alike abstractions of my own mind, and have no pretensions to the same definitive certainty."[36] A sort of disgust, described in language very close to that which Hume had used in alluding to the immense numbers of mankind, oppressed him.

In this time of ferment he returned to an old love, poetry, writing that he "would go to the farthest verge of the green earth to learn what it was or was not." He asked Mary to be mediator: if Plato or "the laureled lovers of the British Muse, harp in hand, sit on your misty mount . . . conjure them."[37] Imagination once banished as a "daemon" was being summoned back.

Mary—the imaginative principle at some level to Waldo—obliged with a letter he not only saved but seems to have used elements of in the opening chapter of *Nature* almost a decade later. Poetry, she wrote her nephew, in some cultures "comes mournfull and terrible in the clouds of the north" and "blood and pestulence . . . and the dust of antient urns make rich the laurels of modern bards." But this is not the poetry that she and Waldo worshipped:

> Not so with him [the poet] to whom this celestial Guest has appeared in a garb which is conjectured to be original and native. She has not come with sword and fire . . . dragons and gorgons—nor even with sylphs and fairies . . . nor bows and arrows—but bearing the olive and palm, decked with the humblest flowers which grow wild in the mountains; often with the staff of the wanderer, sometimes in rainbows—the loftiest gifts of nature . . . to concentrate around her altar the *souls* of men.[38]

The American poet, in short, was to deal not with the wars, myths, or fairy tales of Europe, nor even with the romanticism of American Indian life—another mere fact of external origin—but

---

[35] For a different view of this stage of Emerson's development, see Whicher, chap. 1.
[36] *J*, 2:101–3.
[37] *J*, 2:105, 110.
[38] MME to RWE, 1826, HMS.

with inner life, a life stripped of the past because it was conceived by a regenerate soul in nature.

Poetry had "entranced him into the sanctum sanctorum of nature—where there is a perpetual millenium—yet she has her festivals and arrays herself in magical vestments. When the seer and yellow leaf of Autumn lies motionless," Mary went on, rising to her vision, "when the aged trees lift their naked arms to the dun and sullen clouds, when the sun seems to tarry in the Heavens and takes no note of the earth, marks no sign on the dial, gives no form to the shadow of man, then—" The fragment breaks off.

But her reader was able, in a sense, to finish it for her. Almost a decade later, as he began writing *Nature*, the language had changed but little, as the "perpetual millenium [and] festivals" of autumnal nature become in Emerson's version the "perpetual youth [and] perennial festival" that the poet—still the same "guest" of God Mary had named him—enjoys among the trees and skies of winter.

It is fascinating to see, in the dialogue between the aunt, now autumnal and "seer" at fifty, and the youth of twenty-three, the seeds not only of verbal parallels but of the program that Waldo was to develop as he thought about the relation of the present to the past, of America to Europe, and the role of the American poet and bard in articulating these relationships.

THIS WAS a creative period for Emerson, but his new ideas did not encourage him. On the contrary, he grew increasingly lonely, depressed, and regressive. In May he wrote that "the friends that occupy my thoughts [are] not men but certain phantoms." Happiness was a butterfly, and the boy who caught it, "crushed blood and dirt betwixt his fingers."[39]

A sonnet, written in effect to death, looks backward to the effusions of his adolescence as it begins, "My days roll by me like a train of dreams / A host of joyless undistinguished forms. . . ." Revealingly, the persona of the poem as it rises to its climax is identified with a bride, a child, and death—all images regressing to an earlier frame of mind:

> On me on me the day forgets to dawn
> Encountering darkness clasps me like a bride
> Tombs rise around and from each cell forlorn
> Starts with an ominous cry some ghastly child

[39] *JMN*, 3:25, 26, 29.

Of death & darkness, summoning me to mourn
Companion of the clod brother of worms
The future has no hope and memory mild
Gives not the blessed light that once my woes beguiled.[40]

As the time of his licensing on October 10 approached, his mood grew darker, his health weaker. A month before that date he wrote, "The days blow me onward into the desarts of Eternity. I live a few strong moments in the course perhaps of each day." His role in life was passive, he shaped his "fortunes . . . not at all," and the sacrifices he had made for his "friends"—i.e., his family—he now thought reflected no credit on himself. "It is low and ridiculous to be the football of vulgar circumstances and never by force of character to have surmounted them."[41]

Two weeks later—the same day on which he wrote Mary of his exciting but disquieting insight into "modern philosophy" and the freedom it granted from church history and biblical tradition—his journal recorded not excitement but depression: "Health, action, happiness. How they ebb from me." Soon thereafter he wrote: "Die? what should you die for? Maladies? What maladies? Dost not know that Nature has her course as well as disease? . . . fangs and weapons for her enemies . . . ? Die? Pale face, lily liver! go about your business and when it comes to the point then die like a gentleman."[42]

He did go about his business; less than three weeks later he received his "approbation" and preached his first official sermon in the pulpit of his uncle Ripley at Waltham where he had, nine years before, begun work as a teacher. His effort was successful, but his body was halting in its work. Nature might have her course, but disease was running faster. Perhaps philosophy would in future provide a stronger clue to lead him out of the labyrinth, but the conflicts at present were overwhelming. He did not yet feel a full sense of possession of his own life, yet he was called on to preach, heal, and lead. To accept a vision of religious insight that made subjectivity all-important while denigrating the value of centuries of the exemplary lives and works of honored men—and to adopt moreover such a vision while it seemed "emasculat[ing]" in its passivity and inwardness—was impossible.

From long buried and unconscious levels were returning old shadows, old voices of the phantom children of "death and darkness

[40] JMN, 3:36.
[41] JMN, 3:44.
[42] JMN, 3:45, 46.

... summon[ing] him to mourn," and rendering him rather the "bride" of death than the groomsman of dawn and the day. The stresses were great. As they increased, his breath grew shorter, his body weaker. Six weeks after he had preached his first sermon as a full-fledged minister, Emerson embarked on a voyage to the South, hoping to return in better health, fearing that he might not.

Chapter 10

THE HOUSE OF PAIN

"He has seen but half the Universe who has never been
shown the house of Pain."

—RWE to MME, 1827

W HEN EMERSON boarded the *Clematis* in the last week of
November 1826, bound for Charleston, South Carolina, he
was embarking with borrowed money on the kind of trip
the poor made only when life was at stake. He did not really know
his destination or when he would return.

Despite its importance, Emerson never named the disease that
had changed his life. Whatever his reasons may have been, the result
of his studied silence has been that obscurity and confusion have surrounded the issue. Some biographers ignore his illness almost completely; others refer to it very briefly, as "symptoms . . . in his chest";
others imply hypochondria. Some merely assume—correctly but
without evidence—that it was tuberculosis, but do not inquire into
the circumstances surrounding so major and usually tragic an affliction.[1]

This result is ironic, for Emerson triumphed over his sickness
in a way that both expressed and shaped his character. It was,
moreover, a significant part of his early life; he could not have ignored an illness that had decimated his family—his father, older
brother John Clarke, and two younger brothers, Charles and Edward, were all afflicted or killed by it. How Emerson managed this
disease and survived it are important matters.

Recent research has resolved much of the mystery. We now know
not only what he suffered from, but also who his doctor was, where
that doctor was trained, what the mysterious and seemingly casual
but repeated "operation" he performed was, and why it did not give
more than temporary relief. We can also be reasonably certain that
Emerson's other major symptoms (the partial loss of sight, the lame-

[1] Holmes, p. 41; Rusk, p. 119; Whicher, p. 3; Bishop, pp. 168–69; Allen, p. 94.

ness, and probably his later relapses as well) were aspects of the same illness.[2]

The story has been told in detail elsewhere, and only the most important aspects of it need attention here. The main clue in resolving the mystery lies in Ruth Emerson's reference to "Dr. Reynolds," for Edward Reynolds (1793–1881) was already Boston's best-known eye surgeon. A year before he treated Emerson he had co-founded the Massachusetts Charitable Eye and Ear Infirmary, and he became known as the father of American ophthalmic surgery. It was he who performed the "operations" that Ruth mentioned.[3]

Reynolds had been trained in England, where the famous James Wardrop was at the leading edge of contemporary research. Reynolds brought back with him Wardrop's methods for treating both cataract and inflammation of the eye. Wardrop had established that there was a specific condition, which he called "rheumatic inflammation" of the eye, or *ophthalmia rheumatica*, that was generally accompanied by arthritic pains in other parts of the body. "Mr. Wardrop's procedure" was his answer to the inflammation. Known as ophthalmo-paracentesis, this procedure was simply the first step in the operation for cataract, involving puncture of the cornea and evacuation of the aqueous humor collected behind it. Since the cornea has no nerve endings, the operation is painless, and the bacteriostatic quality of human tears acts against infection. The fibers of the eye close up without leaving a scar, and Wardrop and his followers recorded repeating the procedure on a single sufferer as many as seventeen times. The procedure was used widely for many years, but since it treated only the symptoms of the illness and not its cause, it could have no permanent effect, and it fell into disuse by the 1860s.[4]

[2] Evelyn Barish, "The Moonless Night: Emerson's Crisis of Health, 1825–1827," in *Emerson Centenary Essays*, ed. Joel Myerson (Carbondale: Southern Illinois University Press, 1982), pp. 1–16. This source contains a discussion of knowledge of tuberculosis in the early nineteenth century, of uveitis, and of the differential diagnoses for Emerson's arthritis.

[3] Alvin A. Hubbell, *The Development of Ophthalmology in America: 1800 to 1870* (Chicago: Keener, 1908), p. 70. I am indebted to Mr. Charles Snyder, Curator of Rare Books and Librarian of the Massachusetts Eye and Ear Infirmary, and author of a study of Reynolds, for sharing his knowledge with me.

[4] George Frick, *A Treatise on the Diseases of the Eye . . . Including the Doctrine and Practice of . . . Surgeons*, ed. Richard Welbank (London: J. Anderson, 1826), pp. 63, 71; Daniel M. Albert and Nancy Robinson, "James Wardrop: A Brief Review of His Life and Contributions," *Transactions of the Ophthalmological Societies of the United Kingdom* 94 (1974): 907, quoting J. V. Solomon, *Tension of the Eyeball: Glaucoma* (London: Churchill, 1865).

Reynolds's reputation upon his return to the United States was based on his expertise at the cataract operation; he would naturally have regarded this as the only possible "operation" for Emerson, whose other symptoms all fitted the profile his English mentors had trained him to look for. He also knew that the other two extant eye procedures (there were then only three intraocular operations in use) were not relevant to his patient's case. It seems reasonable to infer, therefore, that given Emerson's rheumatic symptoms this was in fact the operation that Reynolds twice performed.

Assuming this, one can understand better why Emerson should have recovered from the operations without either much difficulty or great benefit, for references to his weak eyesight continued sporadically thereafter. One may perceive too why the procedure was mentioned so casually as an "experiment," why it could be repeated, and why it did not have lasting benefit. While the procedure could alleviate the pressure of fluid behind the eyeball, it did nothing to alleviate the underlying disease of which the uveitis was a symptom.

Of particular interest is the connection Wardrop established between this set of symptoms and rheumatism. (The term "rheumatism" was an archaism among professionals by the second decade of this century, and *ophthalmia rheumatica* before then.)[5] He observed that the eye disease seemed to alternate with or strike soon after a rheumatic attack, especially after exposure to bad weather or sudden change of temperature, and most typically in the spring—just the season when Emerson's crippling attack of March 1826 was reported. Other symptoms, apart from the pain in the head and swelling of the eye, were a temperature that rose in the late afternoon and evening, impaired appetite, increased pulse, and "evacuations always changed in quality." It is not known if Emerson had all these other symptoms (although diarrhea plagued him during his unhealthy summer of 1832), but they are also symptoms of tuberculosis. Eye afflictions have long been associated with tuberculosis.[6]

What is clear is that by the fall of 1825, Emerson was under treat-

---

[5] C. A. Wood et al., eds., *The American Encyclopedia and Dictionary of Ophthalmology* (Chicago: Cleveland Press, 1919), vol. 10, gives *ophthalmia rheumatica* only as an archaic sublisting of the disused "rheumatism." *Ophthalmia rheumatica* does not appear in the *National Medical Dictionary* (1890) or the *Dictionary of Medical Science* (1895), although both include rheumatism.

[6] James Wardrop, "On the Effects of Evacuating the Aqueous Humor in Inflammation of the Eyes, and in Some Diseases of the Cornea," *Medico-Chirurgical Transactions* 4 (1813): 142–87. See also "Account of the Rheumatic Inflammation of the Eye with Observations on the Treatment of the Disease," *Medico-Chirurgical Transactions* 10 (1819): 1–15. Cited hereafter as Wardrop (1813) and Wardrop (1819); Wardrop (1819), p. 8.

ment for uveitis associated with other tubercular symptoms, and when he wrote to William that what Dr. Dalton "nicknamed rheumatism" had slain its tens and crippled its hundreds he had good reason for fear. Modern medicine would agree that, in view of his other symptoms, Emerson's uveitis may have been aroused as a tubercular allergic reaction, probably to stress.[7]

It was not Emerson's eye or joint trouble, however, that caused his southern journey, but the outbreak of pulmonary symptoms and apparently an alarming loss of weight. Oddly, he denied that his complaints had been diagnosed, and minimized them in his only specific description of his symptoms, written to William in early January 1827: "I beseech you however not to be in any particular alarm on my account. I am not sick; I am not well; but luke-sick—and as in my other complaints, so in this, have no symptom that any physician extant can recognize or understand. I have my maladies all to myself."

Waldo then gave a precise description of his ailment: "I have but a single complaint,—a certain stricture on the right side of the chest, which always makes itself felt when the air is cold or damp, and the attempt to preach or the like exertion of the lungs is followed by an aching. The worst part of it is the deferring of hopes—& who can help being heart sick?"[8]

His weight had evidently also fallen, probably alarmingly, because even in February, three months after he had embarked, he weighed only 141½ pounds, a low figure for a man of six feet, and he reported that he had been gaining. In mid-March, three weeks later, he had gained almost ten pounds. If 152 were closer to a normal weight for

[7] In what follows I am indebted to Dr. Martin Wohl, of Harvard University Health Services, Dr. Mark M. Altschule, president of the Boston Medical Library, Prof. Barbara G. Rosenkrantz of the departments of Public Health and the History of Science of Harvard University, and Dr. Donald Stern of the Harvard University Medical School for valuable discussions. I am especially grateful to Drs. Rosenkrantz and Stern for reading the manuscript. Any errors of course are my own.

In stressful situations, the adrenal glands produce additional amounts of the steroid hormones, among whose many effects is lowered resistance to infection. Experts on the subject believe not only that tuberculosis allergy may produce uveitis, or a nonsuppurative swelling of the eye, but point out that 79 percent of the sufferers tested for uveitis proved either to have or have had tuberculosis. See Michael J. Hogan and Lorenz E. Zimmerman, *Ophthalmic Pathology: An Atlas and Textbook*, 2d ed. (Philadelphia: Saunders, 1962), pp. 373–74; Paul B. Beeson and Walsh McDermott, *Textbook of Medicine*, 14th ed. (Philadelphia: Saunders, 1975), pp. 371–73; Frederick Harold Theodore and Abraham Schlossman, *Ocular Allergy* (Baltimore: Williams and Wilkins, 1958), pp. 13, 15, 327, 340.

[8] *L*, 1:184.

him, a reasonable estimate of his initial weight loss by November, the month he had left Boston, might be fifteen to twenty pounds, or even more. In May on his return journey, he wrote to his aunt, "I am not sure that I am a jot better or worse than when I left home in November. Only in this, that I preached Sunday morning in Washington without any pain or inconvenience. I am still saddled with the villain stricture and perhaps he will ride me to death."[9]

In view of all this, Emerson's remarks to William that he had "no symptom any physician extant can recognize or understand" is surprising. In fact, it cannot have been true, for Emerson had related to his brother, as he must have done to his doctors, the classic symptoms of pleurisy. Then as now pleurisy was understood to be a sign of mild, chronic, or "indolent" tuberculosis. Technically an inflammation of the serous membrane enveloping the lungs, pleurisy is not a disease in itself but the name of the chronic chest pain that is made worse by bad weather and exertion of the voice. The pain is caused by lesions that remain on the surface of the lung after an outbreak but that usually remain localized. Samuel Morton, in fact, began his 1834 text, *Illustrations of Pulmonary Consumption*, with a long description of pleurisy precisely because it was known to be a feature of many cases of consumption. In it he described exactly the one-sided pain, aggravated by every motion of the body, but especially by coughing, speaking, and efforts at full respiration. He knew too that morbid changes in the pleura "do not necessarily involve the life of the patient . . . they are often followed by restoration to health."[10]

"To health"—but only to relative health. Tuberculosis could not be cured. It could only be arrested. Although it was the most familiar of all causes of death, ignorance and fear about the subject were great. Part of the fear sprang from the widely held belief that consumption was almost invariably fatal.[11] Waldo had contracted a disease that had already attacked his father and killed one brother. It was clearly eating away at Edward. To live with a chronic case of tuberculosis made extraordinary demands on consciousness, insight, and self-discipline. If anxiety, obsessive modes of thought, and de-

[9] *L*, 1:192, 198.

[10] Author's personal communication with Mark D. Altschule, M.D., 1977; Samuel George Morton, *Illustrations of Pulmonary Consumption* (Philadelphia: Key & Biddle, 1834), p. 10, cited hereafter as Morton. See also Arnold C. Klebs, ed., *Tuberculosis: A Treatise by American Authors on Its Etiology, Frequency, Semeiology, Diagnosis, Prognosis, Prevention And Treatment* (New York: Appleton, 1909), p. 807, cited hereafter as Klebs.

[11] P. C. A. Louis, *Researches on Phthisis*, 2d. ed., trans. W. H. Walshe (London, 1844), p. 472.

pression had become habitual, they must be eliminated. This was a disease that left no choice: one must change or face death.

Nothing was known about the bacterial causes of tuberculosis, and the proposed treatments ranged from the bizarre to the pragmatically sensible. But contemporary medicine had a great deal of experience with the disease, for it was extremely common. Oliver Wendell Holmes, whose biography first drew the veil of silence over Emerson's illness—a silence the more striking from a man whose primary vocation was medicine—told his students in 1867 that "every other resident adult you meet in these streets is or will be more or less tuberculous. This is not an extravagant estimate, as very nearly one-third of the *deaths* of adults in Boston last year were from phthisis."[12]

It is virtually certain that Emerson's doctors would have both diagnosed and informed him of his pleuritic consumption.[13] In traveling to the South Emerson was following the treatment of choice for cure of the disease, which was absence from sources of stress and the passive exercise afforded by a sea voyage. Even early in the century there was a consensus that stress—called by various names—was a predisposing factor that must be eliminated for a good prognosis.[14]

As W. W. Hall, a mid-nineteenth-century writer put it, "We then have arrived at a great fact that depressing mental influences are a 'cause' of consumption."[15] Earlier a German doctor named Avenbrugger had described his dissection of the tubercular bodies of many young conscripts who, shipped to a foreign country, became "hopeless of returning to their beloved country, sad, silent, listless, solitary, musing, and finally quite regardless of all the cares and duties of life. . . . The body gradually wastes away under the pressure

[12] Oliver Wendell Holmes, "Scholastic and Bedside Teaching," *Medical Essays: 1842–1882*, vol. 9 of *Works* (Boston: Houghton Mifflin, 1892; reprint, St. Clair Shores, Mich.: Scholarly Press, 1972), p. 294.

[13] Author's personal communication with Prof. B. G. Rosenkrantz, 1977. Two publications on the subject, circulated among medical readers but overlooked in studies of Emerson, were published in the twentieth century. Lewis Moorman, M.D., diagnosed Emerson as tuberculous, but damaged his case by an equation of Emerson's "genius" with what he called "the ecstatic workings of the toxins of the tubercle bacillus": "Tuberculosis and Genius," *Bulletin Of The History Of Medicine* 18 (Nov. 1945): 361–70. See also Arthur C. Jacobson, *Genius: Some Revaluations* (New York: Greenberg Publications, 1926).

[14] Modern practice holds the same: "We would encourage cheerfulness of spirits and occupation of the mind," Edward Smith, *Consumption* . . . (London: Walton & Maberly, 1962), p. 285.

[15] W. W. Hall, *Consumption* (New York: Redfield, 1857), p. 41.

of ungratified desires." They died, he concluded, "of the disease called nostalgia"—of which consumption was, in effect, a symptom.[16]

Stress, of course, had been a major factor in Emerson's life for several years. Avenbrugger's words—"sad, silent, listless, solitary, musing"—echo Waldo's own just before the outbreak of his disease, when he saw himself as passively blown onward by the days "into the desarts of Eternity," "hope [was] fled," and he felt "summon[ed] to mourn / Companion of the clod brother of worms." Brother, indeed, to the brother already gone before him to the earth whose funeral he remembered sadly. Perhaps at that time he identified also with the fate of Edward, so visibly wasting away before the horrified eyes of his family.

Given this and his other afflictions, Emerson's joint pains were probably also tubercular in origin. Tuberculosis of the bones and joints was very common, and the hip was the second most frequent site for its occurrence. Predisposing factors would be a family history of tuberculosis, developing primarily before one reached thirty—just the era when his lameness set in.[17] Remission with a tendency to relapse—also present in Emerson's case—was not infrequent; true spontaneous cure was rare.

The basic treatment in Emerson's day and afterward until the advent of drugs and safe surgical conditions was the same as for consumption: rest, good nutrition, and a worry-free environment. Emerson's case would seem to fit the particulars for an early stage of arrested tubercular arthritis, although such a diagnosis can only be guessed at. Stress, of course, would also have been involved in activating Emerson's other symptoms, and the arthritic pain in his hip (sometimes his knee) remained chronic throughout his life.[18]

[16] Cited by Morton, p. 46.

[17] Theodore B. Bayles, "Psychogenic Factors in Rheumatic Diseases," in *Arthritis and Allied Conditions*, ed. Joseph L. Hollander and D. J. McCarty, 8th ed. (Philadelphia: Lea and Febinger, 1972), p. 230 and passim, cited hereafter as Hollander. See also Klebs, pp. 735, 745.

[18] For the "striking" tendency of joint tuberculosis to cure itself, see William Osler, *Principles and Practices of Medicine* (New York: Appleton, 1892), pp. 194, 246; W. Watson Cheyne, *Tuberculous Diseases of Bones and Joints*, 2d ed. (London: Oxford University Press, 1911), pp. 120–22, 146, 169; Cheyne also stresses the body's tendency to resist this disease. See also N. Senn, *Tuberculosis of Bones and Joints*, 3d ed. (New York: Oxford University Press, 1952), pp. 2–3, 53, 55, 61, 72, 74–75, 102; Glenn M. Clark, "Tuberculous Arthritis," in Hollander, pp. 1242–54; Metro A. Ogryzlo, "Ankylosing Spondylitis," in Hollander, pp. 699–723.

THERE REMAINS the question of why, given the evidence concerning his disease, Emerson should have denied that it had a name or diagnosis. (William would surely have guessed the truth, whatever his younger brother told him.) Perhaps the answer is that the Emersons as a family knew it only too well, and the denial may have expressed a deeper family pattern of repressing painful knowledge. Thus Ruth could write of Edward's "hidden disease" and describe its ravages, but just as she had not used the word "food" in reproving William's praise of what she termed Harvard's "accommodations," she did not permit herself to suggest consumption by name. Mary, by contrast, was able to utter harsh truths: "Alas for Edward's health," she wrote, "For your sake whom he loves so well, I hope and for all of us; he will do well. But don't expect it."[19]

What is now clear, at any rate, is not only that Emerson suffered from a lazy or "indolent" form of tuberculosis, but that it was also almost certainly the cause of his other afflictions of eyesight and joints—all of which were chronic, lasted well into his life, and flared up under stress. In short, he lived productively most of his life with a body riddled by a frequently mortal disease. Yet this is not the most important fact about it. A deeper truth lies in what it taught him: that talent and energy would count for nothing without patience, self-discipline, a persevering will, and lucidity. Most of all, he learned that these moral qualities would be useless until he could exert a centripetal force powerful enough to separate himself from a destructive environment, draw a magic circle around consciousness, and create a space in which his inner life could grow. Within such a field, insight and the lyric power of his work would take root. When his mind became, in a Miltonic phrase he liked, "its own place," his creative energies were freed.

WHEN Emerson arrived in St. Augustine in mid-January 1827, he found it unlike anything he had known. Instead of the polar skies and lung-piercing winds of Boston, there were gentle air, short shadows, and a sense of ease. Water stretched to the low horizon; light was everywhere. A couple of streets followed the shore of a bay whose surface rippled in the sun. Little low houses, hung with balconies and galleries, their walls glinting with coquina-shell mortar, shaded streets dotted by flowering bushes. At the center was a palm-shaded square dominated by the Catholic cathedral, a handsome,

[19] RE to MME; 1826, HMS; MME to RWE, 1825, HMS.

baroque, and curvilinear structure, nothing like a New England church, with red-tiled roof and iron grillwork. Emerson lodged a few blocks away in a small house at the south end of town, furthest from the old Spanish fort.

The outpost was essentially still a foreign enclave, having belonged to the United States for only six years. Except for a generation of English rule, it had slept through a quarter of a millennium as a remote outpost of the decaying Spanish empire. Once it had dominated the trade routes between Spain and South America; in 1827, the entry to its harbor almost silted over, it presented the anomalies and charms such Caribbean enclaves have long offered the gaze of more righteous visitors from the North.[20]

In reaching this southernmost point of the country, Emerson had gone as far as he could in every sense. Only twenty-three but heartsore and uncertain, he was a minister whose aching lungs impeded him most when he tried to preach. His difficulties, he acknowledged, were "physical and metaphysical" both. In a sense he was, like his new environment, a bankrupt of history—but of a different history—that "sucked eggshell" of Calvinism, as he later called it. What he needed for a while was a place not only where the air was warm, but where things mattered less. In St. Augustine, he found it. Where life had changed little, metamorphosis began.[21]

THE JOURNEY had not been auspicious. He had delayed sailing until just after Thanksgiving, perhaps to give the now shrinking family a last holiday together. Two weeks later, bypassing New York and William, he had arrived at Charleston, South Carolina, seeking contact with one or two of his former classmates. But although he lingered there for most of a month, the weather was unrelentingly cold, and the pain in his chest, which he felt "chiefly by night," continued to worry him. By early January he had realized that if he were to recover he would have to abandon even his present tenuous ties and go further south, where he would be completely a stranger.[22]

He wrote to William of his symptoms, but he did not mention the

[20] J. T. Van Campen, St. Augustine: Florida's Colonial Capital (St. Augustine, Fla.: St. Augustine Historical Society, 1977), pp. 1–72, cited hereafter as Van Campen; J. Leitch Wright, Jr., British St. Augustine (St. Augustine: Historical St. Augustine Preservation Board, 1975), pp. 1–54; Albert Manucy, The Houses of St. Augustine (St. Augustine: St. Augustine Historical Society, 1978), pp. 7–17.

[21] L, 1:184.

[22] L, 1:179n.–180; L, 1:184.

pain that is part of pleurisy and often intense. The older brother, for whom poverty at times meant going hungry, could not have helped and would only have been further depressed at such news of the family malady. To internalize anxiety while sparing others its effects seems to have been a characteristic of the Emerson family's psychological culture. It was a stoic system of defense built on denial and probably learned early under Ruth's tutelage. But it could be adaptive only part of the time.[23]

Though denying that his doctors recognized his illness, Waldo now added a significant new assertion, saying that the worst of his condition was the "deferring of hopes—and who can help being heart sick?" He had "not succeeded in overcoming certain physical and metaphysical difficulties sufficiently to accomplish any thing in the way of grave composition, as [he] had hoped."[24] Acknowledging both the illness and the depression he had long kept to himself may have been a milestone in his management of himself and his disease. It was perhaps no coincidence that within a few weeks of writing this letter, he decided to go further south, made the voyage, and began to feel immediate relief.

Other insights, too, were arriving. Just a few weeks earlier he had written to his older brother that he was experiencing a surprising sense of estrangement and that it was not entirely unwelcome. After less than a month of travel, he wrote that "it is really the most extraordinary event I remember to have happened to me—the entire separation for good and evil which a few hundred miles of one and the same country have effected between us. . . . it 'puzzles all analysis.' "[25] They had previously lived apart for two years when William had been abroad without this effect, but Waldo himself had never traveled. Now he had left home psychically as well as physically, and he was aware of the importance of his sea change.

[23] Samuel Bradford, a boyhood friend of the Emerson sons, shared William's garret room in New York where he lived over the firm in which he was reading law, and describes the straitness of their circumstances. Bradford had failed in business in Boston and gone to New York in hopes of recouping his fortunes by starting anew there—not a unique pattern. A good friend of William, he said of him, "a better man I have never known," but felt that he had never been "appreciated" and remarked that he had had only "a fair practice." He described him as a man of "feeble" health and "quite reticent." Clearly the upheavals William suffered in his career did not leave him the stronger for the struggle. Samuel Bradford, *Some Incidents in the Life of Samuel Bradford, Senior, By His Son. Also, the Autobiography or a Brief Narrative of the Life of Samuel Bradford, Junior, to January 1, 1879* (Philadelphia: privately published, 1880), pp. 63–64.

[24] *L*, 1:184–85.

[25] *L*, 1:179.

With a largely Catholic population that combined Spanish, "Minorcan," British, Creole, and black strains, St. Augustine had no commercial or industrial base for its economy. Oranges were grown, tended by slaves, but there was no real farming, as the vast tracts lying inland from the shore were swampy and insect-ridden. Most visitors and all supplies and mail arrived by sea. The port, founded in 1565, had grown in its early days as a base for Spanish colonial operations, but St. Augustine had fallen into somnolence long before it was annexed by the United States in 1821. Government officials, would-be settlers, remnants of the old armies, and a few invalids like Emerson made up the largely idle white population.[26]

It was this idleness and its effects that most surprised and amused Emerson, and his style sprang to life, growing both more free and more serious as he observed his new world. In a community of eleven or twelve hundred, he reported with nice precision, "what are called the ladies of the place are in number, 8." No one seemed to work. "What is done here? nothing. It was reported one morning that a man was at work in the public square and all our family turned out to see him. What is grown here? Oranges." He found over the gate of the old fort a Spanish inscription—but no one he asked had ever read or knew anything about it. By the city gates he saw the gibbets from which hung empty cages, shaped like mummies, in which living wretches had been "left to starve to death." His old preoccupation reawakened, in his journal he sketched these frames, which had recently been exhumed still full of bones, and then apparently rehung.[27]

He also observed the intertwining of the local forms of government and religion, which appeared to him equally corrupt, but whose activities he merely reported with minimal comment. In this small community, men played multiple roles. When Emerson attended a meeting of the Bible society he noted that its treasurer:

> by a somewhat unfortunate arrangement, had appointed a special meeting of the society and a slave auction at the same time and place, one being in the Government house and the other in the adjoining yard. One ear therefore heard the glad tidings of great joy whilst the other was regaled with "Going, gentlemen, Going." And almost without changing our position we might

[26] Van Campen, pp. 52–62.
[27] *JMN*, 3:115; *L*, 1:189; *JMN*, 3:116.

aid in sending the scriptures into Africa or bid for "four children without the mother who had been kidnapped therefrom."[28]

The ironic distance he had absorbed in part from Hume and his own keen sense of the ridiculous, not free since his adolescence, returned, awakened in a culture that must have struck him as grotesque when it was not wicked. "There is something wonderfully piquant," he wrote:

> in the manners of the place, theological or civil. A Mr. Jerry, a Methodist minister, preached here two Sundays ago, who confined himself in the afternoon to some pretty intelligible strictures upon the character of a President of the Bible Soc. who swears. The gentleman alluded to was present. And it really exceeded all power of face to be grave during the divine's very plain analysis of the motives which probably actuated the individual in seeking the office which he holds.

In this setting, he was not particularly surprised to be told by a North Carolinian of the "monstrous absurdities of the Methodists at the Camp Meetings in that state. He related an instance of these fanatics jumping about on all fours, imitating the barking of dogs and surrounding a tree in which they pretended they had '*treed Jesus* . . . !' "[29]

If Emerson seems to anticipate Mark Twain here, he sometimes also foreshadowed Graham Greene. The local priest fascinated him. "This exemplary divine," Emerson noted, had lately been arrested for debt and imprisoned, but not before he had attempted to defraud further one of his creditors, a Mr. Crosby, of an additional six dollars by asking him to give change for a ten-dollar bill: " 'If you can change ten dollars for me, I will pay you the four which I owe you.' Crosby gave him six which the father put in his waistcoat pocket, and, being presently questioned, stoutly denied that he had anything from him. But Crosby was the biggest and compelled him to restore the money." Nevertheless, the priest subsequently said mass at the cathedral. Emerson went to hear him, "for his creditors have been indulgent and released him for the present." The same cleric, Em-

[28] *JMN*, 3:117.
[29] *JMN*, 3:117, 115.

erson reported later, "represented at a masquerade the character of a drunken sailor with the most laudable fidelity."[30]

But although the town in all its *bizarrerie* was entertaining and had a tonic effect on his style, there was no one to talk with, and Emerson spent much time alone. He needed that isolation, however, and the use he made of it was reflected in his language soon after he had thus reached his journey's end. Perhaps it was not without some unconscious significance that he had come as close to the edge of his country's limits as it was possible to go, for his geographic position found an echo in his inner sense of his own boundaries.

Behind the entertaining chat of the letters one senses that the shape of a new and gradually sharpening vision of himself was emerging. It was a not undramatic figure, clothed in the clerical black that simultaneously excluded him from ordinary amusements and signaled another role as he moved on the margin of two worlds. In this persona he wrote to Charles just over a week after his arrival: "Whosoever is in St. Augustine resembles what may be also seen in St. A. the barnacles on a ledge of rocks which the tide has deserted; move they cannot; very uncomfortable they surely are,—but they can hear from afar the roaring of the waters and imagine the joy of the barnacles that are bathed thereby."[31]

The image is deliberately comic in its bathos, but it is also apt. The graceless barnacles, stuck to their places, bereft of the inflowing waters of life but conscious of their neediness, "hear from afar the roaring of the waters" and can imagine the joy of those freer creatures of their kind. In the same way the unsaved soul, stuck on the ledges of his human body but aware and awake, can envision his deliverance. In case Charles missed the point, Emerson dilated on it: "The entertainments of the place are two,—billiards and the sea beach; but those whose cloth abhors the billiards—why, theirs is the sea beach. Here therefore by day do I parade, and think of my brother barnacles at a distance."

The rest of the letter, interestingly, not only conjures up and blesses a vision of his distant but virtuous brother, but also articulates, perhaps for the first time, Emerson's own claim to the prophetic role he had so long admired and wished for, but not assumed: "Thus you see that the poorest of us hath his ideal; a small grey-coated gnat is wagoner to the Queen of Fairies, and we who walk on

[30] *JMN*, 3:116; *L*, 1:189.
[31] *L*, 1:187.

the beach are seers of prodigious events and prophets of noble na-
tures."

He made the prophetic claim disarmingly, but he made it: "*We
who walk on the beach are seers and prophets*" (my emphasis)—choosing as his ground that strip of territory belonging neither to one
world nor to the other, neither to terra firma nor to the uncharted
sea that Emerson elsewhere associated with godly power.

The same images and vision dominated a letter he sent to William
describing the changes in his physical and spiritual condition. He
had been in St. Augustine for less than two weeks, but his stricture
was relieved, and his health was improving. Concluding his description of the sluggish ways of his environment he added, "Here then
in Turkey, I enact turkey too," alluding to a Byronic image of an
Eastern pasha. But as in his letter to Charles, his language projected
a sense of the sharp contrast between himself and his surroundings:
threatened by dissolution yet indissoluble, living on the margin of
opposing forces, whether of beach and wave, life and death, or the
present and the eternal:

> I stroll on the sea beach, and drive a green orange over the sand
> with a stick. Sometimes I sail in a boat, sometimes I sit in a
> chair. I read and write a little, moulding sermons for an hour
> which may never arrive. For tho' there may be much preaching
> in the world to come[,] yet as it will hardly be after the written
> fashion of this pragmatic world, if I go to the grave without
> finding vent for my gift, the universe I fear will afford it no scope
> beside. So pray for the perfect health of your loving brother.[32]

One is struck by the Miltonic assurance of the phrase "my gift,"
as by "we who walk on the beach are seers and prophets." Emerson
is a seer because he can literally see more in that place, from which
he can look both ways. His ground, that strip of land ever shifting
between land and water, is the borderline of two states, precarious
and unstable, but opportune. On this margin, to be sure, his imagination had often dwelt. The Magician from the Dead-Sea-shore
must have crossed it; the bearded islander from the Land of Not had
known it; even Isaac and his father had come over that strand when
from "far far oversea" they had made their way to William's court.
Emerson seems now to have begun to know that at some important
level of his consciousness he was to stay there, that it was his place—
uneasy, shifting intertidally between the human and the less or more

[32] *L*, 1:189.

than human, but vital with the possibilities of hidden life and metamorphosis.[33]

As an image, the sea with its shore was to become powerful in his
writing, just as its analogical state of mind, the contained tension of
living with ambiguity, was to become both habitual and profoundly
fruitful. He has become "matter out of place," less polluting, however, than sacred. For he is at once the green orange rolling ran-
domly toward and away from the waves through the agency of the
stick, passive in the universe but open to it, and the agent controlling
the stick, the self that both wills and directs life: a green orange on a
beach, a New England minister wandering the subtropical coast.
"Sometimes I sail in a boat, sometimes I sit in a chair." Supported
by, almost one with the elements, he participates in them, able to
hear the "roaring of the waves" and increasingly to articulate the
meaning of what he sees and hears. One reads these phrases in light
of the earlier imagery of sleeping, darkness, entombment, and tunneling, and recognizes that Emerson feels he has at last awakened;
he now knows that he can hear and see both things and their signs,
both appearance and reality. Experience, though narrow at this moment, was deep.

FOR the next month or so, Emerson consolidated his gains. Six
weeks later he noted repeatedly that he weighed 152 pounds.[34] But
his journalizing and letter-writing had dropped to a low ebb: inner
change, when Emerson was in its grip, absorbed his energies, and
he had little to say. Early in January he had excoriated himself (using the third person) for "hypocrisy" and "habitual guilt," asserting
that consciousness of sin, of the discrepancy between his morals and
his mind "betoken some future violence." Because there was a tendency in the universe toward harmony, he warned, "If the string
cannot be made to accord, it must be broken." The attitude was self-
punitive, but he did not name the source of this guilt and anxiety; it
is unlikely that he even knew it.[35]

But by late March and April he could articulate to Mary his new
state of mind and the nature of his "hypocrisy." It appears to have

---

[33] Compare Julie Ellison's description, pp. 76–77, of Emerson's mature style, which is
specifically not dialectical because it "accumulates but does not progress," discussed in
the Epilogue. This period of illness and recovery seems to have marked the beginning of
that resistance to synthesis.

[34] *JMN*, 3:75; *L*, 1:192; *JMN*, 3:77; *L*, 1:194.

[35] *JMN*, 3:60.

been a harder name for what now would be called ambivalence. Illness and exile had taught him something. The near confrontation of death had made his choices more clear. "He has seen but half the Universe," he wrote to his aunt, "who has never been shown the house of Pain." He had been a dreamer and self-indulgent: "The decay of his hopes, the manifested inefficacy of efforts into which he has pushed the pith and resources of all his nature; the suffering and the grievous dependence on other men which suffering brings with it—these things startle the luxurious dreamer, and alarm him with necessities never experienced before."

It is not clear what he meant precisely by "the lesson of resignation hard to learn, and I believe . . . seldom taught the young"; Emerson was not specific as to the form of these necessities and the nature of the false goal he thus renounced. On the practical level, I believe it meant giving up worldly ambition, recognizing that he could not expect the success he had inchoately dreamed of as a youth while filling the particular intellectual role and critical stance he had chosen. The identity he had long framed as an ideal had little to do with reality. In a broader sense, however, what it all added up to was becoming self-reliant. This journey was, I believe, the core experience of that conversionary process.[36]

Emerson wrote to Mary of his renunciation in the kind of terms they shared, comparing himself to a young martyr not ready for death at the stake because he had not yet been tested in the world: "Many a man has died with firmness who yet had never broke his spirit or rather sublimed his spirit to such resignation. Resolution was on his face but regret sat on his heart." Emerson, however, had gone beyond that wavering point, he told his aunt, for suffering and necessity "suggest the possibility of relations more intimate and awful than friendship and love. They bring to light a system of feelings whose existence was not suspected before; they place him in a connexion with God that furnishes a solution of the mystery of his being."[37]

The key words of this passage are "intimate," "love," and "friendship": they defined Emerson's deepest needs, and this letter suggests finally that he had gained enough distance from himself or from egotism—had "sublimed his spirit" enough—to see the extent and power of these needs. His lifelong ambition had aimed fundamentally not so much at "fame" as at being rewarded for his special "ge-

[36] *J*, 2:180.
[37] Ibid.

nius." Because of that genius, he was to receive the love of the world and the approval of social and professional arbiters, of all the patriarchy that had long stood in his fantasy for the dead and living past. He had been taught by Mary to believe in the uniqueness of his voice and moral insight, and he shared her vision of himself as Abdiel, the Miltonic angel who stood alone against the host of Satan. Perhaps he was beginning to recognize that he could not have it both ways, and to understand where the conflict lay. The figures of fantasy who had engrossed him had been rewarded by applause. Abdiel had had his Milton; Massillon had preached to a frenzied court. In the same way, his own Vahn, grandson of Odin, and even his silent Isaac, had had as witnesses kingly or patriarchal figures whose mere acknowledgment constituted confirmation of their being, affirmation of their worth. In his fantasy, heroes had been recognized. It was this welcome that Emerson had wanted more deeply and irrationally than anything else. It may have been this need that he was now beginning to recognize and surrender.

It was probably no accident that on this voyage home, just a few days after he wrote to Mary, Emerson wrote of his first conscious sense of love for another man, Achille Murat, a brief but moving contact. He had already met the recently married Murat in St. Augustine, where they had boarded together, but no reference to him occurs in his writings of the time. Chance, however, appears to have thrown them together on the ship, where they shared a cabin and much serious talk. Murat, a nephew of the exiled Bonaparte, was intending to settle in the South as a planter. An atheist, he and Emerson could have shared little common experience, but both were men of open, inquiring minds. An entry in Emerson's journal, written in April on his journey northward, is lit up by the sudden and intense attraction and records an expanded and renewed assertion of the new independence he had expressed more circuitously to Mary a few weeks earlier:

> Let the glory of the world go where it will. . . . No man can serve many masters. The night is fine; the stars shed down their severe influences upon me and I feel a joy in my solitude that the merriment of vulgar society can never communicate. . . . I lead a new life. I occupy new ground in the world of spirits, untenanted before. . . . Strange thoughts start up like angels in my way and beckon me onward. I doubt not I tread on the high-

way that leads to the Divinity. And why shall I not be content with these thoughts and this being which give a majesty to my nature and forego the ambition to shine in the frivolous assemblies of men where the genuine objects of my ambition are not revered or known?[38]

One is struck by the tone of strength and certainty in this discussion of his direction in life. Equally strong was the tone in which he celebrated the acquisition of his new friend, in another entry written while lying up in Charleston on his way home.

A new event is added to the quiet history of my life. I have connected myself by friendship to a man who with as ardent a love of truth as that which animates me[,] with a mind surpassing mine in the variety of its research, and sharpened and strengthened to an energy for *action* to which I have no pretension by advantages of birth and practical connexion with mankind beyond almost all men in the world—is yet, that which I had ever supposed a creature only of the imagination—a consistent atheist. . . .[39]

His own faith was "indestructible," but "meantime I love and honour this intrepid doubter. His soul is noble, and his virtue . . . is sublime." The experience of this new and compelling friendship probably strengthened Emerson's sense of his own worth; although in his shipboard journal he seems to have been comparing himself with Murat, for once he did not come out the loser.[40]

Although they never met again and exchanged only one or two letters, that encounter became for Emerson an exemplum, the very type of friendship and the meeting of true minds.[41] Gradually over the years it acquired almost a mythic quality. Six, nine and ten years later he could write that traveling with Murat had been worth all the bad journeys he had taken with others, that Murat had been one of the small band who had "ministered to my highest wants" and

[38] *JMN*, 3:78.

[39] *JMN*, 3:77. See John Q. Anderson, "Emerson and Prince Achille Murat," *Boston Public Library Quarterly* 10 (Jan. 1958): 27–37. Anderson presents a flamboyant, "coarse," and changeable man in Murat. He had married a grandniece of George Washington in July 1826 and settled with her in Tallahassee. They were briefly in St. Augustine while traveling north when they met Emerson in their shared lodgings. He and Emerson became friendly only on the voyage north, however, when they shared a cabin during a difficult trip that took almost nine days, instead of the normal two-and-a-half.

[40] *JMN*, 3:78.

[41] *L*, 1:202; *J*, 2:187–91.

that one ought to meet great men not in public, but as they had done, confined close together "in the cabin of a ship."[42]

Apparently this contact with its feelings of mutual admiration and affection marked an epoch in his life. Long pent-up emotions had suddenly found their vent. Emerson's very deep capacity for attachment had evidently been stirred to life and met an answering spirit. Clearly in an important way he was a different man now. His social role or status was no different from what it had been when he had left Boston five months earlier. But now he could feel his freedom. He could, in Nietzsche's phrase, accept his right to his task. Emerson was now a licensed minister, literally launched on his career and earning money by occasional preaching as he traveled. He stood on an equal footing with his new acquaintance, however disparate their social roles or status might outwardly be. His adolescent fear of intimacy with a friend of his own sex had disappeared. Love for another man could be a strengthening and not a threatening experience.

It is likely that there was a deep connection between Emerson's new ability to experience true friendship and his wish, framed as a rhetorical question, to "forego the ambition to shine in the frivolous assemblies of men." Both involved the acceptance of a new or adjusted sense of his own identity. What Emerson projected giving up in this moment was not trivial. All his life he had dreamed of glory. He knew his talents as a speaker, and gravely had schooled himself so that his natural seriousness had become in public a somewhat awesome, visionary dignity. Undoubtedly at some level of consciousness he had perceived that in the growing republic and as the scion of New England's "aristocracy" he would, once possessed of a pulpit and its access to public print, be the professional match of any of his contemporaries. Given his imagination, intellect, and the originality of his language, it was within his grasp to be a great preacher and to stretch the model handed down by Channing and Buckminster. Certainly he could surpass that of his father, whose pulpit manner had been less than stirring. In that role, even his poetic gifts were not secondary—on the contrary, they had been essential to all great divines since Ecclesiastes.

Moreover, Emerson was a man who knew his talents, although deep, to be comparatively narrow. His was not the easy social manner and convivial nature of the worldly rising man, nor despite his wide and constant reading did he see himself specifically as a scholar.

[42] *JMN*, 4:242; 5:160, 319.

His gifts of language and insight were aided by an extraordinary capacity for concentration, not so much on the object of study as on the object of his vision. In all the great variety of objects and moods on which Emerson's journal reflects, there is one subject important to success that he virtually never mentions; singleness of purpose was not a matter for anxiety or discussion because it was virtually his ground of being.

But even with energies so focused, knowing his goal was not the same as knowing how to reach it: that was the rub. He had always assumed that he would find his role within the church. Now he was beginning to grasp that to be a man of faith, his relation to that institution might have to be tendentious, problematic, and contingent. He had a year earlier successfully avoided confrontation with Norton and his other examiners, but it is unlikely that he had fully recognized the long-range implications of that tactic. Now on the threshold of his vocation, he had to accept that he could never, so to speak, enter the hall of that "assembly" and join the party. For Emerson to describe a future as a minister as an "ambition to shine" in some frivolous way may today seem odd, but from his point of view it was no misnomer. That was precisely his aunt's vision of her brother William's career. Undoubtedly it was also Waldo's. The intimate relationship between established Congregationalism in Boston and wealth and privilege was simply a fact of life. Social and conventional professional success in his vocation had to be counted as one.

For years he had been asserting his independence of "the universe," naming himself "God's child" and affirming his self-sufficiency in the face of an indifferent cosmos. He had felt essential human loneliness with special pain. Orphanhood in a world from which God had retreated was for him more than a metaphor. But these pronouncements of independence had been rather cryings out, defiant denials of fear, than assertions of faith. In St. Augustine he had finally understood and accepted what his stance must be. He could not then have known that within the next decade he would become first and briefly a conventionally successful clergyman and then a leading and influential rebel, but he was preparing for just that role.

WHERE he had derived the new strength to accept this position is not certain, but much of it must have come as Emerson learned from experience and pain that he could face the worst and be freer for it. In the warmth and languor of St. Augustine, past social pressures

and anxieties must have seemed as distant as the haze at the horizon. It was easier to distinguish real from imaginary threats, to understand what was productive and what merely defensive in his activity. The end of his life could be very close. In a matter of months or a year or two, he, still only twenty-three, could disappear like the green orange foundering in the waves. The prospect of death, as Dr. Johnson said, wonderfully concentrates the mind. Like poverty, it reduces choice—but also confusion. What is possible is what one does. For Emerson, unimportant issues shrank to their real size and could be let go. With acceptance of new tasks and the need to enact them, the shameful sense of dependency began to vanish. Needing less brought autonomy and balance.

He was beginning to grasp what he later expressed in the essay, "History," that the voice of the prophets he longed to hear would come only as his own inner voice. The approval of the "bards and criticks," bestowers of the "fame" for which he had thought to bargain, constituted ultimately only another part of himself. And their price, his "bones and sinew," was usurious. It would always be excessive because the aim of such internalized criticism was not growth but safety, not change but stasis.

That inner opponent, in fact, that punitive alternative self that could wipe out or deny all sense of his own worth, became eventually Emerson's most real, externalized enemy. It is not solipsism that one hears in Emerson's later claim, "Great is the Soul, and free," but the voice of a man who has crossed the abyss he called "nonentity" and wishes to help others make that passage. Learning to transcend the self-destructiveness of his years of "misery" and frustration became fundamental to what he had to say and the key to his continuing appeal to his audiences. That achievement was not irreversible, to be sure. His lung ailments flared up under stress in later years, just as new losses, such as the death of his first wife and oldest son, renewed for him temporarily his identification with all that was negative. But the struggle with mortality never ceased to be for him the beginning of learning.

Chapter 11

THE FRUITS OF SUMMER

"When I see a green lane open, I suppose . . . it leads
somewhere . . . all Hume and Germany notwithstanding."
—RWE to MME, 1829

T HE EMERSON who returned from the South in June 1827
was a man very different from the youth who only nine
months earlier had evoked as his persona a "ghastly child of
death and darkness, summon[ed] to mourn, / Companion of the clod
brother of worms,"[1] and who had written while on his trip, "I have
an appetite for pain." What he had seen in his exploration of himself
and the boundaries of his isolation had led him back to the world.
He was twenty-four, eager to work, to be healthy, and to marry.

The doctrine that Emerson was ready to evolve over the next five
years was disarmingly simple and grew partly out of such felt needs.
He had not resolved the problems of theodicy and skepticism that
had paralyzed him for so long; rather he had moved beyond them,
coming to realize that they were both insoluble and, on a certain
level, irrelevant. No one else had slain "this uncircumsized" Goliath
and his party, and it was not incumbent on him to do so. What be-
hooved him was to attach himself to life, and to aid others in finding
their way.

EMERSON'S first move on returning to Boston was to join his
mother and step-grandfather in Concord. Invited by Ezra Ripley to
fill the pulpit there one Sunday in June, an occasion that he must
have felt as marking a personal epoch, Emerson preached a sermon
that reveals much about his new frame of mind. It reflected both joy
in returning to family and home and a conscious rejection of the isolation he had long both endured and sought. The youth who had
defiantly asserted that a possibly meaningless universe could return
to chaos for all he cared, that he would yet be God's child, had be-

[1] *JMN*, 3:36.

198

come a man who early announced in this first address to the people
of his ancestral home that "an immediate connexion and dependance
upon God is too lofty a motive to sustain and console our virtue in
the daily warfare of the world. . . . Our clouded eyes cannot always
see God walking at our our side. . . . We must do as others do. In
short we are virtuous and vicious as social beings."[2]

"We must do as others do." Simple and universal as this formula
may be, for Emerson it was almost a new idea. Our eyes are
"clouded," he said. This was literally true, for his difficulty in seeing
had not ended with Reynolds's operations. But for one whose visual
perceptions were so acute, cloudiness of vision was not only a handicap but a vivid metaphor of deprivation of inner vision that could
only be endured by patience and a kind of determined trust. He had
learned from the failure of his health that the apparent was not necessarily the real and that present pain, emptiness, and depression
would yield to management and willed patience. In the meantime,
he would wait; do as others did; reach out in love and friendship to
other human beings. Implied in the language of the sermon is a new
and genuine humbleness. Ordinary virtue was sufficient because it
was very difficult. Extraordinary and romantic heroism was not necessary.

Under such a dispensation, life was possible. Self-punishing hesitation and self-abnegation had no place in this world. Emerson expressed it to Mary when in March he wrote that suffering had "sublimed his spirit." Having looked at the prospect of real death, he no
longer found pleasure in romantic fantasies about it. Life was his
object.

Above all, life offered the opportunity for love, the most necessary
nurture. Using a metaphor of food and eating for such love, a figure
that henceforth was to grow in power in his language, Emerson
wrote that "we do not eat our bread alone and spread our table in
secret. . . . We dwell in families.[?] We have taken sweet counsel
together. God has united us in family or in friendship. It reaches
farther this mighty sympathy, this golden hoop that binds our brothers in. . . ."[3] Probably his brothers Edward and Charles were in the
audience, undoubtedly his mother and grandfather and perhaps
other relatives were listening also. The contrast in his sense of self,
like the contrast in his language, is extravagant but characteristic of

[2] RWE, Sermons, HMS.

[3] See Greenberger, "Phoenix," for a discussion of Emerson's use of imagery of food;
RWE, Sermons, HMS.

what was to be a lifetime spent between the dichotomies of society and solitude.

Clearly Emerson spoke from his heart of "this golden hoop" out of the joy of his return, as he addressed a congregation for whom it must have been a moving experience. The theme of the opposing claims of society and solitude—the title of the last work he was to complete without assistance—was also the subject of his first sermon: "Compare the wondrous dwelling of the beaver and the bee, with the unprovided rock of the eagle and the lion . . . compare the powers of man when he is alone, with the powers of man in society. In solitude he is weak; in society he is strong. In solitude the mind and body decay. . . . In society, his mind is expanded in its efforts.[4]

Interaction with others was for Emerson a central crux, and perhaps the most fruitful of all the problematic issues he was to know in life. Later, he took the other side. As the late poem "Power" asserts:

> Cast the bantling on the rocks
> Suckle him with the she-wolf's teat,
> Wintered with the hawk and fox,
> Power and speed be hands and feet.

By then the adversity endured by animal and rejected child seemed more fruitful than gentle rearing. But that tough-mindedness still lay ahead. In 1827 isolation implied no kind of nurture.

NOT LONG after giving this sermon, and obviously in search of that wider world in which to grow, Emerson moved away from Concord into Cambridge. He took quarters in Divinity Hall and worked on producing his "stock" of sermons. He had been asked by the congregation of his father's old church, the First Church of Boston, to substitute for Octavius Frothingham, a longtime friend of his mother.[5]

[4] RWE, Sermons, 1827, HMS. For a discussion of Emerson's sermons and doctrine, see David Robinson, *Apostle of Culture: Emerson as Preacher and Lecturer* (Philadelphia: University of Pennsylvania Press, 1982), cited hereafter as Robinson. This excellent study stresses Emerson's place within the Unitarian tradition and deals with some of the complexities of defining that tradition. The present chapter, however, draws on manuscript sermons by Emerson that have not been discussed by Robinson or printed in his source, *Young Emerson Speaks*, ed. Arthur C. McGiffert, Jr. (Port Washington, N.Y.: Kennikat Press, 1968), (Robinson, p. 2). McGiffert published only 2 of the 27 sermons Emerson wrote before 1829, and only 8 of 61 he composed before 1830.

[5] The invitation was relayed to Emerson while he was returning home by his brother Edward, EBE to RWE, 1827, HMS.

During this period and for the next few years, Emerson began to articulate many of the ideas associated with his major works. He was helped by the loan of Edward Everett's sermons, a generous act that must have gratified the younger man, but which also marked him as one of the most rationalistic of his kind, for Everett had given up his pulpit, studied in Germany, and finally resigned a Harvard professorship before entering politics.[6]

Residence in Divinity Hall gave him new food for thought. In place of the notion that he had "an appetite for pain," Waldo's journal now reflected—when he had time to write in it—an acceptance of adversity and an urgency about using time to the fullest. The ideal of the self-reliant man began to take shape as one whose determination "the stars cannot thwart with evil influences."[7]

Supporting such a spirit was hope. He stood his old deathbed fantasy on its head and used it as the theme for a sermon: "There is a story of a man who on his deathbed called to him his profligate son and left him large possessions only exacting of him the promise to spend an hour every day alone. The son kept his word & became a wise & good man."[8]

He realized now that the use of death was to prick one into increased consciousness of life. "The employment of time is the main purpose of life & the main consequence of death is the account that is to be rendered thereof." To achieve consciousness, the mind must be focused, and for that the will must be strong: "He to whom appetite is nothing & pleasure nothing & pain nothing before his immutable will, will find not many impossibilities in his way."[9] Emerson has been criticized by some modern readers for what they see as a stress that amounts to a Nietzschean will to power, but this interpretation takes his term out of context. Emerson had no interest in power for its own sake or the dominance of others. What he wished to share was what he had learned in moving beyond long-standing ambivalence and virtual paralysis. He used such terms as "will" and "power" to describe the force that he ultimately felt, but the process was far more complex than a single term could suggest. The sense of strength he aimed to describe existed, as well, only in a God-centered universe; never did he imagine a sense of self whose only referent was itself.

Emerson was beginning at last to find and define his real subject,

[6] Tyack, pp. 35, 90, 108–9.
[7] *JMN*, 3:93.
[8] *JMN*, 3:96.
[9] *JMN*, 3:97; *JMN*, 3:134.

the progress or growth of the soul—a subject not so different from what psychoanalysis today would call the ego—and step by step he was building his conception of what it was and whence it drew its strength.

Another of Emerson's most characteristic ideas dates from this period: the axiom that consciousness is the central mental activity of humanity, the process without which one can neither discover one's true identity nor nurture the awareness of God's immanence. It followed that the only way to grow freely was to dare to be oneself, and those who did not so dare he now began to recognize and censure. The famous strictures he was to raise in 1838 against the unlived life evident in Barzillai Frost's bad preaching he had already complained of in 1827 when he wrote:

> I attended church . . . & the image in the pulpit was all of clay and not of tuneable metal[.] I said to myself, that if men would avoid that general language and general manner in which they strive to hide all that is peculiar and would say only what was uppermost in their own minds after their own individual manner, every man would be interesting. Every man is a new creation. . . . But whatever properties a man of narrowed intellect feels to be peculiar, he studiously hides; he is ashamed or afraid of himself; and all his communications to men are unskilful plagiarisms from the common stock of tho't & knowledge and he is, of course, flat and tiresome.[10]

Living at Divinity Hall gave him new opportunities to observe his fellow men. Of an unfortunate "young c." Emerson wrote:

> I would write a sermon upon the text men are made a law unto themselves to advise them to fear & honour themselves. . . . Now here is young c. I am afraid to trust him. He is such a chameleon & borrows his key so implicitly from those that are better than he & obviously curbs the expression of bad feelings out of regard to them that I should fear to leave him alone. I should feel no security for his dependant or inferior that they should not suffer incivility or tyranny. If you could only make him *reverere sui*.[11]

The aim of knowing the self (insight so lacking in "young c.") was to achieve, in a condition of openness, a sort of wise passivity.

[10] *L*, 1:207.
[11] *JMN*, 3:142.

He wrote of that condition occasionally using water imagery to connote the fluid, trusting state of the soul:

> A child is connected to the womb of its mother by a cord from the navel. So it seems to me is man connected to God by his conscience . . . giving him a free agency . . . to work his will in the world. . . . [But God] has kept open this door by which he may come in at all times & visit his sins with distress or his virtues with pleasant thoughts. It is like the hydrostatic paradox as naturalists call it; the Ocean against a hair line of water[,] God against a human soul.[12]

In this image the soul is an unborn fetus, and God is a great placental ocean; God thus is also, perhaps for the first but not the last time in Emerson's prose, a mother.

THESE new thoughts and experiences contributed to what Emerson told his early congregations. Those sermons are close to but not identical with his later thought. By comparison with *Nature*, for example, his position in these sermons, although softened by a lyric quality, was more starkly rationalistic and lacked the elements that seemed pantheistic or mystical to some later readers. Already, however, his approach was primarily ethical and positive; it gave little attention to tradition or biblical authority, much to inner knowledge of God, and almost none to sin.

His doctrine was evolving as a blending of the Arminian and Hopkintonian traditions, that is, of the liberal Enlightenment tradition and the more subjective assumptions mediated first by Mary and then by Channing (who had studied with Samuel Hopkins).[13] From the Hopkintonians Emerson drew his emphasis on the subjectivity of religious knowledge, the overriding importance of inner conviction, and the high ethical value of disinterestedness. From the Liberal tradition came his acceptance of the value of science, of positive knowledge, and of the overriding importance of living ethically in the actual world.

[12] *JMN*, 3:139.

[13] William Henry Channing, *The Life of William Ellery Channing* (Boston: American Unitarian Association, 1880), pp. 8off. Robinson, p. 9, has pointed out that Unitarianism and Transcendentalism were in fact more closely blended than time later made them appear. Both were as one in fighting a "pitched battle" with the Calvinists over the concept of "human potential against the conception of original sin." Emerson was not very different as a Unitarian until his rejection in 1832 of Christology.

Yet he picked and chose among these strains, rejecting both the New Lights' stress on a punitive God and the Arminian acceptance of biblical authority, the value of miracles, and other supernatural revelation. With equal freedom, he discarded from each approach what he disliked, which in each case was their disciplinary features: the Calvinists' fear of hell and the Liberals' reliance on tradition and scriptural authority.[14]

In many ways his was an attractive doctrine, for without yet saying that God was "within," Emerson assumed that humanity could both hear God's voice inwardly and live in a world that God loved and was not prepared to destroy. But such doctrine also represented a delicate balancing act, for it tended to perceive humankind, although not as sinless yet as able to thrive without the disciplinary use of fear, whether of hell or of objectively real discipline. Increasingly, God's revelation was in the world itself, properly studied— until eventually nature itself became Emerson's text. That last step still lay ahead, but already the intellect unaided except by the individual soul was a prophet and witness. He knew the precariousness of his position. He pointed it out in fact to Mary when debating with her about his new acceptance of quotidian life: "Does this reasoning seem to you unsafe?" he asked her—knowing full well it did.

In the place of fear was his evolving doctrine of compensation. The idea of compensation implied that there would be retribution in the world for wickedness without invoking the concepts of hell or an eternally vengeful God. "It is but the Justice of God running thro' the universe," he said of compensation, paraphrasing Bacon on revenge. His context in this early sermon was a reproof of business fraud. Commerce, he knew, was the major activity of his audience, and he spoke to their condition: "Fearful crimes are hunted by fearful remorse. . . . love of money is punished by the care of money." Money was needed for life, but fraud in its acquisition would be repaid one way or another, and in this life.[15]

About the Trinity, Emerson believed that his own father had in the first decade of the century "preserved a studied silence" on this question. The son dealt with the issue early. Unitarianism, of course, was identified with the rejection of the doctrine of the Trinity, but there was no firm consensus on the actual origin of Christ or his precise relation to God.[16] Preaching on "Christ Crucified," Emerson

[14] For a discussion of the varieties of doctrinal differences in New England at the time, see Ahlstrom, pp. 388–428, and Robinson, pp. 7–29.

[15] See chap. 5; RWE, Sermons, 1827, HMS.

[16] Ahlstrom, p. 395.

stressed not Christ's birth, life, or purported miracles, but his influence. The sermon adduced the "affecting" and powerful influence of the "being" whose character "has taken such strong hold of the mind as to divide the opinions of men as to his nature & office . . . [leaving] foundation for the opinion that he was a portion of the Deity & in the opinions least reverent that he was first of men. . . ." Giving equal weight to each position, Emerson sought not to destroy credence but to leave room for difference. Evidently Emerson did not accept Christ as a miracle worker. In this he was consistent with the conclusion he had reached years earlier when at nineteen he had "scouted" the superstitions of the Bible. (Rather charmingly, however, Emerson seems never to have been able to part from his love of the notion of angels.[17])

His model of religion was an inner spirit that infused daily acts. This too, of course, was central to his later posture. Specifically, religion was not "austere macerating monkish observances," ritual fasts, prayers, penances, and compulsive churchgoing. "Becoming the well known member of all religious societies" was not religion. Its manner did not "befit the gloom of cloisters and the solitude of desarts." Rather, it was "cheerful social masculine generous. It is inquisitive of the ways of man[,] inquisitive of the works of God. It walks about doing good in the streets of cities. It scorns appearances. It uncovers the vestures of fortune to get at the heart."[18]

In short, religion was nothing if it was not expressed in the real world, but his doctrine rejected in Hopkintonian fashion all notion of "means." Not the outer motions of religion but the disinterested benevolence it inspired from within were its marks. Its mode was "cheerful social masculine generous"—words warming to his hearers and expressive, very likely, of a new ideal of the self that was emerging as Emerson's own. Soon he would see nature as a primary mediator of God, and imagery of urban life would disappear from his rhetoric. Now, however, he still identified with the life of the city that had been his own boyhood environment (Concord was a place he had visited, not grown up in), and the "streets of the cities" were where human beings dwelt and acted with whatever religion they had.

Nature, however, was clearly already important to Emerson, for its beauty expressed God's love and moved him to lyric language. In

[17] In this sermon they roll away the stones from the sealed cave before Christ's ascent to "his father in Heaven." RWE, Sermons, 1827, HMS.

[18] RWE, Sermons, 1827, HMS.

a kind of reverse of *Job*, he offered a long encomium aimed at denying that God was a "dread and dangerous Being." "Who is it that
molded the globe in his hollow hand? Who is it that gave the Sun
his commandment . . . decorating the green earth with the blooms
of spring; renovating life with the . . . fruits of summer; calling man
with the almost articulate voice of the autumn winds to pensive meditation . . . ?" Such joy in life was part of his popularity as a preacher.
"Who is it that sends out the morning sun in such festal pomp, &
pours the day shining over lake and field and river glittering under
the sunbeam until the eye of the pious beholder is dazzled . . . Who
is it that sends down the night in its beauty & takes off the bright
veil of the garish day from the glowing adoring firmament?"[19] Shim-
mering through this pious language too is the energy of sexuality, as
the last metaphors suggest. Clearly Emerson was far more in touch
with his own sources of vitality than he had been.

There was to be much development of these positions in future
years, but no reversal of his tendency. Reintegrating the "fine mysticism" his aunt had spoken of came later, and it seemed less Christian when it reappeared.

To some his was a dangerous doctrine, avoiding the Calvinistic
economy of sin and punishment and ignoring original sin, the fall,
and the atonement. But he spoke eloquently to sophisticated congre-
gants who had often themselves left behind serious belief in a vengeful God and a penitential life, and they granted their clergy much
latitude. The language of a contemporary Arminian apologist, for
example, has been described as suggesting that one might "be a
Christian without jeopardizing his social standing." Biblical literal-
ism was identified with the less educated lower classes.[20]

Inevitably, however, he was headed for collision with orthodoxy,
and his ties to Mary were the first to show the strain. She had long
been his best audience and best opponent, but she was more than
that. She had mediated the religious life to him more clearly than
any other figure, and he had studied and introjected her "prophetic
and apocalyptic" voice, making it central to the roots of his own prophetic stance.[21] Nor was he ever to be wholly free of her influence if
by that is meant not so much specific doctrines as a way of examining
life.

[19] RWE., Sermons, 1827, HMS.
[20] Wright, p. 248.
[21] *JMN*, 5:323–24.

In his mid-twenties, however, it was crucial to establish that as an adult he was not to be a Uilsa, or even a Vahn. The Merlins and Sphinxes he invented later worked their magic on the complex and problematic world of reality, not of romance. Although in the long run Mary's life remained for him the epitome of a certain kind of religious vocation, it was not a goal. The protected and quasi-hermetic mode she had chosen was uniquely adapted to herself. Moreover, the very fact of her longtime influence inevitably meant that in achieving his own autonomy he had to move away from his aunt.

Evidently Emerson had begun to do so; in a letter of November 1827, only part of which survives, he challenged her on two topics he knew she would least yield on. One was his preference for a rational over an enthusiastic or mystic mode of belief, and the other was his choice of a social rather than a privative mode of witness. That the letter had rankled (its offensive portions are missing) is evident from two references to it in her correspondence with him as late as four and six months later. Hers to him of May 2, 1828, implies that they had been wrangling over the issues and that he had apologized for some language she took as personal criticism. "My thanks for the sensibility you express," she wrote to him with a sarcasm that borders on savage indignation, "at my being hurt to be tho't by you distraught. But after all I do appear so to other folks . . ."[22]

Apparently she had found in his words an allusion to her reputation for being "distraught," or eccentric, and she asserted both that more sympathy would have made her act less bizarrely, and that in the past Waldo had understood and loved her better than others. It is unlikely, however, that he had meant his comment in the sense she took it. To be unable to adjust the conflicting claims of feeling and reason—the mistake he had mentioned—was not so much a personal failing of Mary's as the conventional error, from an Enlightenment or Kantian position, that characterized religious enthusiasm in the age of new thought.

In addition to this, however, he had also announced his own choice of prudence and rationality over enthusiasm and mysticism:

> We are not to be bound by suggestions of sentiment, which our reason not only does not sanction, but also condemns. T'were to throw our pilot into the sea in compliment to the winds. And when the mystics tell me, as the mystics will not hesitate to do, that there is sin in every good work until I have the assurance

[22] MME to RWE, HMS.

clear as the sun in heaven of a new connexion of God with my
soul, of a new birth, or what not, I shall give them no regard.

His own father could not have put the Arminian position more
flatly, or fenced better with his enthusiastic sister. "Does this reasoning seem to you unsafe?" he asked, knowing well it must. But to him
it would now seem a "crime" if he were to "surrender to the casual
and morbid exercise of the sentiment of a midnight hour the steady
light of all my days, my most vigorous and approved thoughts, [and]
barter the sun for the waning moon."²³ Interestingly, he concluded
by saying that his difficulty "consists in finding the proper mean . . .
in adjusting life betwixt reason and feeling." (He thus acknowledged
what was certainly true, that he too found difficulty with the problem of which he accused Mary.)²⁴

Mary's response was characteristically acerb. Mysticism was a gift
of God: "The lover of beauty will not desire to analyse the mystic
mistress of his heart . . . its source is God. . . . If the Angel of 'midnight' who is commissioned to turn the starry mirror of reflection
has oftener visited him—it may be that truth is more clearly dis-
cerned then [than] in the sunny influence of vigorous thoughts and
business."²⁵

Extending his metaphor, Mary undoubtedly identified herself
with the angel of midnight who ought to be his guardian and conscience. His contempt for midnight reflections, moonlight, and mysticism were met by her satire on "vigorous thoughts" and "sunny
influences." Her message was always the same: that only the angel
of midnight—the voice of conscience that spoke of inward things—
should be heeded.

Basically, what she feared was that Waldo might be embracing an
Arminian hubris, a dangerous modern loss of humility that would
lead him away from salvation. "The shipwrecks w'h so often float
over the sea of human life are held to be those of self-[courting] virtue mour often . . . than of the dependant mendicant." It was better
to remain conscious of one's secondariness, one's dependency on
God. "That the good find themselves everlastingly debtors for existence can never be disputed nor derived but by Lucifer." In her Miltonic vision, to reject spiritual dependency was a work of Satan.²⁶

They argued philosophy in the language of poetry, consciously

²³ J, 2:222–23.
²⁴ J, 2:221–23.
²⁵ MME to RWE, 1828, HMS.
²⁶ MME to RWE, 1828, HMS.

loading it with the metaphorical freight of post-Reformation and post-Calvinist disputes. Mary feared rudderless shipwreck, and took refuge—when being the angel of midnight seemed inappropriate— in the image of humankind as "worm"—poor and neglected, but a member of God's kingdom. Emerson, on the other hand, was to make a destinationless voyage his image of humanity's fearful but exhilarating freedom: "Do not require a description of the countries towards which you sail," he was to write, "the description does not describe them to you, and tomorrow you will arrive there and know them by inhabiting them."[27]

In this and similar arguments is summed up the fundamental clash between modern and traditional ontology, between perceptions of humanity as "barely existing creatures" dependent forever on the Almighty, and as creatures forced into a freedom that might not give them control over their destiny but that required them nevertheless to confront it. His later and powerful concept of the "Central Man," second to no one, was to be the direct opposite of—and defiant response to—such Calvinistic thought. Perhaps Mary deserves some credit for the useful clarity and vividness with which she had put the opposite doctrine.

The rift between them was not personal, but it represented, as Emerson said, the separation of two great eras of thought, now drifting apart. Her life, he wrote, was "a fruit of Calvinism and New England, and marks the precise time when the power of the old creed yielded to the influence of modern science and humanity."[28] But already in 1828 he had understood that enthusiasm was not enough, that inner conviction of the light was not all-sufficient, that "the great multitude of the best men who have lived and left a name [were] what the enthusiast calls 'cold and prudent Christians'—Bacons, Lockes, Butlers, Johnsons, Buckminsters."[29] Emerson did not see himself as a "cold and prudent" Christian, but he was ready to apply his talents in the world and let them grow. It was time to put himself where he could connect with others.

A few months earlier, he had written to Mary in August in the old vein wishing to have her old almanacks "before they are a legacy." That was the last demand he was to make for her writings in which his tone would be hyperbolically greedy. Privately, he noted to Sarah Ripley his only extant contemporary criticism of her: "Aunt

[27] "Over-Soul," CW, 2:283.
[28] CW, 10:399.
[29] J, 2:220.

M is a kind of she-Isaiah who quotes as wildly as she talks."[30] His new stance was less to wish her assistance in peering into invisible mysteries than to attain a kind of wise quiescence. He was "curious" what the higher criticism might reveal about Jesus, but was content, given his eyesight (and his personal inclination, surely), not to inquire minutely. "To ask questions is what this life is for,—to answer them the next."[31]

Probably Emerson's best statement of his position during this era was in a letter he wrote to Mary not long after his marriage. There he asserted, not in an argumentative but in a lyric vein, the modern proposition that religious truth was both progressive and relative to its age. What he could understand was true for himself only and as an approximation. Nevertheless, the world seemed full to him of God's revelations. "All that I see is full of intelligence and all that I know is *my* approximation to the idea of God." A "green lane" must lead somewhere—Hume and the skeptics notwithstanding. The moral laws held "perfectly" and were proved constantly by analogies found with nature; "every man's life is to him the idea of a Providence. And moments are remarked in his memory of intercourse with God." Intuitive knowledge of God, analogical evidence of Providence in the material world, a flooding sense of God's presence—these would henceforth be sufficient for his proofs. The texts of the past, the Bible, and traditions of the church were outmoded: "The best man of our time is a nobler moral exhibition than the *God* of a much ruder time."[32]

Mary attacked him angrily. After complaining of his "Kantism" and of the "revolting" deism she heard from William and Sarah Ripley, she concluded with a sarcastic summary of his beliefs: "I . . . consider these negations as spawns of infidelity and bastards of metaphisiks."[33] Norton himself was not so fierce when he criticized "The New School in Literature and Religion" and "The Latest Form of Infidelity."[34] But her anger could no longer rouse him. Long before this outburst, Emerson had determined to ask only real questions; for that, experience of life was essential.

[30] *L*, 1:208, 242.

[31] *J*, 1:221, and *L*, 1:208.

[32] *J*, 2:273-74.

[33] MME to RWE, 1829, HMS.

[34] "The New School in Literature and Religion," *Boston Daily Advertiser*, Aug. 27, 1838; *The Transcendentalists*, ed. Perry Miller (Cambridge, Mass.: Harvard University Press, 1950), pp. 193-96; *A Discourse on the Latest Form of Infidelity* . . . (Cambridge, Mass.: John Owen, 1839).

MARRIAGE

"Let us live together first."
—Ellen Tucker to RWE, 1829

WHILE HE was maturing these ideas, Emerson pursued his goal at a steady pace that made up for lost time. Within three months of his return he began preaching regularly. At age twenty-four he was the head of the family with many people dependent on him. Ultimately, Emerson's success in life would have been impossible without his shaping capacity, his sense of timing, and his judgment about when to follow and when to resist the paths taken by others.

Managing his health was a crucial test of that judgment, for his greatest problem was the slow uncertainty of his recuperation. Recent preaching showed that he was not yet strong enough to undertake a minister's normal workload.

Sometimes, if only in passing, he was tempted to find another profession. In pleurisy inflammation around the lungs makes speaking and even breathing painful. By late June 1827, Emerson had been home for most of a month, but he wrote to William one Sunday night that he was "all clay, no iron. Meditate now and then total abdication of the profession on the score of ill health." He could not yet project his voice enough to preach twice without suffering; the day had done him in, and he had had to refuse a reengagement for the next week. If he could not plan even a week ahead, how would he live? He looked no worse, he reported, than when he had met William in New York, "but the lungs in their spiteful lobes sing Sexton & Sorrow whenever I only ask them to shout a sermon for me." Carrying out parish work would have been beyond his strength.[1]

Pushing himself evidently only heightened the disease. He would have to learn to curb his ambition and make sure that one step forward was not followed by two backward. It is a commonplace of biography to assert that Emerson's life was saved by his lack of com-

[1] *L*, 1:201.

petitiveness or ambition, an impression he contributed to by criticizing the family's "ill-weaved ambition." On the contrary, Emerson
was intensely ambitious, though not competitive in personal sense.
He was also a totally determined fighter, not of persons but of the
practical obstacles that stood in his way—a characteristic for which
he has never been given credit because he preferred to paint quite a
different picture of himself as "inapplicant, time-wasting Ralph," the
persona of dreamer and writer he adopted early in dealing with his
older brother William. In fact, real waste of time—time spent on
unproductive personal or social trivia—was foreign to him. He rejected not high goals, but obsessiveness in their pursuit. What saved
his life, most probably, was his rare capacity to learn from experience
and to change both his behavior and emotional response to stress—
something few are able to do. For the rest of his life Emerson
schooled himself in the hard training of patience; what may have
looked like slowness or lack of energy was in fact the successful strategy of survival.

Medicine alone could do nothing for tuberculosis, or for most
other diseases.[2] Far more than today, it was up to the ill person to
get well. Emerson made this his business. "Heat is my best medicine," he wrote in August, but in winter, after months of work,
travel, and bad weather, he learned to adjust his means:

> I don't write because with all my leisure I've none. I am writing
> sermons. I am living cautiously yea treading on eggs to
> strengthen my constitution. It is a long battle, this of mine be-
> twixt life & death & tis wholly uncertain to whom the game
> belongs. So I never write when I can walk or especially when I
> can laugh. . . . But scamper scamper; this fine day . . . is dying
> away & I have not walked to the end of the rope of my rheu-
> matism so have little more time for brotherly love, for tho it is
> strong as death yet wd I not have death prove the stronger and
> so I must fight inches with him.[3]

Later Emerson wrote more specifically than ever before to William, perhaps fearing for the process he saw taking place in Edward
as well: "I am very much disturbed . . . at the idea of your Sickness.

[2] Dr. James Jackson, later one of Emerson's own doctors, taught his Harvard students
that only quacks pretended otherwise; they could "care for" their patients; they could not
" '*cure* a patient . . . nature heals, art helps.' " Oliver Wendell Holmes, *Life and Letters of
Oliver Wendell Holmes* (New York: Chelsea House, 1980), 1:82.

[3] *L*, 1:211, 227.

. . . Have you forgotten that all the Emersons overdo themselves?"[4]
One infers that there was a well-grounded family tradition attributing the early deaths of father and grandfather to excessive stress and
overwork. Today also such a family history would be considered om-
inous, and Emerson was right when he warned William: "Don't you
die of the leprosy of your race—ill-weaved ambition. Pah how it
smells, I'll none of it." It was not the ambition that was wrong, but
the ill-weaving of it, its excesses and failures of self-knowledge.

> Why here am I lounging on a system these many months writ-
> ing something less than a sermon a month for my main busi-
> ness,—the rest of the time being devoted to needful recreation
> after such unparalleled exertions. And the consequence is—I
> begin to mend, and am said to look less like a monument &
> more like a man. I cant persuade that wilful brother Edward of
> mine to use the same sovereign nostrum. If I have written but
> five lines & find a silly uneasiness in my chest or in my narvous
> system to use the genuine anile word (& the old women are
> almost always right—I take them to be the antipodes of the Gar-
> mans) I escape from the writing desk as from a snake & go
> straight to quarter myself on the first person I can think of in
> Divinity Hall who can afford to entertain me, i.e., on the person
> whose time is worth the least.[5]

The "old women" who were almost always right about health and
the "narvous system" was doubtless an allusion to Mary. Waldo was
asserting that he was learning to hear and respond to his body's sig-
nals, to manage and change his moods through therapeutic measures
both mental and physical. Discipline, and the capacity to control
anxiety and negativity were crucial in his battle between life and
death. "I always take as much exercise as my hip can bear and always
at intervals & not in a mass," he added. "He who would *act* must
lounge."[6] The arthritic pain, tubercular in origin, had become
chronic and was to reappear in his left knee during the summer and
fall of 1829. Waldo had learned that he must constantly move the
affected joints and not let them grow worse.
  One can hardly underestimate the influence of the tragic careers

---

  [4] *L*, 1:233. Their father, while preparing for services, had suffered a hemorrhage from
which he never fully recovered, and their grandfather had died on a Revolutionary battle-
field at the age of thirty-three from a fever contracted while serving as a volunteer chaplain.
  [5] Ibid.
  [6] *L*, 1:227, 233.

of his siblings and his own experience with sickness on Emerson's thought. William would remain in New York in "feeble" health with what was never more than a "fair" legal practice, rising at length to a minor judgeship. Edward was obviously extremely sick, rather "excitable," driven by manic hopes but with an uncertain future; he could work only part of the time and was to suffer a violent mental breakdown from which he never fully recovered. He would be dead by age thirty. Charles was still in college in 1827, but he was to sicken and die of consumption only two years after Edward in 1836. Bulkeley, who appears to have been the only healthy brother, was grown now and less manageable, given to such vagaries as wandering on his own for weeks through New Hampshire, offering singing lessons.[7] Two other siblings had died young, but Waldo had been old enough to remember them. Waldo not only loved and identified with his surviving brothers, he supported them financially for years.

He must have seen in their lives powerful object lessons. To retreat, as three of them did, into virtual unbelief and unwelcome secular pursuits was no solution. It begged the question, denied deep psychic needs and sources of insight, and left them ambivalent and even disgusted by their profession. Edward, for example, wrote once that he "hated" his work at the law, while William also apparently preferred lecturing on literature to working at his new profession. If life was to be an unending battle, Emerson may have felt, he would at least fight it on ground of his own choosing. If religion had changed, while its official professors had not, it was for them to defend their interpretations, not for Emerson to flee the ground. Moreover, he had grown very realistic through struggling with his disease: if even survival must be fought for "by inches," he may well have recognized that neither religious faith, nor love, nor any thing of value in life would come easily.

SINCE he was not yet strong enough to sustain a full-time appointment, Emerson set himself to "supply" preaching, part-time work in which he filled the pulpits of absent ministers. By the fall of 1827 he was given a circuit by the American Unitarian Association, which to compete with the evangelical sects sent missionaries to the parishes that lay outside the Boston area. The term "missionary" is a misnomer from the modern point of view, however, because the

[7] *L*, 1:202.

souls Emerson was presumably converting represented, he reported, the "intelligent men" of the region.[8]

"Supply" preaching was actually an excellent way for a young candidate to begin his career, for it provided a modest but adequate income of ten dollars a week (fifteen in Boston) and gave him the opportunity to meet a wide variety of men and women and learn about the world of his parishioners. In the last months of 1827 Emerson, always a good traveler whatever his state of health, covered hundreds of miles, west to Greenfield, north to Conway, and south to New Bedford. He found himself in good company, welcomed by community leaders, with some of whom he began enduring friendships.[9] Living among this group he gained social insights and experiences that would have been impossible for the chronically depressed Emerson of even a year earlier. Previously the Emerson name had won him little more than charity and a chance to compete for scholarships. Now it would seem to those meeting him to imply a promise of worth.

By now, his personal qualities would also have recommended him. He was tall and thin with a face dominated equally by his mother's large and aquiline nose and deep-set, intensely blue eyes, their gaze still powerful in his middle age. Even an inexpert sketch from the period reflects a face of intensity and sensitivity that did not yet show the sadness perceptible in the photographs of his later years. His voice was rich and had a fascinating sort of hesitation that suggested the care with which he chose his language. He spoke rather little but with dignity.[10] He was attractive. He was also extraordinarily intelligent and perceptive. For all the occasional awkwardness he never tired of lamenting, he was a welcome addition to society, worth cultivating and encouraging. Sarah Ripley, married to a clergyman and well able to judge, testified to Emerson's standing when she reported to Mary in December that their nephew (and her husband's one-time assistant) was "the most popular preacher among the candidates, and all he wants is health to be fixed at once in Boston." Such popularity did not surprise them. Mary had written to Waldo of "your manner so peculiarly happy in impressing what you said in the pulpit."[11]

He cultivated that manner, for he had given much thought to style and what he named "intellectual Voice": "A man's *style* is his

[8] *L*, 1:213.
[9] *L*, 1:217.
[10] Holmes, p. 38; Cabot, 1:64.
[11] Thayer, pp. 40–41; MME to RWE, 1827, HMS.

intellectual Voice only in part under his controul. It has its own
proper tone and manner which when he is not thinking of it, it will
always assume. He can mimic the voices of others, he can modulate
it with the occasion and the passion, but it has its own individual
nature."[12]

Public utterance was his métier: "I aspire always to the production
of present effect, thinking that if I succeed in that I succeed wholly.
For a strong present effect is a permanent impression." He urged the
subject on his brothers, criticizing Charles for not engaging directly
with his audience and Edward for not "electrif[ying]" his hearers.[13]

ONE of the pulpits in which his voice was welcome was that in Concord (sometimes known as New Concord), New Hampshire. William Kent, [Jr.], the organizer of the new Unitarian church there,
wrote to the association that Emerson had been "a man of force and
popular address" who had increased his audience every time he
preached. Not only Kent, however, had befriended Emerson. On his
visit there in December 1827 he met his future wife, Ellen Louisa
Tucker.[14]

She had been brought up in Boston as the daughter of a well-to-
do merchant, Bezaleel Tucker (1771–1820), who happened to have
been one of William Emerson's parishioners at the First Church. Ellen (1811–1831) had moved with her mother to New Hampshire
when the widowed Mrs. Tucker became the second wife of Colonel
William Austin Kent.[15] (One of the deep experiences Ellen and
Waldo shared was the loss of a parent when young.) Kent, a banker
and landowner, had given the new church he and his son were spon-
soring the ground it stood on. When Ellen and Waldo met she was
still only sixteen, but by all accounts charming, intelligent, and
pretty; Waldo thought her "very beautiful, by universal consent."

[12] *JMN*, 3:26.

[13] *L*, 1:211, 238–40, 210.

[14] *L*, 1:222n.

[15] Tucker bought a gallery pew in 1802 for $125 and traded up in 1808 when the
move to a new building at Chauncy Place gave him access to a better site on the ground
floor for an additional $400. However, he at once "disposed" of this to another parishioner
for an unrecorded sum. Whether he then ceased to be a church member is not certain, but
the inference is clear that he was a man socially and economically on his way up through
trade, and that alliance with the Emerson family would have added honor to his. See
Richard Pierce, *Publications of the Colonial Society in America*, no. 40, *The Records of the
First Church in Boston 1630–1868* (Boston: Colonial Society of America, 1961), 2:607,
636, 638–40.

She was fond of poetry, liked to write verse, and as he wrote a year later, "She has character enough to be religious." She was also an heiress, having inherited money from her father. They met on December 25, 1827, and Emerson remained in Concord until early January.[16]

Their correspondence from the period following this meeting, if any, has not been published, but Emerson wrote Charles while still on this visit that brothers were not enough: he wanted friends:

> Brothers, even if I had decent ones, can never in any manner answer this purpose. . . . If you could see me as I uncomfortably draw my pen thro this sheet bent over my knee with a stranger by my side you would guess how great must be the inconveniences. . . . how sincere is the want I have expressed. My quarrel is with my race which will not give me what I want either in the shape of man or woman.[17]

This last remark is sometimes quoted out of context as suggesting misanthropy. On the contrary, it shows that Emerson now recognized that something crucial was missing in his life. Perhaps the "stranger by my side"—a stranger, but one in whose presence he could write intimate letters—had helped him notice that brothers could not be all in all forever. The next day, he planned to visit the Shaker community nearby—which happened to be one of Ellen's interests in that small town of thirty-five hundred souls. Both were probably sorry when he left, and glad when he was able to return for more work in May and June.

He was beginning to receive offers of permanent appointments. One from suburban Brighton he spurned: "One should preach bucolics there," he commented to William.[18] Concord, New Hampshire, also wished him to return and stay several months on his own terms, and Kent's request to the Unitarian association was clearly based on Emerson's success as a preacher rather than on any more personal tie. Waldo, however, had other and wider opportunities. In June one of the best of these came when he was invited to supply the pulpit at Boston's Second Church, whose minister, Henry Ware, Jr., under the shadow of his own tuberculosis, was soon to retire to the less demanding work of a Harvard professorship. Emerson took the offer, and work and care kept him in Boston most of the summer

[16] *L*, 1:256.
[17] *L*, 1:225.
[18] *L*, 1:234.

and fall of 1828, since Edward's recovery from his second breakdown in June was slow, and his condition fluctuated for some time.

That summer Waldo was supporting two brothers in institutional
or other care at once.[19] Despite these strains, Emerson continued to
mend. He must have wished his preaching at the "Old North" to be
his best, for if he could win continued tenure there he would have a
pulpit from which his voice could surely be heard. But ill health and
the ministerial life seemed inextricably interwoven, as Ware's ill
health suggested.[20]

By December 1828, however, a year and a half after his return from
Florida, things had become more hopeful. The family was in better
shape: Bulkeley had been able to do useful work where he was
boarded and had earned some of his keep. Edward, too, seemed sta-
ble, and William's news was also encouraging. It was time, Waldo
determined, to bring matters to a head with the Second Church. He
had been engaged there for about half a year; after consulting with
Ezra Ripley he decided, as Rusk put it, to make a "strategic withdrawal": "It is well understood Mr. Ware wd. shortly resign. . . . I
did not think it very delicate to hang on longer; if the parish was to
be regarded as open for candidates I was monopolizing. So having
spoken with Dr. Ripley I told them I wd. come away at the end of
November."[21]

The church wished to put off making a decision. Emerson spoke
not of forcing their hand but of the indelicacy of "monopolizing"—a
nice distinction, made in discreet, clerical style. Emerson always felt
that his social manner lacked polish and ease, but in dealing with
authority he had developed a certain finesse. The results showed the
strength of his tact. In January 1829 the Second Church voted sev-
enty-four to five to engage Emerson as Ware's replacement, and he
was sufficiently well informed and adept at counting votes that he
could report to William not only the names but the motives of the
recalcitrant fraction.[22] The politics of these matters was not trivial.
Not merely a favorable vote but a solid majority was important if the
ongoing relationship was to prosper. Emerson had promoted this by

[19] Emerson received some unsought contributions from old friends, but the burden was
his. William tried at least once to help, but he was more likely to need a loan than be able
to make one. *L*, 1:253, 251.

[20] *L*, 1:249.

[21] *L*, 1:253; Rusk, p. 130.

[22] *L*, 1:260.

the clarity with which in December he had defined his role in relation to the church committee. In many social matters he continued
to feel himself graceless, but on issues he deemed important, he was
idealistic but not naive in dealing with the world. It was this competence that enabled him later to live in Concord as a heretic but not
an outcast, a radical critical of official theology but still a man to be
reckoned with, who stood his ground and although without a pulpit
was able to go on preaching, lecturing, and growing in influence.

Before this result had occurred, however, Emerson had traveled
on December 6, 1828, to Concord, New Hampshire, taking Edward with him. He also brought along that lover's necessity, a gift
book. Within ten days of his arrival, he was engaged to Ellen Louisa
Tucker.

He was very happy.

HE HAD good reason to be, for Ellen, although still an unformed
young girl, was to be the "romance" of his life, a figure who from the
beginning he idealized, and to have been loved by his ideal, however
tragically short their life together, was of deep and healing importance.[23] To William he wrote on Christmas Eve, a week after the
engagement:

> I thought I had got over my blushes & wishes, when now I
> determined to go into that dangerous neighborhood again on
> Edward's account. But the presumptuous man was overthrown
> by the eye & the ear and surrendered at discretion. He is now
> as happy as it is safe in life to be. . . . She is 17 years old, & very
> beautiful by universal consent. Her feelings are exceedingly del-
> icate and noble.[24]

A month later he described to William her "character": "Well then
she is perfectly simple though very elegant in her manners; then she
has common sense; then she has imagination & knows the difference
between good poetry & bad; then she makes fine verses herself, then
she is good—& has character enough to be religious. Then she is
beautiful, & finally I love her. If my story is short, it is true.[25]

Others less prejudiced agreed that to win her was "success."
Charles was enthusiastic and came to care much for her, while by
coincidence Mary heard the news early through another channel,

[23] *L*, 1:318.
[24] *L*, 1:256.
[25] *L*, 1:259.

which described Ellen and Waldo's "success" in gaining her. Mary paraphrased it as "giving a most brilliant account . . . of her worth, and living, in fine, an Angel."[26] Ellen's letters reveal that if she was not an "Angel," she deserved as much of this praise as might reasonably be expected of so young a girl. She was intelligent, sensitive, and perceptive, not without humor, and she probably was considerably more aware of the quotidian world of social relations than her suitor, even though he was eight years her senior, whom she liked to call "Grandpa."[27]

She had been raised not in the Calvinist but in the genteel tradition described by Greven. She liked to wear fashionable clothing—which she argued was less trouble than dressing plainly; she loved music and liked to sing. She had her own horse named Marmion (sometimes known as Byron). As the step-daughter of a leading banker, her life in the village was necessarily circumscribed by the activities of her mother, her sisters, the suitors who called on them, and the books she came across. Her instruction had not been wide, and after their engagement she was touchingly eager to learn from Waldo, while he was more than willing to set his new pupil to reading—in history, of course, and French.[28]

On her own, she enjoyed whatever freedom she could, riding out on Marmion, or going with friends on an errand of mercy to visit some destitute Indians nearby, finding them in worse condition than she had imagined. She also liked to tease her fiancé, but she could laugh at herself as well, noting after writing a cliché, "Oh the metaphorical droppings of a girl in her teens." But she was as much in love with Waldo as he was with her; she understood his worth and was eager to learn from him.[29]

Waldo wrote to Mary in January 1829 of both his engagement to Ellen and his appointment to the pulpit of the Second Church. He reminded her that she had promised him success, but there was a note of disbelief in his tone, as if he could not fully trust the reality of this change in his fortunes.[30] Her response, however, was not warm, both because she feared change and loss and because she dis-

[26] MME to RWE, 1829, HMS.

[27] *One First Love: The Letters of Ellen Louisa Tucker to Ralph Waldo Emerson*, ed. Edith W. Gregg (Cambridge, Mass.: Harvard University Press, 1962), pp. 21, 26, 27 and passim; cited hereafter as Gregg.

[28] Ibid., pp. 13, 43.

[29] Ibid., p. 13; ibid., p. 12.

[30] *J*, 2:360.

liked the threat that Ellen's wealthy background posed to a humble spirit. She wrote to Sarah Ripley:

> Well, my dear Sarah . . . I've heard of Waldo's success. This is the boy I used to like the better for your liking. But he is gone, for me; no romance,—all common, fat prosperity; not the poet, reckless of scholarship, glad to get his bread anyhow. He will be as busy as a bee, yet as cautious as if he were a tailor making patterns. And the fair Ellen, so goblin like, will be obliged to take the tune and encounter of the times.[31]

In many ways the letter is the essence of Mary at her most recalcitrant—placing responsibility for her own lifelong sponsorship of Waldo on Sarah's shoulders, critical when others were happy. But it is also her most plangent statement of the antinomian ideal she had set up for Waldo of minister-hero-poet, equally reckless of material gain and orthodox approval. She probably feared in Ellen's wealth and his own new appointment Waldo's entrance into the same fashionable life her brother William had led and, she thought, been lost in.

Nevertheless, she came around and softened enough to warn Ellen against all spiritual and intellectual attainments, as they might lead to pride. She included in her proscriptions pride in maternal love (unless it involved "great sacrifice"), and the study of French and chemistry. Ellen must nevertheless be strong: "The man that God has blest you with is devoted to the highest and most urgent office. Lean not on him for resources—but urge him on. . . ." "I hope you don't paint nor talk french," she finished, "Hope you'll be a unique. and *love* poetry—that musick of the soul."[32]

THAT SPRING Ellen moved with her mother to Boston to be near her fiancé. Ordained in March, by June 1829 Waldo was made chaplain to the state senate—a post his father had held before him, carrying honor if not additional emolument. His salary, which began at twelve hundred dollars, rose by prearrangement after Ware's final departure to eighteen hundred. This was an adequate salary, but with Edward, Charles, and his mother as dependents, he was in ef-

[31] Quoted in Thayer p. 40.
[32] MME to ETE, 1829, HMS.

fect supporting four adults living in separate homes.[33] Nor was he
underworked in his new position. With ordination had come parish
duties, and within a few weeks in March he had made, he said,
"more than fifty pastoral visits and am yet but in the ends and frontiers of my society." Charles reported to William that "Waldo grows
more and more eloquent every Sunday [but] he visits his people
without any other guide or introduction, than his own knowledge of
the street wherein they live. And thus he has sometimes made long
calls, kind and affectionate, on families who had no other claims to
his attentions, than that of bearing the same name with his parishioners."[34]

Even if this happened only once or twice, it suggests both Emerson's good nature and how unskilled he was at the day-to-day matters of parish work.

Clearly he was in need of a wife with the sort of social skills that
Ellen, backed by her mother, possessed. From the beginning, however, their lives were shadowed by Ellen's ill health. Already she had
lost a father and brother to the same disease that was the scourge of
Waldo's family. Her mother and a sister suffered from it; worse, she
too had already shown signs of it. Immediately following their engagement she suffered a hemorrhage, and Waldo helped to nurse
her. He had to leave Concord to meet his other obligations, but he
returned when he could. By the summer Ellen, who had returned to
New Hampshire, was still unwell, and a remarkable letter from her
describes the atmosphere in her house, so full of sickness. The usual
accounts stress Ellen's charm, youth, and innocence. Attention to
her language, however, shows that it is already dense with internalized feeling; beneath the surface of joke and wit lie painful insights
about the end she foresaw, feared, and yet hoped to escape:

> The house is inhabited by solemn spiritlike dancers—We meet
> on the stairs and greet each other with a low whisper—we pass
> in the entry and wink long and expressively—We glide into
> each other's chambers with the charitable intent of enlivening
> the melting hours but as we are all of the gliding race when we
> reach our neighbors chamber we are not sure not to find them
> at home—they have just glided into ours—and so we meet in

[33] Just how highly he was valued and how different the pay scales were between a
prominent Boston church and a new, rural one is evident in the fact that the pay for the
post Emerson refused at New Concord was only $600. This was earned by Moses George
Thomas, a contemporary of Emerson at the Harvard Divinity School, who married his
step-sister-in-law, Mary Jane Kent. See Kent Family Archives, New Hampshire Historical Association, cited hereafter as NHHA.
[34] L, 1:270n.

the entry again—-Now what an idea this must give you—of the utter vacancy of souls content to live inactive and sink without resistance with the body[.] This would be making a serious matter of it—I was laughing about it when I sat down to write to you and told the girls we seemed liked dancers that had wearied the musicians. . . .[35]

Such phrases, written as if from within the tomb, must have horrified him. "The utter vacancy of souls content to live thus inactive and sink without resistance with the body. . . . We seemed like dancers that had wearied the musicians." The imagery is of empty motion, continuing by inertia like dolls in a music box after the rhythm of life had ended.[36] Emerson must have felt that if there was to be any hope for Ellen, already fearful of "gliding" and "melting" away, he must take matters into his own hands. Setting aside his career and arranging for a substitute to take his pulpit, he went to New Concord in early August, probably with a plan. Ellen had frequently written of having taken short rides on her horse without ill effect. Together with Mrs. Kent, who came along, they arranged a twelve-day trip in two carriages through the mountains of New Hampshire.[37] Since Mrs. Kent had once planned to meet a crisis of health in two of her daughters—Margaret was "raising blood"—by projecting just such an extended trip to Massachusetts, Rhode Island, and Connecticut, she may have actually originated the idea.[38]

A ramble so organized would, in fact, provide the treatment of choice for consumptives: fresh air, passive exercise, and change of locale. It was a risk, but the alternative was the continued confinement in fine weather of a fundamentally high-spirited girl of seventeen, lonely for her fiancé and fearful of dying, to the imprisonment of what he thought of as her "hot little room." The trip was successful—so much so that it was followed by another on which they took her step-sister. By the end of this second journey, Ellen had spent nineteen days out of some six weeks traveling with her fiancé and family, and every sign suggested that the experience had been beneficial.

Not only her health had profited. Traveling together had cemented their relationship, and as Ellen wrote, "I think of you *all the time*. . . . We have tried a short journey together and like so well that we think of taking a *longer*—." Emerson and the Kents had reason

[35] Gregg, pp. 73–74.
[36] *L*, 1:279.
[37] *JMN*, 3:158–62; *L*, 1:275–79.
[38] William Kent, Sr., manuscript, NHHA.

to think that he could impart to Ellen the sources of his own strength and hopes of recovery, especially since not only she but apparently her mother and sister had also benefited from his regime. Plans for the wedding went ahead.[39]

During a brief separation at the end of August, a flurry of letters discussed their plans, strongly supported by Mrs. Kent. Ellen instructed her suitor to write formally to her stepfather, presumably about their nuptials. She also quashed, evidently after consulting with her parents, "the ugly *insurance* business," which appears to have been Waldo's wish to insure his life on her behalf.[40]

Ellen had a certain force of her own and also her mother's support, and she did not hesitate to coach Waldo in how to manage the older people around them: "Write to Pa just so as the scheme says—I think he will yeild and be glad to live with his better half on these terms." The "scheme" was the not inconsiderable proposition that the Kents should move to Boston for the winter, taking lodgings with Waldo and Ellen to manage the housekeeping and minimize Ellen's cares. Only people of means and considerable devotion could have rearranged their lives as the Kents did for Ellen.

With both so ill, one may wonder why the marriage went forward

[39] Gregg, pp. 86, 88–89.

[40] "I am glad we have done with the ugly *insurance* business—bad on every account— Mother never liked it I raved about it," Ellen wrote him, and she especially feared to alarm the executor of her father's estate, Pa (Pliny) Cutler who evidently had the power to put obstacles in their way (Gregg, pp. 91, 93, 94). Henry F. Pommer, *Emerson's First Marriage* (Carbondale: Southern Illinois University Press, 1967), p. 16, writes that the subject Ellen raved about was "probably her will," but he gives no evidence for this and does not discuss it further. It is not clear why "ugly *insurance* business" should need reinterpretation as "her will."

Allen, p. 143, expands this: "Almost any conjecture we might make on this mysterious debate would be unfavorable to Emerson, though possibly all he had done was to urge Ellen to make a will."

However, if insurance means insurance, the reverse might be true, and the incident might rather be interpreted favorably to Emerson. Ellen feared Mr. Cutler might have been made to "think you were doubting yourself and would be justified in doubting too. . . . whereas now the good man owns how fair our earthly prospects are" (Gregg, p. 94). Asking to have a will (not her word) made in one's own favor implies the opposite of self-doubt, and it does not sound like Emerson, who was not avaricious but was chronically self-doubting. Insuring (the word she used) one's life is for the benefit of another, but it might suggest the "doubting yourself" that Ellen feared Cutler would see in Emerson. Given his chronic and often fatal disease, moreover, it would have been a reasonable suggestion for him to make—though likely, as Ellen thought, to make an executor like Cutler think twice. Insurance would be an "ugly business" to Ellen because it would formally acknowledge the possibility of death that her marriage aimed at denying ("how fair our earthly prospects are").

at all. There were probably several reasons. They were of course very much in love, and Ellen was a petted and favored child who got her own way with her mother's assistance. More deeply, her parents must have reflected that if these two people could not marry each other because of their disease, then they could marry no one. The alternative for Ellen was continued life as a single but now unmarriageable woman in an isolated village. Given the widespread illness in her family, invalidism was likely, and death—hastened perhaps by depression and disappointment—more than possible. On the other hand, she was at least as likely to recover as Waldo's wife, especially in view of her parents' willingness to shoulder the young couple's homemaking duties. And her mother must have been deeply determined that Ellen should have a chance at happiness. She had buried one husband, and her son had died of consumption. Now her two daughters were coughing blood, and she herself was also sick. (She and Margaret in fact died of tuberculosis a few years after Ellen did.) Having lived with tragedy, Mrs. Kent had had plenty of time to think about life and death. Clearly she decided that a marriage of two loving people, even a brief one, would be better than none. Besides, no one could predict the length of anyone's life. Married, Ellen and Waldo could share the burden of their sickness and, with Emerson's careful husbandry, possibly prevail over it as he had managed his own condition.

They were aware of the risks involved, as Ellen's letters show, and communicated openly about the possibility that one of them might die, helping each other accept these fears. Ellen tried to answer this when she wrote, "The 'ever present thought' I can echo heartily. Few let them love ever so ardently and purely, have the happiness to lie down in the earth together." Five days before their wedding she wrote, "For my sake I would say—let us die together but the world is scantily furnished with such as thou art. . . . and . . . but stop—let us live together first—and then we will talk about the rest."[41]

Little is known of Emerson's state of mind in the period just before his marriage, apart from his commitment to Ellen and her health, for his letters to her are missing. But sometime during that summer he used a sheet of paper torn from his father's sermons, which still bore William Emerson's jottings, to inscribe the following poem, which he never published:

> I am not ⟨born⟩ I thank the gods
> Born a slave to priests or Kings

[41] Gregg, p. 96.

Both were bad but what's the odds
To be the thrall of thoughts or things
There's blood alike on crown ⟨cap⟩ & mitre
Pronounce who can which ⟨throne⟩ cap is whiter

⟨Ellen⟩

My humour poor & proud disdains
The monarch's crown & friar's frock
My blood shall warm my proper veins
Nor stain the altar or the block
This cup of life is not so shallow
That we have drained the best
That all the wine at once we swallow
And lees make all the rest.[42]

On the one hand, the sonnet is appropriate for a young man look-ing forward to a full life despite its cares and oppressions. The speaker is cocky: "What's the odds"—for he is in thrall to no one, while all secular and religious authority share in the blood guilt of oppression: "There's blood alike on crown & mitre / Pronounce who can which cap is whiter." In the octet he asserts that he will avoid guilt by abjuring both power and the moral glory of martyrdom; he will instead celebrate life, and drink the the full cup of wine that symbolizes both actual and eternal life and thus cannot be emptied by his act. Read in this fashion, the sonnet asserts reconciliation to life, and specifically clerical life, in which he will drink the wine of communion.

But there is also a darker subtext in the blood that stains the cap, the mitre, and the crown; the blood of his own veins that will *not* stain the block; and the blood of Christ that as priest he will sym-bolically create. It is no accident that Ellen's name is interjected after the sestet, for he surely was thinking of her when he thus celebrated his good fortune. He had seen her hemorrhages, as he perhaps had seen his father's. Marrying Ellen was a consummation of all he most desired. They were deeply in love. But the fear, mentioned only to be promptly denied, that in his good fortune "all the wine at once we swallow / And lees make all the rest," speaks for itself.

Entering his father's profession, he quite literally took a leaf from his book to write this poem. He had already assumed his roles as chaplain and priest and was soon to be a husband. The sonnet with its anger at the oppression of "priests and kings" suggests an inerad-

[42] *JMN*, 3:154.

icable quantum of guilt, of fear of his father's fate, and perhaps of retribution for his own success. He had written to his aunt in January 1829 that he feared he would have to pay a tax for his success; that irrational guilt seems to have hung on. Whatever may be one's interpretation, the literal consumption of his father's manuscript in the production of this poem suggests powerful currents of feeling that the student of Emerson's life cannot ignore.[43]

How to drink the cup of life while avoiding guilt was no small issue, now or in the future. It was a symbol central to his crisis in 1832 when his refusal to continue serving communion—"to eat or drink religiously"—led directly to his resignation from the pulpit. He might struggle to come to terms with social roles and to accept traditional symbolism for a time, as this poem suggests he wished to do. But in the long run, the materials he dealt with were laden for him with associations too full of unresolved conflicts for the acquiescence to endure fresh losses. He might marry Ellen, "so goblin like," and seem to his aunt to be heading for a life of conventional success. But the disjunctions and ambiguities of his poems suggest that the deepest currents of his nature would carry him elsewhere.

Five months after his marriage he wrote quite differently:

> And Ellen, when the greybeard years
> Have brought us to life's evening hour,
> And all the crowded Past appears
> A tiny scene of sun and shower,
> Then, if I read the page aright
> Where Hope, the soothsayer, reads our lot,
> Thyself shalt own the page was bright,
> Well that we loved, wo had we not.
>
> When Mirth is dumb and Flattery's fled,
> And mute thy music's dearest tone,
> When all but Love itself is dead,
> And all but deathless Reason gone.[44]

For lovers of Byron, as of each other, it was an appealing poem. One is struck, however—as in Ellen's letters—by its being written as if from the foot of the grave, for the speaker looks down the long

---

[43] This poem is written in a notebook bound into a spine that had been used by William Emerson for volume 39 of his sermons. The page, a loose one already containing William's jottings, was tipped into the spine at the end after the fresh leaves of the notebook had been inserted. See *JMN*, 3:119.

[44] *CW*, 9:94–95; cf. *JMN*, 3:181–82.

perspective of approaching time to imagine the point when both shall have died, "and mute thy music's dearest tone" (a complex line, perhaps the poem's best). On September 28, 1829, Waldo returned to Concord to be married. Charles was his best man. The ceremony took place in the Kent house, amid due festivities, on September 30, 1829. Ellen died a year and five months later.

Chapter 13

ADAM'S ANSWER

"Mortality makes us queasy. What have I to do with death?"

—RWE, 1832

EMERSON'S married life was even briefer than it seemed, for within six months Ellen had begun to fail. A springtime trip as far south as Philadelphia did not help, and by their first anniversary Emerson's prescient remark to Charles, made after her first loss of blood, that he feared she was "too lovely to live long" was being proved right.[1]

It would be desireable to know how Emerson experienced his marriage subjectively, but he left little direct evidence, and speculation would be unproductive. Letters between the couple do not survive, and his journals for this period are essentially notebooks for his sermons, impersonal and not spontaneous. Family correspondence tells of the couple's journeys and the household they set up with Ruth Emerson in Brookline, but Emerson's tone, while consistently affectionate and cheerful, is unrevealing. He may have felt fear and anguish, but he appears to have used his sensitivity and skill as a writer to render his voice unequivocal.

He had good reason to do so, for the brothers to whom he wrote, William and Edward, were poor and ill. It would have been wrong to share his burden with them. He helped them financially, as he now had a significant income, but Ellen, weak as she was, needed servants, and their combined resources supported a household of six persons, together with the costs of visiting relatives and of the two vehicles they maintained. (Emerson was for a period unable to walk because of a flare-up of his tubercular arthritis, now settled in the knee.) For his wife's sake also, he could not afford to yield to the darkness. His tone in referring to her was positive until the last months, when he either omitted comment on her condition or at last, two weeks before her death, told Edward she was even sicker than

---

[1] *L*, 1:259n.

he. Such silences were typical of his periods of private stress. One knows that they loved each other and feared for the future; further speculation would not clarify what must have been a period of increasingly tragic suffering.

Ellen died in February 1831 at the age of nineteen. Waldo's grief was extreme. He began the habit of walking every morning to her grave, a distance of several miles, an obsessive act that culminated when he recorded that he had "visited Ellen's tomb & opened the coffin," a bizarre act of which he said no more, but which suggests the depth of the regression to which his bereavement had plunged him. This indeed was shaking hands with death.[2] The intensity of his reaction suggests that this recapitulated for Emerson other, earlier losses: his older brother John Clarke, his father, his sister Mary Caroline. Each death in turn, but especially his father's, had left him less able to cope with such separation except by repetition, and it seems probable that both the extremity of his grief after Ellen's death and his withdrawal from the ministry in 1832 were conditioned to a considerable extent by his special vulnerability to such loss.

Illness, too, was reawakened by this period of stress. Throughout the summer of 1832, while he meditated giving up his pulpit, he was plagued by a diarrhea he could not shake, a symptom that tended to accompany indolent tuberculosis and that even long afterward would return, together with inflamed lungs and accompanying infirmity. (Charles, in fact, reported that Waldo suspected the diarrhea was related to an unnamed "worse thing."[3]) Waldo's prescription for himself that summer was long country walks and minimal stress—the process that had gradually restored his health in 1827–28.

With the inevitable focus on digestion came a return of the old anxiety about eating, and one is struck by the fact that when in September he announced to his parish that he must either cease to administer communion or leave the pulpit, the sacrament that had become the crux of all his other dissatisfactions with his role in the church involved eating. The sharing of food symbolically representing a dead person, however holy the ritual, now seemed repellent to him.

His "Lord's Supper" sermon judiciously and persuasively summed up historical and logical objections, and he was at pains there to stress that Jesus's words did not name the bread and wine

[2] Haskins, p. 112; *JMN*, 4:7.
[3] *L*, 1:353n.

as being in any way transformed into something else. But in a letter
to Mary he put his position more succinctly and pungently: "I remain of the same mind not prepared to eat or drink religiously, tho'
it seems a small thing, and seeing no middle way, I apprehend a
separation." One hears not only echoes of "Here I stand, I can do no
other"—so lacking from the deliberately unprovocative sermon he
gave the next month but in fact quoted in his journal[4]—but also his
sense that appetite was in some fundamental way opposed to religion
and the spiritual life, and that their conjunction was repellent. As he
put it in his explanatory homily, the symbolic act was "every way
agreeable to an Eastern mind [but] disagreeable to my own feelings."

To a mind trained to see its own hunger as a source of shame and,
conversely, the ability to live with it unsatisfied as evidence of moral
strength, the connection drawn by ritual between faith and appetite
might well seem obscene. At this time of stress, communion was
both intellectually and viscerally repugnant to Emerson. It was "a
painful impediment. To eat bread is one thing; to love the precepts
of Christ . . . is quite another." His language resounds with disgust;
he has tried to "deaden this repulsion," it is "painful . . . foreign . . .
unsuited" and Eastern. It is sensual, a vestige of middle eastern Se-
mitic cultures, not of what Haskins called "the best methods of a
well-ordered New England home." His parishioners would have understood this appeal, for they shared his descent from generations of
puritanical child-rearing practices, and many of their mothers like
his own had practiced "wise economy," fed their children on bread
and milk, reproved their talk of roast beef dinners, and covered their
infant fingers with mittens designed to end the gratification of suck-
ing.[5]

Above all, what Emerson sought at this time was a sense of inner
change. Leaving the pulpit was only one step in a continuum he
called "the growth of the true self." What drove him forward was the
need to shatter old ways of thinking, old habits and thoughts now
perceived as obsessive and enslaving. Within a year of his morning
pilgrimages to Ellen's grave he wrote instead: "Think of living. . . .
Don't tell me to get ready to die. . . . The only preparation I can
make is by fulfilling my present duties. This is the everlasting life.
To think of mortality makes us queasy. What have I to do with
death?"[6]

[4] L, 1:354; JMN, 4:53.
[5] "Lord's Supper," CW, 11:19.
[6] JMN, 4:40–41.

THAT PROCESS got underway during Emerson's nine-month trip to Italy, France, and England in 1832–33. The voyage to and through Italy lasted almost three times as long as the three months Emerson spent in France and England, but scholars have stressed the end of his journey, when he met a variety of famous men. It is likely, however, that the real turning point for Emerson came in the long months of surprise and thought he experienced before he crossed the Alps.[7] Meaning at first to visit Edward in Puerto Rico, Emerson, following some deep leading, almost literally at the last moment instead booked passage on a different ship, and sailed to see the "Wide World," as he had named it in his early journals.

What seemed like an impulse sprang actually from the deepest kind of aim. Shortly before embarking, he had described the gulf between his public and private experience:

> And then will our true heaven be entered, when we have learned to be the same manner of person to others that we are alone, say the same things to them, we think alone. [A vain and awkward man is embarrassed and ungracious in the presence of others.] The reason is, himself is a peppercorn & his relations to other people are the whole world in his imagination. The only remedy must be from the growth of his true self.[8]

The freedom to utter publicly what was most private and important was crucial to the success of his work; achieving that freedom was the true agenda of his voyage.

His mood as he crossed the sea was peaceful and reflective. His health began to improve almost at once, despite a rough crossing, for the distance the sea placed between himself and the sources of stress always gave him ease. He found ways to be alone while confined with other people. "I rose at sunrise and under the lee of the spencer sheet had a solitary thoughtful hour," he wrote, "all right thought is devout." As they sailed south and east, the weather improved and with it his mood: "We have sauntered all this calm day at one or two knots the hour & nobody on board well pleased but I. And why should I be pleased? . . . I will be pleased though I do not deserve it."[9]

He began the trip with a true American swagger and the old anxiety about the weight of history. As they coasted through the Mediterranean, he addressed Europe impertinently as the "Place of His-

[7] See Evelyn Barish and Evelyn Hofer, *Emerson in Italy* (New York: Henry Holt, 1989).
[8] *JMN*, 4:66.
[9] *JMN*, 4:104, 105.

tory," a "slumberous old giant" who could not bestir himself in
these, his "chair days." "Sleep on old Sire," Emerson wrote in his
journal "[while] we your poor spawn thrust our inquisitive eyes into
your towns and towers and keeping rooms. Here come we and mean
to be welcome. So be good now, clever old gentleman."[10] His tone
expressed juvenile, cocky aggression as he thrust old Europe back
into his fireside chair. This, however, was only a temporary defense;
it turned into delight almost as soon as he reached port.

He arrived first in Malta, "the little end" of Europe, where American ships often called first on Mediterranean voyages. After a few
weeks of virtual incarceration in quarantine, he sailed to Sicily and
became at once conscious that he trod where Dis had stamped his
foot and the classical battles of history had been fought. All of it
stimulated and pleased him, and the openness of his attitude made
him a willing student and lover of what he saw. It was common for
most American travelers to be critical, even contemptuous of things
Italian, especially in religious matters. Emerson by contrast was an
immediate enthusiast.[11] His attitude was set in Malta at the great co-
cathedral of St. John:

> I yielded me joyfully to the religious impression of holy texts &
> fine paintings and this soothfast faith though of women & chil-
> dren. How beautiful to have the church always open, so that
> every tired wayfaring man may come in & be soothed by all that
> art can suggest of a better world when he is weary with this. I
> hope they will carve & paint & inscribe the walls of our
> churches in New England before this century.[12]

The cathedrals exhilarated him and put into perspective the
"meanness" of New England churches: "How could any body who
had been in a catholic church, devise such a deformity as a pew?" He
saw the serenity and attractive austerity of the lives of the "handsome
and courteous" barefoot monks, one of whom called offering hospitality, which Emerson accepted with gratitude but an observant eye.
Their whipcords hung by their beds, and the promise of "perpetual
indulgence for the living and the dead" inscribed over a church door
seemed to him "almost too frank, may it please your holiness." But
"I hardly pass a monastery but I ask them on what terms they will
receive me for life." He liked every religious man he encountered,
and particularly the pope, whose audiences he attended and whose

[10] JMN, 4:104, 109.
[11] JMN, 4:116; Paul Baker, The Fortunate Pilgrims: Americans In Italy 1800–1860
(Cambridge, Mass.: Harvard Univ. Press, 1964).
[12] JMN, 4:117.

ritual processions at the Vatican, accompanied by glorious music, he found beautiful and moving.[13]

He quickly developed a good eye for art, noticing in Venice, for example, that Canova in a famous statue had "seated Madame Bonaparte in a chair with the same beautiful form I admired in the Caffè at Padua." The Caffè, a universally admired building only two years old, was the work of Pedrocchi and furnished in the same Directoire style that governed Canova.[14] By his own admission he "haunted" the Vatican and its vast art collections. He was guided by both Goethe (whose *Italienische Reise* accompanied him) and Byron, whose *Childe Harold* shaped much of his political and artistic perceptions and which he quoted continually.

In this place of history, Emerson was aware that his own history was weighted with the double freight that included Ellen's loss. As he traveled it became easier to come to terms with it. In February when he reached Catania, he sketched out a poem mediated by her memory. Its language suggests that he was ceasing to see the past as an impregnable storehouse locked against him of all goodness and power, and that he was coming to feel instead a kind of beneficent flux between past and present, with each day capable of bringing its own revelation and sublimity.

> We are what we are made & every following day
> Is the Creator of our human mould
> Not less than was the first. God
> Gilds a few points in each several life
> And every varied leaf is sketched each with a new design
> A spot of purple & a streak of brown
> . . . .
> Not many men I suppose see any pleasure in
> The fogs of close low ⟨woods⟩ pine woods in a river
> town Yet unto me not star's magnificence
> . . . nor Rome
> nor Paris. . . .
> hath such a
> soul a resurrection of the happy past
> As comes to me when I see the morning in
> such low moist roadside where blue violets peep [?]
> as [?] magic remembrances out of the black loam[15]

[13] *JMN*, 4:117, 125; *L*, 1:365, 367.
[14] *JMN*, 4:184.
[15] *JMN*, 4:130.

The "black loam" is the earth shed off from Aetna, which rises snow-covered all year over Catania and much of southern Sicily. This Wordsworthian poem is one of reconciliation with the meaning of the present moment, for its humble, private, and particular beauties, celebrating the return of the capacity for love that comes with the return of spring. The memory of Ellen is alluded to indirectly through the imagery of violets, but directly invoked in the two lines he added later at Naples. She was still to him an exquisite flower, but violets bloom and wither early in spring. His choice of image suggests he had accepted the reality of her brief life and early death. With this reconciliation came new poise; as he traveled, other peoples' cultures and great cities lost their power of erasure and seemed less to be thrust backward and chaired, more to be heard and consulted.

Emerson continued to meditate on and make more deeply his own the vision reflected in this unfinished poem; later in the month when he reached Naples he both revised the poem and had an experience of which he wrote a year later: "Remember the Sunday morning in Naples, when I said, 'This moment is the truest vision, the best spectacle I have seen amid all the wonder[,] and this moment, this vision, I might have had in my own closet in Boston.' "[16] That morning was probably March 24, 1833, when he had heard "an insipid and inane" sermon and had gone back to his hotel, angry as always at bad preaching, but also suddenly seeing how "we are always beginning to live, how perfectly practicable at all times is the sublime part of life, the high hours, for which all the rest are given."[17]

He had said it better in the poem he began in Catania. Of that city he had written: "Town of lava of earthquakes. The mountain is at once a monument and a warning. Houses are built, streets paved with lava; it is polished in the altars of the churches. Huge black rocks of it line the shore, & the white surf breaks over them."[18] The warning was to be read in the face of death, the always-smoking Aetna; the monument lay scattered everywhere in the black, basaltic stones, mute testimony of the many it had slaughtered. The message was to turn instead, as the Italians did, to life.

HE WAS not alone on his journey, for as he traveled he met several young American artists with whom he shared lodgings and travel

[16] *JMN*, 4:320.
[17] *JMN*, 4:148.
[18] *JMN*, 4:130.

arrangements and from whose knowledge of art he profited. He chose their company over that of more the respectable, bourgeois travelers with whom he began his trip. The latter were "such as did not help me." In the company of artists he "haunted" the Vatican and other places until in his dreams he wandered "amidst statues & fountains, and last night was introduced to Lord Byron!" In that month of intense experience his ideas developed, and he articulated them so freely that one man he met, a Philadelphian with whom he shared a coach for some weeks, later reported that Emerson's "pantheistic ideas" had so affected him that they had unsettled his religious faith.[19]

With his new friends Emerson explored Italy in a spirit of increasing exhilaration, and found Rome a revelation with its many-layered history literally laid open. The very flowerpots, he noticed, stood on "blocks made of the capitals of old columns, turned upside down," and the foundations of the houses incorporated fragments of old temples. He became an insatiable sightseer; "Much will have more," he said, eager for everything, hastening from the central icons of early nineteenth-century art—the Laocoön, Raphael's *Transfiguration*, and Michelangelo's *Moses* among many others—to less-known works and places. (In Bologna he observed the celebrated Hercules, a baroque work in which a heroic, beautiful, and naked male figure sits in twisted posture over a fountain supported by four nymphs, each pressing her breasts upward so that the viewer expects but does not find them to be gushing. The mildly erotic effect produced his comically repressed comment, "Good enough—but why so famous?" The purer and less playful representations of female beauty in the Medici and Canova Venuses, however, received his profound admiration.)[20]

Generally, first-time travelers in Italy were content to admire the well-known set pieces of classical and Renaissance art, rarely straying beyond received opinion. Emerson of course began with these works, but he also pursued and trusted his own judgment. He was uniquely moved by two less-noticed works: one a painting by Andrea Sacchi of *The Vision of St. Romoaldo*, the other the head of "Justice" on the tomb of Paul III in the Vatican by William de la Porta, whose design was then attributed to Michelangelo.[21] "One is

[19] *L*, 1:375; *JMN*, 4:159; W.S.W. Ruschenberger, *A Sketch in the Life of Thomas Stewardson, M. D.* (Philadelphia, 1833), p. 8.

[20] *JMN*, 4:160, 150, 180–81, 168.

[21] Ann Sutherland Harris, *Andrea Sacchi* (Princeton, N.J.: Princeton University Press, 1977), p. 23. All the works admired by Emerson were also praised by Reynolds, who had

greater for knowing that such forms can be," Emerson wrote, as well as, "where in the Universe is the archetype from which the Artist drew this sweetness & grace? There is a heaven. . . . I shall remember it all my life." These works repay examination, for with striking similarity the faces of both express a singular and attractive remoteness from the orginary world. Each seems to be looking inward, contemplating something of extraordinary beauty that has been taken within to meditate upon.[22]

The intensity of Emerson's response suggests the fervor with which he was searching for what the art seemed to represent. He had been conscious as he traveled that he had not yet found his voice. For all his years of sometimes compulsive writing, "the thing set down in words is not affirmed," he had now realized, and the affirming voice was his craving. He wanted not merely to see the sights, but to see with what he called "the Anointed Eye," the seer's eye.[23] He was learning, that spring of his thirtieth year, that the vision he sought would come to him in proportion to his focusing on life and accepting what Italy had to teach him.

In Florence for a month he met Walter Savage Landor, the first of the literary figures he sought out on this journey. Their visits were pleasant, but Emerson was disappointed in the man. He was offended—as he wrote in an essay published some years later—by Landor's "freaks" and "cold and gratuitous" use of lewd language. As he traveled he was still looking for a prophetic guide, a figure external to himself, and he articulated his sense of need repeatedly: "My great want is the very one I apprehended when at home, that I never meet with men that are great or interesting. There are such everywhere . . . but a traveller . . . never learns even their names." And, "I would give all Rome for one man such as were fit to walk here, and could feel and impart the sentiment of the place. That wise man whom everywhere I seek here I hunger and thirst after."[24] To be unfulfilled spiritually was to be hungry—still an unacceptable condition.

Toward the end of his five months in Italy, as he was leaving Florence, Emerson noted that he had climbed up into a colossal statue of Father Apennine: "I got up into his neck & head & looked out of his

been instrumental in forming Anglo-Saxon taste. Sacchi was also praised by Sir Joshua Reynolds, *Discourses [on Art] Delivered to the Students of the Royal Academy*, ed. Roger Fry (London: Sealy & Co., 1905), 2:439.

[22] *JMN*, 4:159–60; *L*, 1:379.

[23] *JMN*, 4:106, 113.

[24] *JMN*, 4:173–75; "Walter Savage Landor," *CW*, 12:337–49; *L*, 1:371, 374.

ear. Fine mountain scenery to the frontier of the Roman state."[25] The moment, despite his conscious humor, suggests a condition one might call traveler's synaesthesia, sought for the same state of heightened perception as poetic synaesthesia produces. Yet it is also an image of Gulliver among the Brobdingnags. His language suggests a testing of the limits, a marking of the frontiers of his vision. Looking out of the giant's ear he was comically small, but only so in relation to a colossus of sixty feet, sited atop one of the windiest and highest ridges in the region.

The more articulately he searched for the "wise man," the closer he was to realizing that no such figure would cross his path. Envisioning the teacher he needed, however, led Emerson closer to incorporating him, and eventually he knew that the guidance he longed for would proceed only from his own unaided vision. He had now seen "great, great Rome" and felt not intimidated but enlarged by it. In Florence also, walking up the piazza of Santa Croce, "I feel as if it were not a Florentine no nor an European church but a church built by & for the human race. I feel equally at home within its walls as the Grand duke, so *hospitably* sound to me the names of its mighty dead. Buonaroti & Galileo [entombed there] live for us all."[26] He had come seeking the "growth of the true self": clearly, that had begun.

EMERSON left Italy in early June aiming for England and its literary men, but he stopped in Paris for a month. He found the city expensive, busy, and sexually immoral, but he profited intellectually there significantly, for it helped him crystallize ideas that were the result of his long and silent years of thought. This occurred when he visited the Jardin des Plantes and studied the "Cabinet of Natural History," an exhibition arranged by the botanist Jussieu, based on the work of Cuvier. It was a revelation so exciting that it struck him like a consummation: "It . . . makes the visiter as calm & genial as a bridegroom. The limits of the possible are enlarged, & the real is stranger than the imaginary." Stretched out in all their beauty were displays of wonderful birds, shells, blocks of minerals: "quartz, native gold in all its forms of crystallization, threads, plates, crystals, dust; & silver black as from fire. Ah, said I, this is philanthropy, wisdom, taste—to form a Cabinet of natural history."[27]

[25] *JMN*, 4:180.
[26] *JMN*, 4:175.
[27] *JMN*, 4:198–99.

He had found an objective correlative of his own thought. He had long been looking for evidence of those occult ties between humans and nature that Madame de Staël had said once existed, those "more than Eleusinian mysteries" to which he had referred in his 1821 essay. In 1832 he had already concluded that study of the natural world—whether of stars or sea shells—would support his faith where biblical miracles would not. Reflecting on the writings of the naturalist James Drummond he had written, "Not a white spot but is a lump of Suns, the roe, the milt of light and life. Who can be a Calvinist or who an Atheist? God has opened this knowledge to us to correct our theology & educate the mind."[28]

With ground so prepared, what Emerson saw in Paris was sure to prove fruitful. Now he saw "not a form so grotesque, so savage, nor so beautiful but it is an expression of some property inherent in man the observer, an occult relation between the very scorpions and man. I feel the centipede in me—cayman, carp, eagle, and fox. I am moved by strange sympathies, I say continually, 'I will be a naturalist.' "[29]

In these cabinets of natural history organized by the human hand he saw factual evidence of divine order, an order that the long but random catalogue of human events, revealed in its human history, had denied him. When Emerson said, "I will be a naturalist," it was a promise he meant to and did keep, for to him that profession was not the actual collection of tangible objects—on the contrary, he deliberately collected nothing. For Emerson to be a naturalist meant meditation on the meaning, the moral taxonomy of nature. To a man in search of religious insights, this was at last a fit subject for thought, a promising field.[30]

What he saw in Paris did not begin, but clearly recapitulated, the long process of reconciling himself with the nature that Mary had so long mediated with only partial success. The woods he had found "not half poetical enough" when guided only by the romantic impulse (not poetical enough because they yielded no insights, only pleasures) he could now begin to explore, seeking in them his spiritual home.

This reconciliation also helped him to let go the burden of history, to shuck it from his shoulders. History, theology, and Europe had long been one thing to him, together constituting the dead weight

[28] *JMN*, 4:24.

[29] *JMN*, 4:199–200. F. O. Matthiessen, *American Renaissance* (Oxford: Oxford University Press, 1941), p. 15, credits Bliss Perry with first noticing the passage. See also Rusk, pp. 187–89.

[30] *L*, 1:372.

of the past that had tyrannized modern thought but now offered it nothing except the end-stopped misery of millennial expectations. To see in the material world such beautiful evidence of order and development implied something better. The lessons of history were at best chaotic and at worse so bloody and cruel that they tended to induce either skepticism or total unbelief. This evidence of God's mind organizing tangible reality was a relief, for it suggested instead that His lessons were open-ended.

EMERSON was still occasionally conscious of his personal deficits and could comment with eloquent misery: "Sometimes I would hide myself in the dens of the hills, in the thickets of an obscure country town, I am so vexed and chagrined with myself,—with my weakness, with my guilt." But such moods were ebbing, and it was more common to feel that "we grow wiser by the day and by the hour," as he wrote to Charles.[31] In London in July, just before the meetings with the several literary lions for which his trip is best known, Emerson declared his readiness to take them on. While still in France he had considered:

> the singular position of the American traveller in Italy. It is like that of a being of another planet who invisibly visits the earth. He is a protected ⟨seer⟩ witness. He sees what is that boasted liberty of manners—free of all puritan starch—& sees what it is worth—how surely it pays its tax. He comes a freeman among slaves. . . . He is not now to be answered any longer in his earnest assertions of moral truth by the condescending explanation that these are his prejudices of country & education. He has seen how they hold true through all the most violent contrasts of condition & character.[32]

Compared to the Emerson who strolled the beach in St. Augustine, this persona is far more clearly defined, a "witness" who comes not to ask but to commune, observe, and even judge. His borders seem more firm, less permeable, and his region is not so much intertidal as airborne, stratospheric. For good or for ill, Emerson had also accepted on this trip his "puritan starch." The morals, specifically the sexual mores, of the Italians and French did not persuade him that theirs was a superior mode of life. He might perceive New En-

[31] *JMN*, 4:74; *L*, 1:372.
[32] *JMN*, 4:78.

gland manners and morals with a more sophisticated irony, but he accepted his framework of moral reference with clarity. "We are what we are made," he had written in Catania; with that acceptance, he could go on to other matters.

His encounter in Florence with Landor had been interesting but not profound. The meetings with the aging Wordsworth and Coleridge he reported with a mixture of respect and sardonic humor, for each had well-settled opinions and public roles to express; dialogue was not to their purpose. Emerson came away glad he had met them, but not impressed. Wordsworth had appeared an elderly man in "goggles," who recited his poetry and thought that "schools do no good . . . Sin, sin is what he fears." The interview with Coleridge was more substantial, but also comical:

> He burst into a long & indignant declamation upon the folly & ignorance of Unitarianism[,] its high unreasonableness & took up B[isho]p Waterland which lay (laid there I think for the occasion) upon the table & read to me with great vehemence . . . notes writ by him[self] . . . As soon as he stopped a second to take breath, I remarked to him that it would be cowardly in me, after this, not to inform him that I was an Unitarian . . . Yes, he said, I supposed so[,] & continued as before.[33]

Only the last, Thomas Carlyle, was of his generation, and only he seemed authentic to Emerson. By the end of his trip Emerson had spent hours with England's chief romantic poets, and he judged them very coolly.

> Many things I owe to the sight of these men. I shall judge more justly, less timidly, of wise men forevermore. To be sure not one of these is a mind of the very first class, but what the intercourse with each of these suggests is true of intercourse with better men, that they never *fill the ear*,—fill the mind—no, it is an *idealized* portrait which always we draw of them.

Right or wrong, his judgment was firm: "Not one of these is a mind of the very first class. Especially are they deficient all these four—in different degrees, but all deficient—in sight into religious truth."[34] He loved Carlyle, felt him "amiable," but with these dismissive words he was glad his traveling was done. He had felt like a "protected witness" or seer, a "being from another planet" invisibly vis-

33 *JMN*, 4:222, 408, 409.
34 *JMN*, 4:79.

iting the earth. Now he was ready to return and make use of his new
knowledge.

A FEW DAYS later he was at sea, and ideas held in reserve while
traveling were surfacing. "I like my book about nature," he wrote
briefly, "& wish I knew how & where I ought to live."[35] This quiet
remark belies the significance of the moment as he mentally began
the book that was to help shape his culture. The practical questions
resolved themselves after his return as he preached by invitation in
different pulpits and finally, a year later, settled into Concord and
began work on his first book. It is not within the scope of this discussion to examine his early works in detail, but certain points worth
noting about their origin and appeal are now clear.

One of these is that *Nature* is a manifesto, especially in its often-
quoted and powerful opening pages, that bases itself on rejection of
two elements prominent in Emerson's experience: death and history.
Because his writings are always interwoven with assertions of trust,
readers tend to see Emerson as he would have them see him: cheerful, optimistic, content to float effortlessly on his sea of faith.[36] But
that was one mood only, one-half at best of the impulse of his "peculiarly faithless faith," as Harold Bloom has called it. Its opening
tone is actually that of a rebel, an angry man long held down who
has at last found his voice and his point of attack. "Our age is retro-
spective," the famous opening begins:

> It builds the sepulchres of the fathers. It writes biographies, his-
> tories, and criticism. The foregoing generations beheld God
> and nature face to face; we, through their eyes. Why should not
> we also enjoy an original relation to the universe? Why should
> not we have a poetry and philosophy of insight and not of tra-
> dition, and a religion by revelation to us, and not the history of
> theirs?[37]

Readers tend to focus on the stunning demand for an "original
relation to the universe," but the weight of this assertion rests on its
conviction of being justified—with the certainty of the convert—in
its aggression toward an enemy that is now known and must be
swept aside, that cast of mind that looks backward because it has
been appropriated by the weight of the past: history itself.

[35] *JMN*, 4:237.
[36] "Over-Soul," *CW*, 2:283.
[37] *CW*, 1:3.

"Why should we grope among the dry bones of the past or put the living generation into masquerade out of its faded wardrobe?" These were real questions for Emerson, not metaphors. He had literally opened a sepulchre, his wife's coffin, and gazed, perhaps even "groped" at the bones it contained. Once past that extraordinary act, Emerson must have wondered at himself. His language suggests that he looked back at that obsessive need with an enormous desire to distance himself from every internal process that had produced it. He had also dismembered his father's manuscript volumes and literally inscribed himself on the very pages of his father's writing. And for much of his life, time and vital force had been wasted imagining magical powers and assuming that wisdom and insight were locked in the graves of those who had gone before and would not share their secrets. "We must pick no locks," he was to say later. But for years he had sanded his fingertips and looked at the past with greedy eyes, for like his aunt's chest of "almanacks," it contained what he needed to thrive.

By the mid-1830s he understood that it was he who had worshipped at a false shrine. Wrong traditions, wrongful authority, wrong ideas had held him back: "Let us demand our own works and laws and worship." This is in part the anger of revolt, of the man kept out of his heritage and determined to claim it, not only for himself but for others. What he wanted, however, was neither a share of that repressive power nor a redistribution of the wealth of the past, but denial of its currency. All the accumulated works of humanity he defined as mere "art"—and then dismissed: "His operations taken together are so insignificant, a little chipping, baking, patching and washing." Sweep them away, like so many shards, and a naked unaccommodated man was left, alone with himself and nature.[38]

BUT the destructive impulse was only a small portion of Emerson's message. It was his passionate understanding of and desire to communicate what was life and what was death that made his language powerful; it was his urgent need to teach how to distinguish between them that moved his audience. Emerson is not known for speaking of death or fear in his writings—quite the contrary—and of course to have done so directly or in any orthodox fashion would have been anathema to him. It was precisely Calvinism's manipulative use of these issues that had in the early 1830s crystallized his anger against

[38] *Nature, CW,* 1:5.

its doctrines. By the end of the decade, Emerson would become a magnet in Concord, and his second wife would complain at the quantity of young rebels she found at her door and table, shoeless and bearded, who partook of their hospitality while turning up their noses at the butter. These "come-outers" did not flock to Emerson because he projected an image of sweet mildness, but because his criticism expressed their own discontent with the social norms and social repression. Nor did he have to speak directly of anxiety or mortality for them to understand that he had faced the same abysses as they and had found a way to get across them.

He offered a choice, making clear and simple the nature of the divergent paths before them. What he urged was the absolute necessity of choosing to live now, not later, and at almost any risk; this became the single most fundamental message of Emerson's early writings, so pervasive—and persuasive—that it could supercede other demands for logical or thematic structure. He cast the message in his consistent imagery of solid earth and uncertain abyss, as here in "The American Scholar": "We know whose words are loaded with life, and whose not . . . I run eagerly into this resounding tumult. I grasp the hands of those next me, and take my place in the ring to suffer and to work, taught by an instinct that so shall the dumb abyss be vocal with speech."[39]

"The dumb abyss" had been made vocal with speech by Uilsa, many years before, but at too frightening a price. Now that he had met its terrors, he could speak from the other side. To be alive meant to be able to grow, and he was everywhere concerned with growth: "So much only of life as I know by experience, so much of the wilderness have I vanquished and planted, or so far have I extended my being, my dominion."[40]

EMERSON later lectured on "The Philosophy of History" and published "History" as an essay; he had been engaged with the subject for many years. But he was not a philosopher of history. It might be more accurate to think of him as an early theorist or observer of the ego, a student of what makes the soul or psyche whole, how it grows, and what thwarts and baffles it—a forerunner of such ego psychologists as D. W. Winnicott and Erik Erikson.

Like the thinkers who came after him, Emerson advocated seeing

[39] *CW*, 1:105, 95.
[40] *CW*, 1:95.

over repressing. More, not less sight was needed, and courage to look. He condemned those afraid to live in this "age of Introversion" for their desire to avoid vision and new consciousness: "Sight is the last thing to be pitied." Theirs was "the discontent of the literary class . . . that they find themselves not in the state of mind of their fathers, and regret the coming state as untried; as a boy dreads the water before he has learned that he can swim." Once past fear of the water—induced by fear of the father—one will swim; once past the fear of blindness—another real, not metaphorical experience—one will have that insight.[41]

When he called, "Give me insight into today, and you may have the antique and future worlds" he was adverting not to others' failings, but to his own earlier longing for just such other secret worlds; his language has the rebounding energy of the coiled spring. And when he catalogs what one would really "know the meaning of—the meal in the firkin, the milk in the pan; the ballad in the street; the news of the boat; the glance of the eye; the form and the gait of the body"—he is giving images whose power comes from their very commonality and openness, symbols of that true mystery which lies not in esoteric but in universal things, accessible and sensuous— food barely taken from nature, bodies one can hear, see, touch.[42]

Similarly, the Harvard Divinity School address turned on the same passionate dichotomy, cutting to the core of the ethical choices facing his audience. What was alive was good; what was frozen or dead was evil, precisely because it was dead. Evil did not rest in specific wrong opinions, or even acts; it was not the monster snake he had once imagined, nor was it hubris or daring, romantic defiance. On the contrary, "Good is positive. Evil is merely privative, not absolute; it is like cold, which is the privation of heat. All evil is so much death or nonentity."

This definition of evil has been debated over the years because of its unorthodoxy and because to common sense it seems to deny reality to evil in the world. But it should now be possible to understand how complexly Emerson came to hold this view, and how much was left unsaid. He was not ignorant of the problem of evil— on the contrary, it had consumed his attention, paralyzing him for years. But his interest in it had become pragmatic rather than purely philosophical. He wished to know how to advocate right action, and

41 *CW*, 1:109–10.
42 *CW*, 1:111, 112.

he resolved the problem of theodicy not so much by denial as by deliberate simplification.

His real enemy lay within the self. The answer to passivity and depression was to find the glass half full, not half empty. The stoicism he had once adopted lacked creative power. Life was too serious a struggle to grant the opposing side even a hearing; his formulation was an ethical imperative designed to indicate that one must act. He equated evil with death to demonstrate that shrinking from commitment and life meant moving toward death, being enwrapped in its chill. Active error might be corrected, but sluggish despair and anomie could not be quickened.

Out of the opposite tradition had come preachers like Barzillai Frost, merely "spectral."[43] It was the spectrality of such men and teachings that always aroused Emerson's rage, the sense he intuited of their being haunted by surrender to non-being. Summing up the causes of a decaying church with its wasting unbelief, he said, "Society lives to trifles, and when men die we do not mention them."[44] In the society he sketched, irreparable loss was followed not by grief or rage, but by repression, silence, and the cold superficiality that masks despair. "When men die we do not mention them." So it had been, he thought, in his own family after his father's death. For all the silence around him—perhaps because of it—he now believed that such silence was inimical to all vital force. The violent tone of liberation in the most contemporary sense of the term is always surprising in Emerson when one considers both his outwardly conventional life and the culture from which he sprang, but it seems evident that long and deep thought about what he had both learned and mislearned in his own life were behind the propulsive force of such preaching.

He accepted entirely the repressive proprieties of his day on the subject of sexuality, and said virtually nothing about it. But on subjects that until very recently have been and remain a modern topic of repression, death and what is called the death wish, he was profoundly sophisticated. A great part of the energy of his early writings is devoted to defining, diagnosing, and prescribing against it. There were different emphases and occasions for the message but the shape of the statement held clear: recognize that life is experienced only through action, through which alone we learn who we are, what we

[43] CW, 1:137–38.
[44] CW, 1:143.

want, and what we can do. Imitating good models teaches nothing—go alone.

He was urgent because he understood what few do: that most people do not want, or are not able to wish wholeheartedly to live, or to be fully alive. They do not think they deserve it, or have the right to such power. Emerson shared with them his concrete knowledge of a subject few others would or could touch upon, that "divided and rebel mind," that ambivalence or self-distrust that governs "because our arithmetic has computed the strength and means opposed to our purpose." He asked, "Why should you keep your head over your shoulder? Why drag about this corpse of your memory, lest you contradict somewhat you have stated in this or that public place?"[45]

Hence history must also be discarded because its apparent lessons must be inauthentic. There is, properly speaking, no history, only biography. For if there was one thing Emerson had learned from his own study of history, it was that it had no pattern of meaning. Every mind must know the whole lesson for itself, must go over the whole ground. One cannot *learn* history: one can understand the past only to the extent one understands oneself. What one learns from others are only facts, arranged by some other mind. Emerson does not recommend that one should not read, or not read history, but that to be a good reader, one must be a creator—in fact, a prophet: "When the voice of a prophet out of the deeps of antiquity merely echoes to him a sentiment of his infancy, a prayer of his youth, he then pierces to the truth through all the confusion of tradition and the caricature of institutions."[46] Clearly by the late 1830s, Emerson felt that the prophet's "anointed eye" and affirming voice had become his own.

He has been criticized, and not without justice, for his ahistoricism. But if Emerson's influence tends in this direction, he did not write out of a merely "flaccid," or ignorant, or too cheerful optimism.[47] If anything, it was because he had long despaired of the

---

[45] "Self-Reliance," *CW*, 2:48, 57.

[46] "History," *CW*, 2:27.

[47] See Sacvan Bercovitch, *The Puritan Origins of the American Self* (New Haven, Conn.: Yale University Press, 1975), pp. 161, 173, and passim; cited hereafter as Bercovitch. He criticizes in Emerson "a teleology that eliminated the tension between process and fulfillment" and a rhetoric that "annihilated division," and "enabled him to dissolve all differences between history and the self." Elsewhere, Bercovitch chastises Emerson and other "classic" American writers for "uphold[ing] America even while they "most bitterly assailed their society" (p. 191 and chap. 6) remaining "middle-class," and wishing to cure its diseases rather than to revise its basic tenets and "change the profit system" (p. 187). It is true that Emerson identified with America and thought it possible to chastise

historical schemes he had studied and saw them as reducing humanity to alienation and thing-ness that he turned against history. A vision of social reformation based on cataclysmic change of external
forms would have not have seemed persuasive to him. "Montaigne,
or The Skeptic," best expresses his mature and very dark vision of
the nature of progress.

The early death of Emerson's father was a tragedy, and the years
of attention it absorbed in fantasy and ambivalence could have been
wasted. But it forced him to think deeper; he made it a seed; it made
him a seeker. He so named himself, in fact, when he wrote to Mary
that "I belong to the good sect of the Seekers."[48] Emotionally he had
the sense all his life that something was missing, and in consequence
he was more than usually open to new and undogmatic ideas. To be
a seeker was for him more comfortable than to be complacent in a
faith. In his youth such a stance led him to pursue the secrets he
projected onto the supernatural. Later he looked in history. But a
seeker by definition is one who is not satisfied, who has not found
and may never find the object of desire. Emerson's power—if not his
genius—arose from his intellectual courage in grasping and accepting the unknowableness of the matters that interested him most.

He was intensely conscious of living at the beginning of a new age.
The scion of New England's oldest intellectual traditions, his rejection of the past made him both a paradox and an avatar of an expand-
ing nation who was to be peculiarly useful to generations of Americans yet to reach their new country's shores. He made a place for
himself in that age but lived on the margin of things, twelve miles
from Boston in the village of Concord, from which he could maintain
his critical stance. By the 1850s, he had made himself a "stink in the
nostrils" of Brahmin Boston, as his younger friend the English poet
Arthur Hugh Clough put it.[49] The dichotomy, the choices that he
laid before his audiences, never fully disappeared as the fundamental
element of his thought, although the colors by which the choices
were seen altered as Emerson grew older and himself changed.
Greater irony, greater disappointments, greater knowledge of the
strength of nature and of society to defeat human aspirations were
pressed upon him.

But the darknesses on the whole deepened without diminishing

what he loved. See *The American Jeremiad* (Madison: University of Wisconsin Press,
1979).

[48] *J*, 2:211; see also *L*, 1:205 to William.

[49] *The Correspondence of Arthur Hugh Clough*, ed. Frederick L. Mulhauser, 2 vols.
(Oxford: Clarendon Press, 1957), 2:340.

the power of his thought. "I hold our actual knowledge very cheap," he wrote at the end of "History." "Hear the rats in the wall, see the lizard on the fence, the fungus under foot, the lichen on the log. What do I know sympathetically, morally, of either of these worlds of life?"[50] It was Emerson's gift to be able to hear the rat in the wall, to see the lizard, fungus, and lichen—those symbols of quick life moving toward decay and entropy—at the same time that he wondered about the worlds of life that contained them. While he could sustain within himself such opposite visions, could apprehend so powerfully the uses of ambiguity, his gift and prophetic voice did not desert him.

[50] *CW*, 2:39.

EPILOGUE

"The schism runs under the world."

—RWE, 1867

THIS STUDY has thrown new light on several issues. Two of the broader ones addressed by other scholars are the relation of Emerson's temperament to his work, and the formal qualities—or deficiencies, as some see them—of that writing. Questions of temperament were first stressed by Stephen Whicher, who perceived beneath Emerson's nineteenth-century serene and vatic image feelings of "impotence" and "hopelessness." Though hostile to much in Emerson, Whicher was an original and influential reader, and he affected many who followed him. The eventual implication of this strain of discussion was that some weakness of character kept Emerson from resolving the antitheses his intellect perceived; his reputation is qualified by the sense, unspoken but implied, that had he been more resolute he would have cleared up his doubts and been a more satisfactory man of the modern age.

This book argues for another interpretation. It accepts that Emerson was born into an age in which belief was dissolving but had not yet been surrendered. It would be two more generations before Nietzsche—who honored Emerson and "love[d] his gentle skepsis"—not only glimpsed the abyss but immersed himself in it. In the 1830s and 1840s the American insisted that we "hear the rats in the wall," the sounds of the cracking apart of the continents of belief. "We are lined with eyes," he wrote. In an era when David Hume was still omitted from the syllabus, and even skepticism—much less atheism—could not be openly entertained by public thinkers, Emerson's peculiar genius insisted that he credit his own perceptions. The counterexample of his mother's stance was "to call evil good." Exposure to these maternal hermeneutics from an early date had warned him on the contrary to honor his doubts.[1]

Emerson's achievement has here been seen more clearly by ex-

---

[1] Reflecting on the same moral stance a year later, he rejected its implications. When the soul's intuition conflicted with the New Testament, to "call what it thinks evil, good" would be to "stifle your moral faculty," even if the evil or defect appeared "in the history of Jesus" (*JMN*, 3:212).

amining in detail for the first time some of the events and persons that shaped his double vision, and especially the dark substratum of his experience. He learned to deal with these forces in varying ways, ranging from denial to acceptance, transcendence, and personal change, because to events as tragic and early losses as great as his, reason could not suffice to answer: faith and willed patience were prerequisites to survival.

In particular, one can now recognize the mixture of intellectual, emotional, and physical stresses that produced his early unhappiness. These moods were not monolithic, and they were not evidence of characterological weakness. On the contrary, much of Emerson's real "misery" was rooted in an often fatal disease. He denied it a name, but he faced it, struggled with it, and overcame it—as no one else in his family was able to do—by the extraordinary achievement of changing his ways of living, feeling, and thinking. Saving his own life became of necessity a lifelong exercise in self-management and self-understanding. That it directly influenced (I do not say accounted for) what he said in his mature writings about trust and self-reliance is obvious, but needs to be stated. (His famous and seemingly mysterious metaphor of the "transparent eyeball," so long and so heavily reinterpreted, is also affected by the facts of his illness. To one whose vision was too dim to permit him to read or write for several months on end, the desirability of having a transparent cornea, or "eyeball," would be a self-evident, if somewhat private image.)[2]

More deeply influential even than this sickness, however, was his father's early death, which left the seven-year-old boy outwardly withdrawn and self-doubting, but inwardly guilty, full of *mauvaise honte*, and fueled by an identification with death that contributed to years of withdrawal, depression, and self-doubt. Her husband's death and its after effects were mishandled by his mother, a hard-working and well-intentioned but rigid, repressive, and unaffectionate person who from young Waldo's infancy had given her fourth child little of the love he needed to like himself.

In his maturity, Emerson liked to cite the fable of the stag who cursed his horns but blessed his feet. Because he had to learn to defend his ego consciously, long after the age when most children experience themselves preverbally and extend their self-love into a protective sense of self, the process of psychic growth became a subject

[2] *CW*, 1:10.

he understood very well. Fostering the "growth of the true self," or the soul, was the kernel of all his early public utterances and the essays that made his reputation. Out of the withdrawal into dreams of his childhood and adolescence came the fantastic tales and poems that were the seedbed of his mature writings.

IT IS the relation of his earliest writings to his mature work that at the end of this study seems most intriguing. Here the questions of form addressed by other critics become most relevant, for they affect how one reads him and how useful he is to readers today. Emerson's mature writing is marked by antithesis, and this has made it subject to much criticism, for many readers are dissatisfied with Emerson's form, or lack of it, and have pointed to the connection between this problem and what they see as an excessive tendency in his work toward balanced argument.

Sherman Paul calls that habit "polarity." David Porter speaks of "an essential contradiction" and the binary quality of his intellect, split between an eighteenth-century "rationalist idealism" and romantic organicism, or ideal of the whole. Carolyn Porter uses Marxist terms to describe Emerson's self-contradictions, which constrain him to "swing" between the walls of the real world he has tried to transcend, but cannot wish away. Sacvan Bercovitch considers Emerson's social thought "flaccid" and objects that Emerson's rejection of history renders his thought lacking in "tension." Prior to them all, Matthiessen framed that New Critical reproach when he found Emerson's work formless, marred by a failure of propulsive forward movement in his thought that resulted in a "lack of tension."[3]

I suggest that on the contrary, Emerson's tendency toward antithesis is less a defect than an achievement; that he began quite differently, and that as his consciousness developed, so did the inevitable shape of his style. It is a truism of rhetorical analysis that one cannot separate style and content, the "seesaw" in the voice from the seesaw in the language (to use Emerson's own trope): I suggest that this polarity is not only characteristic but vitally expressionistic.

Let me add in passing, however, that one does not read Emerson because one recognizes him as either a true prophet or a logician; one may not fully accept either his youthful idealism or the "meliorism" (to use Bishop's word) of his maturity. If he is still read today

---

[3] Paul, passim; D. Porter, p. 136; C. Porter, p. 106; Matthiessen, pp. 63, 5–6, 75, 40; Bercovitch, pp. 163, 173.

it is because he is, as Packer has remarked, simply the best American writer, whose fidelity and subtlety of tone and language are unequaled. He called himself "one of the sect of the Seekers" (or as he put it in a later remark: "I am God incarnate; I am the weed by the wall"). He wished to be a prophet, but he was not better than we; he was better than himself, in fact, only in fits and starts, a truth he lamented often enough. But he really was a seer, a see/r in and a see/r out. And he recorded the process of his search in language so intelligent, so delicately tuned to the uncertainties of being in our unanchored and disorderly culture that we go on reading him because his voice is a kind of oboe, an A note against which we tune for authenticity.

Julie Ellison offers a more precise description and a strong explanation of this tendency to antithesis in Emerson's writing, focusing precisely on the very refusal to move forward that for so long has seemed its weak point. That kind of movement, she suggests, has a strategy: it aims at inventing an impossible freedom by destroying stability; it breaks apart in order to make metamorphosis possible. The seeming dialectic so typical of Emerson, she holds, "cannot mean mere alternation, and so necessarily misdescribes prose that accumulates but does not progress. Emerson's writing can just as well be called antidialectic, for its possible unities continually break apart into antagonistic opposites." All his writings are identical in structure: "Whatever the topic, he represents some form of interpretation as an anti-authoritarian, metamorphic act which makes possible a freedom so absolute that . . . it will always (Emerson hopes) exceed its representations."[4] His resistance to synthetic thought is part of his hope for a new vision, a new insight that will stand outside of determined, logical inference.

Yet while this is a shrewd and accurate assessment of Emerson's mature style, it does not describe his early writings. The material that this study has brought to light is not framed antithetically, nor has it postponed resolution while awaiting metamorphosis. On the contrary, Emerson's youthful prose and poetic fictions seek and achieve their transformations in the here and now. They are also characterized by forthrightness, clarity, and a monologic tone. Their thin mysteries are couched in transparently direct language, and all of it, prose or poetry, moves briskly toward closure. The narrator cannot fathom Uilsa's headlong race into the abyss; Isaac refuses to discuss a rejection he acts out but cannot defend; the Land of Not is by definition and history unreachable. The language of these fictions,

---

[4] Ellison, pp. 76–77.

though often lyrical, lacks irony, reserve, and density. One may feel the poignancy of these fables of isolation and terror, but they do not reflect on themselves. Unself-conscious, their protagonists remain part of the world of faerie and perhaps are best described by the same phrase Emerson used to characterize his aunt's best writing: "Inexplicable, as if caught from some dream."

It seems inescapable here to recognize that Emerson became an interesting writer only after he returned from St. Augustine in 1827. The recovery of his health on that long journey, as I have suggested, was inextricably intertwined with a new attitude toward himself and his grand ambition to "shine in the assemblies of men." He renounced that crude aim as he journeyed home, saying that suffering had "sublimed" him. (He used the latter term both in its alchemical and romantic sense.) He was ambitious still, of course, perhaps doubly so. But he began to accept after that date that his lot would lie outside the norms, and that success would not be measured by the standards of his teachers or coequals, those collegians he had once seen passing him on the way and leaving him, a "goose," behind, though hope still held out her "gay banners."

Significantly, the person to whom he confided this sense of change was his aunt. Different herself, Mary Emerson helped him accept his own "difference." It is relevant, too, that the moment of insight into his new sense of destiny coincided with a deep, conscious, and articulated sense of love for a new friend. I do not doubt that part of the change he described to Mary came with his acceptance that the feminine, more open side of his nature, already known to him, was of equal value with its more conventionally masculine aspect.[5]

Apparently it was only after he understood that insight would come not from mingling in the great assembly of men but from remaining at the margin of things, from living between worlds in flux, that Emerson's style matured and deepened. I would suggest that there was a connection between these personal renunciations (his own word) and his capacity to eschew the support of narrative or the structure of logical closure. Certainly, it is only after this watershed year that density and power were added to his lyrical gift.

EMERSON's journal first clearly voiced the coming change during his trip to Italy in 1833. He was to be accused of a sort of iconoclasm

---

[5] As he wrote in 1842: "A highly endowed man with good intellect & good conscience is a Man-woman . . ." (*JMN*, 8:175).

by Andrews Norton, but he did not originate the attack on the idols of belief; it was an accomplished fact by the time Emerson came along and not of his own making. For all his claim for an original relation with the universe, the essential duty Emerson conceived, I believe, was repair, reconstruction, a building up not from the chaos of first creation, but from shards and scraps. He knew early that there lay about him a broken world. It was himself and his brothers he described as the "young men" in the famous passage in "Life and Letters in New England" who felt the "knives in their brain" and knew that by that edge were detached "bone and marrow, soul and body, yea, almost the man from himself."[6] His was a consciousness that had come to being on a landscape not empty of culture, but littered—as he wrote after a long day in Rome—with "old stumps of the past." In Naples, too, he had written tenderly of the same disappointment: "Long ago when I dreamed at home of these things, I thought I should come suddenly in the midst of an open country upon broken columns & fallen friezes, & their solitude would be solemn & eloquent."[7] Instead, he had found himself surrounded by rubble and guided by a thief. The discovery in Italy of the brokenness of things became for Emerson a subtext, a permanent metaphor.

Nevertheless, if he insisted on seeing the damage around him, if he claimed the right to describe the destruction of belief that he had not caused, he did not rejoice in it. An old familiar of loss himself, he could articulate the fading of the objects of faith more readily than others could, but the process was still painful. These mixed feelings probably contributed to the distance of his stance, the coolness with which he armored himself when he confronted such topics, whether philosophically or personally.

That distance also generates a certain confusion in readers' responses to him. When as a student I began reading Emerson, I was charmed by both his language and his ideas. "The alienated majesty" of one's own thoughts, which he spoke of perceiving in other writers, I felt in his essays. But they were alienated indeed. He did not seem to speak to me from a focal point. I did not know his "we" and "us." Emerson told me that man was a god in ruins: the phrase struck me, but I did not believe him. Perhaps Emerson is best understood as a writer bent on refashioning that god.[8] Some see in his references to shrinking, maimedness, and the like an undignified,

---

[6] *CW*, 10:326.

[7] *JMN*, 4:151; *JMN*, 4:143–44.

[8] See Bishop, pp. 145ff., and Packer, p. 94.

unworthy vision of humanity. The problem, however, is not that Emerson denigrated humanity, but that he spoke of chaos and schism with unfathomable serenity, a serenity that today seems suspicious. Modern readers find it impenetrable because the manner belies the substance of his speech. It seems abreactive. Perhaps the damage seemed so great to him that he could allude to it only from a posture of iron poise. If one would find "tension" in Emerson, one should look, I would suggest, beneath that steely, burnished surface.

It may be that what he learned to do to that experience of a world already demystified was analogous to the process that, as he saw, had made art so continuous in Italy. He learned to break up the fables he had begun with or inherited and make of their elements a new environment, one neither empty of culture nor oppressed by the weight of foreign history.

Eric Cheyfitz's discussion of the narrative inherent in *Nature* is a case in point. As a youth of eighteen Emerson possessed in "Uilsa" a highly transparent narrative voice, pure but not of great interest; "monologic" if you will. As he drove himself toward a profession in the church, deliberately suppressing his interest in "Romance," that impulse disappeared from his language. Yet the language and imagery of that tale—the child-hero, the seductive yet fearsome mother, the father-minister lost in the abyss—reappear in *Nature*, as one can see in Cheyfitz's study, an interesting and original examination of this central text. It is as if Emerson had in "Uilsa" erected a glass window to tell his narrative and then, dissatisfied, had dismantled and demolished it. Fourteen years later, ready to write again, he returned to the scrapyard of his own making and, gathering up shards of colored glass, reconstituted his vision. The assertion *Nature* appears to offer seems new, but in its constituent parts, its colors and smaller shapes as they have been teased out, one sees again the old story: the texture is more fine, it is bound together in a different, stronger matrix and fired at a higher heat, but still it is recognizable—the fall, the abyss, the frightening if beautiful mother, the missing, dangerous father.

Emerson's most genuinely creative act, I would suggest, was less his first invention than the long process of breaking down and reconstituting the fable from its elements into a new work. By reusing the language and imagery of his youthful romantic vision, while stripping it of narrative coherence, he freed himself in his first book to write a work of dense polyphony: at once poetic and abstract, personal and ethical, seemingly analytical and deliberately orphic.[9] Seen

9 Ellison, pp. 228–30, again puts it well when she comments on Emerson's refusal in a

in this light, his stylistic achievement has more than merely linguistic implications, for it shows us Emerson in the act of reworking himself. He stands by a hot oven, and there is as much to do as there are memories—abandoned, corroding, misshapen—lying ready to be made if not whole, then at least cohesive.

THIS STUDY began by saying that its origin was the attempt to understand a silence. One can recognize now that his silence appears to have followed the "encryptment" of his missing father. Yet it seems also true that that crypt abutted a place of work, what Mary Shelley called "the filthy workshop of creation" and Yeats named "the rag and boneshop of the heart." Under all the imagery of light, of magic, of seeking, lay a pile of bones, an abyss, a kind of tip that filled only gradually with discarded images, where three bushels of gold rings gathered by Hannibal's army mingled indiscriminately with the bodies of the nine little pigs, with dying martyrs, brothers, sisters, wife, and father. The romances of Emerson's adolescent writing gave way to acts of intellection in his twenties, as he searched for a way to his metiér. But in the long run he became, I believe, a kind of *bricoleur* in Lévi-Strauss's sense, who returned to the place of destruction, the scrapyard of materials he had collected, dismantled, and digested over three decades. From Scott he took, let us say, shards of ruby; from Hume, black lead for the setting and outline; from disease a certain green; from death itself the pressure to inquire; from love a clarity of white light that gave him sight of the beautiful meteor of the snow.

It is interesting from this perspective to contrast Uilsa, daughter of the weird or fatal sisters, whom Emerson invented in his adolescence, with Merlin, the wizard who figures in a poem he wrote more than twenty years later. Both are endowed with magical powers, and both are associated with the Fates. Uilsa is the daughter of Odin and Hela, a Valkyrian Fate who weaves human destiny from the sinews and bones of men slain in battle. Merlin, a figure from Arthurian legend, also mediates Fate and the otherworld. His poem closes with a chant, spoken as if from his point of view:

> Subtle rhymes, with ruin rife,
> Murmur in the house of life,

---

passage from his journals to accept conventional, generic categories. "Emerson's lists in this entry are gestures of acceptance and inclusion, but are critical and ironic too. [The list] implies that new works will be constituted out of fragments of old materials."

> Sung by the Sisters as they spin;
> In perfect time and measure they
> Build and unbuild our echoing clay.
> As the two twilights of the day
> Fold us music-drunken in.[10]

Merlin is a magician not because like Uilsa, a romantic outlaw, he defies and outruns life, plunging into the abyss of nonbeing and the gripe of the serpent, but because he is uniquely conscious of it. In "Merlin" the sounds of life have grown subtle and complex, and its ending is suffused by synaesthesia. Emerson clung to his binary habit of thought, but by the 1840s its content had changed. The antinomies he perceived were more complex, the process of choice less certain. In the later work, Emerson understood that the true mystery was not in the abyss, where consciousness ceases and death begins, but here in the humming room where life spins itself out, and we, too drunk with its music to understand it, are folded for a time like sheep in a cote, "between the two twilights of the day." Life itself is an antithesis by which we are bracketed and confused.

At age seventeen Emerson had raised the despairing question suggested by Hume: "If the system of morals which we hold to be true be a dream, it is the dream of a god reposing in Elysium; and who would desire to be awaked from the sublime deception?" Merlin himself is a fiction, a deception, and in creating him Emerson has not resolved the questions of knowing and being put by skeptical philosophy. But he has imagined a figure powerful enough to live an awakened life. Like Merlin, Emerson suggests, it is possible to hear the song and be its witness.

[10] *CW*, 9:124.

Index

Ahlstrom, Sydney E., 13n.10, 44n.19, 204nn. 14 and 16
alienation. *See* isolation
Allen, Gay Wilson, 7n.9, 37n.1, 76n.12, 90n.45, 177n.1, 224n.40
"American Scholar, The" (RWE), 172, 244
American Unitarian Association, 214
Andover school: EBE's education at, 45, 57–58; established, 44, 58; meals at, 58; orthodoxy of, 150; restricted thought at, 44–45; seminary at, 44–45, 73, 150
Andover School (of evangelism). *See* New Light doctrine
Arminian doctrine, 13, 38, 203, 204, 206, 208
Arnold, Matthew, 6
Arnold, Thomas, 107, 113n.34, 147, 148, 162
art, European: RWE's taste in, 234, 236–37
Augustine, Saint, 6
Avenbrugger, Dr., 182, 183

Bacon, Francis, 204
Bagehot, Walter, 107
Bercovitch, Sacvan, 247n.47, 252
Bishop, Jonathan, 7n.8, 96n.62, 177n.1, 255n.8
Bloom, Harold, 6, 96n.62, 242
boardinghouses: and boarders taken in by RE, 17, 19, 36, 50, 55, 61–62; MME's living in, 47; running of, 61–62
Bossuet, Jacques-Bénigne, 122
Boston Female Asylum, 15, 23–24, 62
Boston Latin School, 73n.2
Boston Patriot, 150
Bowlby, John, 5, 28n.53, 95
Bradford, Mary Russell, 20, 21, 22
Bradford, Samuel (sheriff and father of SABR), 57
Bradford, Samuel, Jr., 186n.23
Brown, Felix, 28n.53

Buckminster, Joseph Stephens, 13, 14, 27n.51, 195
Buddhism: MME's interest in, 47
Burr, Priscilla (friend of WE), 16
Butler, Bishop Joseph, 101, 105
Byron, George Gordon (Lord), 48, 81, 128, 139, 140, 227, 234, 236

Cabot, James Elliot, 25n.45, 37n.1, 51n.37, 55nn. 2 and 3; 61n.18, 73n.2, 75n.9, 158n.1, 160n.6, 215n.10
Cameron, Kenneth Walter, 11n.4, 88n.43, 168, 169n.23
Cameron, Sharon, 31n.60
Canova, Antonio, 234, 236
Carlyle, Thomas, 62, 118, 129, 241
"Central Man," 209
Channing, Edward T., 74
Channing, William Ellery, 16n.19, 45, 67, 105, 127, 135, 146–47, 195, 203
Charleston, S.C.: RWE's trip to, 177, 185. *See also* Emerson, Ralph Waldo: health of
Chauncy, Charles, 13, 14
Cheyfitz, Eric, 7, 52n.40, 87n.41, 256
Childe Harold (Byron), 122, 234
"Christ Crucified" (sermon, RWE), 204–5
Christian Disciple, 149
Christology: RWE's rejection of, 203n.13, 205
Clarke, John, 12n.6
Clarke, Samuel, 101, 127, 155
Clematis (ship), 177
clothing: for Calvinists, 20
Clough, Arthur Hugh, 5, 107, 127n.32, 171, 248
codes: RWE's interest in, 31, 61, 76, 80n.25
Cole, Phyllis, 37n.2
Coleridge, Samuel Taylor, 241
compensation: RWE's doctrine of, 155–56, 204; Hume on, 156
Cooke, George Willis, 38n.3, 61n.18
Cott, Nancy, 5, 45n.24

resondence from WE to, 26; death of,
21, 181, 214, 230; health of, 21, 49,
177; naming of, 12; sent to live with
relatives, 21
Emerson, Joseph (uncle of MME), 38
Emerson, Mary Caroline (sister), 49, 50,
214, 230
Emerson, Mary Moody (aunt): birth of,
38; childhood of, 38–40; correspondence from RWE to, 110, 125, 166,
167, 170, 171, 175, 192, 199, 207,
209, 210, 220, 227, 231, 248; correspondence from WE to, 15; correspondence of, 28, 37n.2, 40, 43, 48, 49, 51,
52, 53n.41, 68, 69, 85n.38, 133–34,
141, 142–43, 173, 184, 207, 208, 215,
221; death of, 38; eccentric behavior of,
36, 42, 85, 141–42, 207; education of,
39, 48; and RE, 16, 22, 40, 41, 47, 48,
49–50, 133; and WE, 40–43, 46, 49;
as feminist, 47–48; founding of Waterford, Maine, by, 151; handwriting of,
41; health of, 47; her influence in Emerson household, 36, 42, 43–44, 50–
52, 55, 65–66; her influence on RWE,
36–38, 52–53, 54, 65–70, 99–101,
109, 132–44, 173, 174, 193, 206–10,
254; inheritance of, 47; journals of,
37n.2, 43, 46, 53, 134–35, 141, 209,
243; her nickname, 52n.40; obituary
for, 50; her objections to RWE's Humism, 108; her opinion on marriage of
RE and WE, 28; rejection of marriage
by, 47; her relationship with RWE
reanalyzed in light of women's studies,
5, 37n.2; religious views of, 44–45, 46–
47, 48, 66–67, 135–42, 165, 203; remarks on humility by, 57; her socialization of, 39–40, 133; social position of,
15, 40; Uilsa's resemblance to, 85; vocation of, 47–48, 207; writings of, 41,
134, 135, 153
Emerson, Phebe (sister), 18, 19
Emerson, Phebe Bliss. See Ripley, Phebe
Bliss Emerson (paternal grandmother)
Emerson, Ralph Waldo: acting done by,
81; as Adam, 27; ambition of, 57, 61,
72, 160, 164, 192, 194, 195–96, 211–
12, 254; anger of, at father, 7, 34, 52,
153; birth of, 10, 14, 19n.25, 24; called

Waldo, 60; clothing of, 55; correspondence of, 25, 31, 37n.2, 49, 54, 57, 60–
61, 63–64, 65, 69, 70, 75, 109, 110,
117, 125, 133, 136, 137, 138, 147,
149, 151, 165, 166, 167, 170, 171,
175, 180, 181, 185, 189, 190, 191,
192, 199, 207, 209, 210, 211, 212,
217, 219, 220, 224, 225, 227, 229,
231, 240, 248; and depression, 30–31,
78, 96, 111, 153, 162, 174, 175, 181–
82, 186; description of, 30–31, 215–
16; drawings by, 30, 82, 91, 134–35,
187; eating habits of, 24–26, 117, 230,
231; education of, 3, 26, 56, 60, 61,
67–68, 72, 75; employed as teacher,
91, 116, 146, 154, 158, 159, 160; employed by uncle, 11n.4, 52, 55, 62–63;
first marriage of, 33, 210, 219–30;
health of, 5, 26, 95, 111, 155, 156,
157, 158–59, 160, 163, 165, 175,
177–78, 179–81, 183, 184, 185–86,
190, 197, 199, 211–14, 230, 232, 251,
254; humor of, 61, 81, 154; life insurance for, 224; as minister, 3, 93, 94,
126, 175, 176, 195, 196, 198–99, 200,
203, 206, 211, 214–16, 217–19, 221–
22, 230, 231, 242; parental criticism of,
25–27; as president's freshman at Harvard, 56, 74, 75; religious views of, 67,
70, 108–15, 130, 145–46, 162–63,
164–65, 194, 201–6, 233–34; response
of, to death of ETE, 230, 234–35; response of, to death of WE, 4, 7, 28–30,
31–34, 52, 77, 81, 82, 93, 95–98, 130,
153, 230, 248, 251, 257; response of,
to death of first son, 31n.60, 92, 96,
197; second marriage of, 244; self-ap-
praisal of, 34–35, 61, 91–92, 94, 126,
154; sexuality of, 75–76, 86, 87, 89,
91–92, 93, 117, 126, 206, 246; socialization of, 43–44, 52, 75–76, 126, 215;
transcendence of, 8; travel by, 177,
184–85, 187–90, 196–97, 232–42,
254; upbringing of, 25, 93; writings
(other than journals) by, 3–4, 31, 61,
64–65, 91, 120, 144, 155, 158, 165,
173, 190, 212, 225–26, 227, 234, 235,
237, 252–54. See also journals of RWE
Emerson, Ruth Haskins (mother): account book of, 17–18; birth of, 16;

D0457368